The HISOFE Dictionary of Midnight Politics:
Expibasketical Theories on Afrikentication and African Unity

Peter Ateh-Afac Fossungu

Langaa Research & Publishing CIG
Mankon, Bamenda

Publisher:
Langaa RPCIG
Langaa Research & Publishing Common Initiative Group
P.O. Box 902 Mankon
Bamenda
North West Region
Cameroon
Langaagrp@gmail.com
www.langaa-rpcig.net

Distributed in and outside N. America by African Books Collective
orders@africanbookscollective.com
www.africanbookcollective.com

ISBN: 9956-792-65-9

© Peter Ateh-Afac Fossungu 2015

DISCLAIMER
All views expressed in this publication are those of the author and do not necessarily reflect the views of Langaa RPCIG.

Dedicated To Afrikentication And African Unity

Table of Contents

List of Tables...ix
Synopsis.. xi
Introduction... xiii

Chapter 1: Conceptroduction And Biggytitlemania: Letting Our Titles Shine From Under............................. 1
CGAM in Brief and the Paradoxical Argument............... 2
The Paradoxical Argument....................................... 3
CGAM and the African Beer-Drinking-Cup-of-Nations...... 4
Defining Midnightism/Tree-Topperism: Is Biggytitlemania Distinctively African?..8
Midnightism and Tree-Topperism............................... 8
Biggytitlemania... 11

Chapter 2: Uniting The Un-United Parts Of Africa: Is The *Grand Frère* Of Theories From Cameroon From One To Many Or From Many To One?............................. 21
The *Grands Coupeurs* of MYR: From Canada to Little Rwanda-Burundi?... 22
Language and Communication Politics: The Left-in-Forest Nightly Meeting..24
The Congo-Issa Story: Learning the Hard Way Is Learning the Best Way?... 36
The *Grand Frère* Theory From Cameroon to Africa.......... 43
The Lockwood Manufacturing Bragger and the Bamileke Money-Harvesters...45
CGAM Regular Visitors and Exploitation: A 99-Sensism Affair?..55

Chapter 3: Fossungu Paffectism And The Unknown Battle With Midnightism: The Revolutionization Of Elections In The CGAM.. **65**
Back-Grounding the Elections Revisionism................... 68
Qualities of a Good Pioneer and the Arrata-Poison Theory..71
Scattering the Wolf-Pack with "No-More-Acclamation"..... 77
Lyslyakoyahism and the Ahidjoist Agenda: Explaining Her Ousting...85
Not Distinguishing Individuals from Relations?.................... 89
Firstohocelectionisn Occasioning Charalicism?...................... 91
Dog-Rule Politics of Exclusion or Not Ready for a Woman as President?... 95

Chapter 4: Getting The Government You Deserve: From Quebec Separatism To CGAM April-Fool Democracy... **101**
The Value of Balanced Critique................................... 104
Death Sociopackism: Confirming the Arrata-Poison Theory?.. 106
Cancellationism Exposes the Politickerizers................... 115
The Pepper Soup and Heineken Government................ 121
The Battles for, and to Recapture, Midnight Power: The 2007 CGAM Elections..126
Separatist-Foolish Dramacracy................................... 127
The Power of the Video-Camera and the Minutes-Taking Fiasco.. 128

Chapter 5: CGAMING MYR'S *Aitwsian* Reinforcement Of The Stereotypes About Africa: From The MIC-Media-Dollarocracy To Onafridism?............................... **137**
The Military-Industrial-Complex and Offspring.............. 138
Is MYR the Hub of *Africanization* and Out of Canada?......... 141
The Zairian Hang-On Rule...141
The Guinean *Wata-Rain* and *Nouveaux* Theses.......…....…..... 148

Are *AITWs* Western But Un-westernized? Some 'After-Elections' Answers from CGAM..................................161
Off-Staging the Briefers...163
Revampinization and the Never-Ending Tree-Topperism in *AITWs*?..167

Chapter 6: From NOSIFE Into HISOFE For Appropriate De-Stereotyping And Afrikentication Techniques: Africa Must Unite Or Die...179
The Tree-Top-Habitaters Theory: Non-Africans Africanizing While In Africa?..179
Carenayahism Crumbling: Any Real South Africans in Canada?..180
Chinalogizing Sovereignty and Globalization: Becoming Big Boys Is Only Way to Fight Big Boys.............................195
Positively Using the Stigmas: Hard Choices, National Humiliation and Viperizationism................................201
Globalization and the Hard Choices.............................202
On Onafridism and National Humiliation:
3-Point Viperizationism..207
Relevantly Surprising Answers to Unnecessary
Questions?...221
Battle for Understanding..223
The Theory of Drunklampostism..................................225

Conclusion..227

Bibliography..233

List of Tables

1. Presidents of CGAM......................................5
2. Chief Whips of CGAM...................................61
3. Secretaries-General of CGAM............................66
4. Electoral Committees of CGAM.......................... 75
5. Treasurers of CGAM................................... 86
6. Financial Secretaries of CGAM.......................... 88
7. Vice-Presidents of CGAM...............................93
8. Social secretaries of CGAM............................. 99
9. Public Relations Officers of CGAM...................... 99
10. CGAM Bylaws Review Committees..................... 133
11. Some CGAM Membership Growth or Admissions (since July 2005)... 156

Synopsis

Building on author's earlier works, and essentially providing Africa with original, critical, and multi-level analyses of the trio of globalization, democracy, and national determination, this book theorizes that African states have to unite in order to have any impact in the global economy, whether it is capitalist- or communist-driven; showing that China, but not African states, did face up with the ineluctable *political trilemma* or hard choices. Brought down to a lower level with the Cameroon Goodwill Association of Montreal (CGAM) as case study, it demonstrates how the CGAM too has grossly failed to make hard choices, preferring politickerization or midnight politics to fossungupalogy (that is, the science of straightforwardness, necessitating the fearless looking at truth straight in the eye). The questions of the book are many but do all boil down to whether or not Africans fear the truth and do not therefore do politics. It is amazing that Africans in the West live in societies where fierce political competitors do embrace each other after one has defeated the other; but they are incapable of looking their so-called friends in the eye and saying, for example: "Man, I think you've totally gotten it wrong this time." Such comportment defines politickerization or negative competition. While attempting some possible responses to the numerous queries it raises, this book basically proffers the science of Four-Eyesism as a discipline that all African schools need to institute and make a compulsory subject: if the vandalized continent would have to be awakened to its realities.

Introduction

Democracy is the faith that the process of experience is more important than any special result attained, so that special results achieved are of ultimate value only as they are used to enrich and order the ongoing process. Africans must therefore be allowed to apply their cultural and historical experiences and talents in working out a pattern of 'government of the people, by the people, and for the people' according to their own understanding and as their own peculiar circumstances demand. Those who do not want the vertical 'Western-Style Democracy' must be given a fair chance to demonstrate an alternative African horizontal democracy. Perhaps what they come up with might be of benefit to politics even in the West, provided that their radical system of horizontal democracy protects the life, liberty and property of citizens, and provided that the people want it [Mentan, 2013b].

Expibasketism is a complex concept. Very briefly put though, you could define expibasketism as that science of drawing from your experience in the field to be able to connect some dots that would otherwise be hard to link up. The term, in short, is shorthand for *basket of experience*. The Chinese are known for never forgetting national humiliation. The Chinese are thus what Michalinos Zembylos would call Greek *Den Xehno* or "I'll Never Forget" (cited in Fossungu, 2014: xii). I am what some critics might now describe as an *African-Chinese*. (Add my Canadian connexion to it and come out with *African-Chinadian*, if you will). Yes, I happily take that because I never forget to learn a lot from a lot of my diverse and sometimes heart-breaking experiences. One thing I must tell you right away though is that expibasketism is not a thing you will find marching along with *visionlessness* or opportunism. It is rather an ingredient of *four-eyesism*. Maybe it is futile trying to teach four-eyesism? Is it inherent or/and something that can be learned? I do not quite know what the experts would tell you here.

But I know that *HISOFE* is the short form for *Higher School of Four-Eyesism*, a unique College with numerous City and Forest campuses from where you will be receiving your written lectures. I have always loved writing, an art which Schmidt (2010: 1) defines as "a process through which we learn to communicate with others." First HISOFE Communiqué therefore: Admission into this School can only be gained by those who have successfully left or can show proof of the genuine desire to graduate from *NOSIFE* which, on its part, means *no-schooling in four-eyesism*. One of the first and enduring lessons I learnt on my first encounter as an aspiring political scientist came from Schmidt (2010: xi) who told me from day one that "What political scientists do best is write." That was scarcely news to me – although it was kind of reassuring to know that I love doing what is considered to be of capital importance to the political scientist that I was aspiring to *officially* be. The really important revelation came when Schmidt (2010: 2) pointed out that "A general rule for writing in political science classes is for students to always ask before they write anything: What are the politics or power relationships existing in a political event?" I have this important question in mind (as always) as I dabble here with the comportment of Africans generally but of Africans in the West (shortened in this book to *AITWs*) – one of whom I obviously am.

Unless the context makes it otherwise, Cameroonians and Cameroon should often be used and read interchangeably with Africans and Africa all through this book; a book that essentially provides Africa with an original, critical, and multi-level analysis of the trio of globalization, democracy, and national determination. It shows that China, but not the African states, did face up with the ineluctable hard choices. In the same manner, the Cameroon Goodwill Association of Montreal (CGAM) has colossally failed to make hard choices, preferring politickerization to a fearless looking at the truth straight in the eye. The tragedy of that pretence of both Africa and Africans is seen in the depth of this book which, in essence, also appreciates and praises *AITWs* for maintaining and fostering a lot of distinctive African communal values even in their homes away from home.

The soul-raking questions raised are many but most of them do boil down to whether Africans are afraid of the truth and do not do politics. This issue is not trivial. What greatly amazes the mind is the fact that particularly *AITWs* live in societies where fierce political foes or competitors do embrace each other after one has defeated the other. Yet these *AITWs* cannot even learn to look their so-called friends straight in the eye and say, for example: "Man, I think you've totally gotten it wrong this time." That comportment is the shortest way of defining *politickerization*. This is a term that the reader can conveniently equate with negative competition or what Ferguson (2010) decries as 'the Fear of Politics'. The persistent questions running throughout the book include: Why are *AITWs* living abroad if they cannot get back home and behave positively differently from those who have never been abroad and who consequently know only the way it is done back home? Do we get out there simply to do *'voluntary slavery'* without learning anything positive from that experience? Didn't someone say travelling alone is a lot of education that classroom lectures can hardly provide? While attempting some possible responses in the six chapters that follow, this book essentially proffers the science of Four-Eyesism as a discipline that all African schools need to institute and make a compulsory discipline: if the vandalized continent would have to be awakened to its realities.

Chapter 1 generally introduces the concepts, such as the CGAM, the need for unity, *midnightism*, *tree-topperism* and *biggytitlemania*. The second chapter looks at what the experts have to say about the difficulty of bringing the so-called un-

united parts of Africa together. Chapter 3 studies the unknown battle with midnight politicians in the context of electoral innovation in the CGAM. The fourth chapter examines the type of government people get as a result of their voting behaviour; while the fifth catalogues some instances of Africans ignorantly reinforcing the stereotypes about the continent. Chapter 6 then advances some appropriate techniques for de-stigmatizing the stereotypes and making positive use of them for purposes of African authenticity and unity. There is a conclusion, no doubt.

Chapter 1

Conceptroduction and Biggytitlemania: Letting Our Titles Shine From Under

I am truly tired of seeing us Cameroonians coming to this part of the world only to enrich other nationalities and races rather than working together to enrich and help ourselves. If you want to get a good grasp of what I am talking about here, just imagine the amount of money our various Cameroonian associations (not to limit just to CGAM) spent yearly on just renting halls [for parties and meetings] here in Montreal. Is our community not large and dynamic enough to at least have, for example, a hall to its name by now? [Peter Ateh-Afac Fossungu, Pioneer President of the CGAM, in a message sent to CGAMers on April 5, 2013 on the occasion of the 10th Anniversary Celebrations of the CGAM].

I am not writing this book as a member of the GAC (Goodwill Advisory Council that is now composed of 'former and current presidents and founding members'), nor as the pioneer and/or emeritus president of the CGAM (see Fossungu, 2013a: 110). Those titles and membership are meaningless to me when, because of negative competition, the CGAM is going in reverse to the ideals that gave birth to it. I write just as a concerned member of the community who would think he may have some ideas on how to resolve the stalemate and some other down-sliding perspectives that are plaguing the immediate community, as well as the larger threats to the larger – Mama Africa – whose own so-called leaders have shied away from making the inevitable **hard choices**, very unlike the Asians generally but China in particular.

All the chapters of this book do most of the time shift gears away from higher government to communal management, specifically using the CGAM's constitutional founding and objectives to show that a lot of positive African communal values are not only maintained and fostered but also mixed with *modern* governance techniques or systems. This is a well-grounded structure through which the concerned *AITWs* were supposed to hone the leadership and other skills necessary for advancing the community, devoid of big titles and low performance. The book thus questions the actual practice and blending of the values and democratic administration of the community. It also harps on the need for Africans to unite in the face of the challenges of the globalized and globalizing world economy. The need for quality and African-loving leaders is of utmost importance. Strategies for awaking the African people to the continent's realities are put forward. I will now give you a short description of the CGAM and one of the paradoxical theories in its regard, before further defining important concepts required for understanding the arguments or theories of this book

CGAM in Brief and the Paradoxical Argument

One of the things I like myself for – assuming that there are even people with self-esteem who do not like themselves – is the fact that expibasketism has aided me not to be dogmatic on/with my knowledge in regard of people. I am therefore able to quickly learn about people with every act (big or small) they pose. I remember the very first day I met a Bakweri Cameroonian called Hans Najeme. We were working in one Montreal factory (Transit, a shoes distribution warehouse) back then when a Bangwa Cameroonian (Moses Z. Nkwenti) presented us to each other. With just a little bit of interaction with the Bakwerian that same day, I knew he was an opportunist. Of course, you too would be opportunistic if you were to ascribe a vision to an opportunist. Neither do opportunists like Joseph-Desiré Mobutu care about set down rules (of healthy competition) that would not provide their endless opportunities.

To such opportunists, home is home only when they are absolute in it. To comprehend these dictators, just hear Ahmadou Ahidjo of Cameroon (the notorious so-called *le bâtisseur de la Nation*) incessantly preaching a bloody North-South divide of the country when power has slipped from him into Paul Biya's hands. Mobutu is also noted for declaring every minute that *'Le Zaïre c'est moi'*. No doubt then that there is no Zaire now for Zaire to be buried in! In this book, I would prefer sticking with Zairian rather than Congolese that I reserve for those from the Congo with Brazzaville as capital. No more further confusion as the one in 'Democratic Republic of Congo' which is anything except a democracy. The many theses of the chapters would couple well with the further concepts definitions following shortly to fortify a paradoxical argument.

The Paradoxical Argument

One of my foremost arguments in this book is that, because of the fear of positive competition in the CGAM, Hans Najeme's rise to its presidency in late 2006 was both *midnightly* accidental and well-planned. Don't spend too much time wondering about this oxymoron or paradox. A *paradox*, according to Hawker and White (2007: 652), is one or both of two things: (1) a statement that is abstract or seems to contradict itself, but is in fact true; (2) a person or thing that combines two contradictory features or qualities. You will see why when you carry on. Just note right now that the midnightistic circumstances surrounding that rise effectively installed constitutional *adhocism* (a form dictatorship) in the CGAM that would shortly thereafter overcome even the majority of the *midnighters*. The heralded December 2007 elections would then be that faction's desperate attempts to regain midnight powers. They would successfully do so; but not without having destroyed everything positive/progressive that the association stood for. Midnight politics and its derivatives like extraordinary-adhocist democracy would be seen taking their toll on the very foundation stones of the association – *sociopackism* or the social packages to members in regard of deaths, births and marriages. There is simply too much that cannot be summarized here, the better thing being for you to just read on and do the discovery by yourself of what midnight politics is all about – negative competition.

The CGAM and the African Beer-Drinking-Cup-of-Nations

A "socio-economic and cultural association [that was] instituted, in the city of Montreal, Quebec, hereinafter referred to as 'Goodwill'" (CGAM Constitution, Article 1), the CGAM is a non-profit association (Article 3) with seat or address in the Borough of LaSalle (Article 4). Duly registered with the Registraire des Entreprises du Quebec as required by law (Article 5),[1] CGAM was founded in July 2003 by thirteen

---

[1] Until May 2013, it was just registered. It has now been incorporated and what this means (according to the 8th president's communication of May 21, 2013) "is that the [ten-year] headache of obtaining an alcohol permit is over and, as an incorporated entity, we can now seek financial assistance from the Government. One thing should be clear [though], we must update our information yearly with the Government especially when the administration changes." Table 1 is provided here for your easy comprehension and information on the association's torch-bearers to date (2014).

English-speaking Cameroonians. Paul Takha Ayah (the association's 2nd president) on 6 August 2013 captured the founding member issue with more recent whereabouts details when he stated that "The founding meeting was attended by 13 persons who are generally referred to as the founding members of the Goodwill Association. These were: Donatus Ako-Arrey (now in Pennsylvania, USA), Emilia Tambong (now in Gatineau), James Tambong (now in Gatineau), Jennifer Semia Tita (now in Quebec City), Lysly Ayah (now in Calgary), Paul Ayah, Peter Fossungu, Scholastica Asahchop (now in London Ontario), Valentine Usongo, Vivian Beng (of blessed memory), Walter Tita, Wilfred Kangong (now in Calgary), [and] Yvonne Kangong (now in Calgary)." These are the few persons, as far as I also know, who were at the Convention, out of about twenty-five members of the English-speaking community in

Table 1: Presidents of CGAM

Name	Year(s)	Name	Year(s)
1st Peter Ateh-Afac Fossungu	2003-2004	6th Florence Ngayap Nankam	2011
2nd Paul Takha Ayah	2005-2006	7th Ignatius Nsom Mbeng	2012
3rd Hans Najeme	2007	8th Caren Osong Ayah	2013
4th Fidelis Folefac	2008-2009	9th Julius Etaya Ashu	2014
5th Edward Ayuk Takang	2010		

Montreal at the time who had been duly invited to be part of this history.

Although formed by English-speaking Cameroonians, the CGAM is however not limited to just that community, being open to 'every Cameroonian of goodwill'. This is a plain fact that could be testified by this other constitutional fact that, although its working language is English, members are free to express themselves in French (CGAM Constitution, Article 2). Thus, there are many influential (in the sense of holding high offices) French-speaking CGAM members or CGAMers. The CGAM basically aims at: (1) fostering solidarity among its members; (2) contributing to the socio-economic and cultural diversity of Canada; (3) providing assistance to its members in times of need; and (4) facilitating integration of new members into Canadian society (Article 3).

How far the association has gone then in terms of its objectives is reflected in the quoted passage opening this chapter. It gives you a clear notion of the lack of unity and of sense of purpose that would have rapidly developed and is stiffly standing in the way of the founding objectives of the association – a kind of reflection of African states since the attainment of 'independence'? It can be really frustrating, viewing where the group normally should be after ten years of existence: especially considering its monumental achievements in the first three years. All this is largely attributed to the *AITWsian* skewed idea of democracy (even while living inside a Western Democracy!) that is completely cut-off from communal progress, being solely a 'democracy as I see fit for attaining the insatiable desires of my fat fall-over *pepsoheinekenistic* belly'. Democracy indeed! Millions of miles indeed away from object! What indeed was the CGAM tenth anniversary actually celebrating: other than the creation of another occasion for pepper soup and Heineken consumption (*pepsoheinekenism*)?

The African Beer-Drinking-Cup-of-Nations (BDCN): It is hard for me to tell the difference between Burundians and Rwandans. I will therefore use Rwanda and Burundi interchangeably in this book as if they were the same. Burundians and Rwandans may not like this because, between them, they know the difference that I am not conversant with. I used to think that any African BDCN would be retained by Cameroon for quite a long time. "As a drug of intoxication," Fossungu (1998d) did thus posit in July 1998, "Soccer competes only with beer-drinking in Cameroon." But I have had to make a radical change of heart since meeting Burundians/Rwandans *en vrac* and in a camp setting. I think Zairians could also be serious contenders for the trophy but I am not so sure because I have not had the same chance to meet them *en masse* and under the same familiar conditions as I have with Burundians: living in a camp setting with so many of them. Zairians I only knew at work in town and without particular acquaintances. While Cameroonians often do the drinking mostly during occasions like *born-houses*, baby-showers, *cry-die* or wake keepings, birthday parties, etc., Burundians go some miles further and also create some of these special events for drinking, most of which are simply routine 'drinking-occasions'. You will be astonished by the number of empty bottles a single Burundian/Rwandan (men and women alike) would be credited with at one seating of just one of these drinking-occasions,. And Burundians, according to a Quebec Government survey, come second only to Cameroonians in terms of *scolarisation* or scholarship in Francophone Sub-Saharan Africa. I don't know if they actually take the same position in the practice of midnightism.

Defining Midnightism and Tree-Topperism: Is Biggytitlemania Distinctively African?

Midnightism and Tree-Topperism

Midnightism: Teena Dewoo Moshumee in her 2013 book (*The Sounds of Silence: Mauritian Tales Told After Midnight*) tells us about Mauritian tales that are usually told after midnight. Specifically it is about Teena who found a pen one day, a beautiful Cartier that her father so delicately kept in soft cotton in a drawer. It was mesmerising and she tried writing with it on that day and has since been writing about Mauritius (her motherland), whether Mauritius is happy or otherwise.[2] I will similarly always write about Africa and *AITWs* because not only *tales* are told after midnight in Africa, it would appear. Politics *in* Africa would seem to have such an after-midnight characteristic or appeal that even *AITWs* just cannot let midnightism go. I would venture to suspect that this is really what distinguishes African *politickerization* from the authentically African politics (as to more of which, see Fossungu, 2013c: chapter 3) that the former has largely displaced, if not completely killed. Midnight Politics or midnightism (for short) can be extremely hard to define since it is always carried out while some of us are having a good deep sleep: either because of the day's heavy rat-race chores in Canadian factories or induced into by what we all know we love to consume. In the final analysis then, is it factory stress or alcohol that would be responsible for our deep heavily-snoring sleep during midnightism's operation? Both are, for sure?

Whatever it is, I think midnightism's definitional problem "presented us with a serious challenge, but also, in our view, an irresistible opportunity" (O'Neil and Rogowski, 2013a: ix). One of such irresistible opportunities would make it possible for

---

[2] See http://www.langaa-rpcig.net/The-Sounds-of-Silence-Mauritian.html

you to be able to get a *sneak-preview* of midnightism. It comes from '*Get a Good Laugh Out of This My Fellow Brothers and Sisters*', courtesy of Baiye N. Orock who sent it to the CGAM Forum on September 22, 2008. "Whether Democrat or Republican," Orock indicated, "I think you'll get a kick out of this!" And here is what he says must set us kicking out of the midnight darkness:

A little boy goes to his dad and asks, 'What is [Midnight] Politics?' Dad says, 'Well son, let me try to explain it this way: 'I am the head of the family, so call me The President. Your mother is the administrator of the money, so we call her the Government. We are here to take care of your needs, so we will call you the People. The nanny, we will consider her the Working Class. And your baby brother, we will call him the Future. Now think about that and see if it makes sense.' So the little boy goes off to bed thinking about what Dad has said.

Later that night, he hears his baby brother crying, so he gets up to check on him. He finds that the baby has severely soiled his diaper. So the little boy goes to his parents' room and finds his mother asleep. Not wanting to wake her, he goes to the nanny's room. Finding the door locked, he peeks in the keyhole and sees his father in bed with the nanny. He gives up and goes back to bed. The next morning, the little boy says to his father, 'Dad, I think I understand the concept of politics now.' The father says, 'Good, son, tell me in your own words what you think politics is all about.' The little boy replies, 'The President is screwing the Working Class while the Government is sound asleep. The People are being ignored and the Future is in deep shit.' Have a wonderful day fellows [paragraphing is altered].

Tree-Topperism: You get a good grasp of *tree-topperism* from an interesting CGAM Table Story. Magnus Ajong supposedly and repeatedly sent out some table-communication several times with no one else's title except the two doctors therein. This one particular instance being discussed came in on December 13, 2011. Refusing to ever refuse looking the truth straight in the face (unlike the politickerizers), Peter Ateh-Afac Fossungu on December 13, 2011 wrote to Magnus Ajong as follows: "Dr. Ajong, I don't know exactly what you're up to since you began sending out this list long ago; but let me remind you that you and Dr. Ntemngwa are not the only two persons that deserve the Dr. title on this list. There may be more that I am unaware of but you, Dr. Ajong, cannot in any way rightly claim ignorance of the fact that there is Dr. Ndonkeu and Dr. Fossungu." According to Fidelis Folefac (who was discussing 'The Future of Goodwill' on January 1, 2012), "This is straight talk which should constitute a framework for the continuous improvement of Goodwill." That is exactly right that this is exactly the kind of straight talk we need. Henceforth, call it *fossungupalogy*, if you will.

But we do not just need to talk about its need but actually practise it. Yes, I will tell you that even in my after-midnight sleep because straight-talking never ever sleeps in me. With this particular fossungupalogy to Magnus Ajong hard on the table then, the whole truth (and nothing but the truth) suddenly had to come down from the *tree-top* where it had been comfortably hiding: since my late father would always fondly tell us that no tree-top can still exist with the trunk already cut to irredeemable pieces. That is the trunk-cutting power of four-eyesism, alias fossungupalogy. The late-father-tale thing is just my usual funny-serious way of saying true things, because two days later, precisely on December 15, 2011 Fidelis Folefac then wrote:

In this email, I will like to offer an apology and secondly provide an explanation as to the occurrence highlighted by the President Emeritus.

Apology

My sincere apology to Dr. Fossungu, Dr. Tita and any other Dr. in the house whom I have failed to adequately address. I take the blame and will ask all of you to kindly find a place in your hearts to let it go. My second wave of apology goes to Dr. Ajong whom I have placed in a 'difficult' situation because the subcommittee list was prepared by me (Fidelis Folifac) and sent to the communication and propaganda subcommittee for circulation. Dr. Ajong, I had no intention to let you go through this.

Explanation

The explanation is no justification to my mistake but simply to put things in context. For some reason, the two gentlemen I failed to address as Dr. are people I address as President Emeritus (Dr. Fossungu) and simply President or Number 1 (Dr. Tita) in our day-to-day conversation. They can confirm this. I am sure this influenced me (negatively) in omitting their well-deserved academic titles. And for [some] reason, I do address Magnus and Michel as 'Dr.' in our day-to-day conversations, I can't explain well.

For records, and as Dr. Tita can testify, Dr. Ajong drew my attention to a similar situation a few days [ago], requesting that either his 'Dr.' prefix is dropped or added for Wally. Action was taken immediately by adding rather than deleting the prefix. As a person, I respect all efforts and will never play down on such things.

Once again, I am sorry for this mistake and hope Dr. Fossungu, Dr. Tita and any other Dr. in the house will throw this mistake over the window. Dr. Ajong, please sorry for putting you in this.

Biggytitlemania

Biggytitlemania means big titles and low performance. To begin to correctly appreciate the significance of the title-question of the second part of this part's title, just think of the way we generally tend to denigrate our traditional African titles and other dignitaries! At this point, you will not afford to disagree with Boh (2013) and Fossungu (2013b) that colonialism is yet to be over in Africa. Africans are kind of cut off from their cultural roots, making progress difficult. That China got to where it is today (and which also justifies the Marxist approach to doing state business[3]), could also be explained through the fact that Mao skilfully localized Marxism and contextualized it in terms of China's tradition. After Mao and his colleagues dressed it up, the communist ideology bore a great resemblance to the ideal Confucian *Datong* society. In Confucian thought, *Datong* is harmony and unity in human society and harmonious relations between heaven, humans, and earth (Wang, 2012: 86). It is well known then that Chinese communism has never been a copycat of (conquered) Russian communism.[4] This may well explain why the latter

---

[3] Therefore, Lindorff (2013) theorizes, it is 'about time American idiocy and paranoia over Marxism got called out'. Marxism or *socialism* (as Mentan (2012) would prefer) is taken in the sense of a community "in which 'the free self-development of each would be the condition of the free self-development of all'. This is an idea to guide us, not a condition we could ever entirely achieve" (Eagleton, 2011). Marxism is central in this book because of two reasons (amongst others), one practical and the other theoretical. Quite apart from the African *socialism*-way of life, the first relates to the practical lesson learnt from the localized practice of Marxism in China, but there is also the theoretical appeal. Apart from its emancipatory project, which Mao did not fail to cleverly emphasize and use (see Wang, 2012: 84-89), the range of political analysis Marxism offers cuts across all the aspects of globalization. It does so through its critically examining how capitalism operates at social, economic and political levels and thereby affects and is affected by the role of the state, international relations, spatial relations and culture (Maguire, 2010: 138; Friedman, 2012; Bojicic-Dzelilovic, 2011; Schwarzmantel, 2012).

[4] Hamid Dabashi quotes Peter Beinart (who is senior political writer for *The Daily Beast*, associate professor of journalism and political science at City University of New York, etc.) as boastfully stating: "In 1989, Americans gloated as the Soviet Union, our former rival for Middle Eastern

'ignominiously fell' at the time the former was rising like never before, leading to headlines, such as: "a rising China counters US clout in Africa" (Edoho, 2011: 104). This Chinese case would give a lot of credence to Tatah Mentan's strong argument on democracy that opens this book and should obviously be read here again, because I agree with him that the question of externally imposed or market-driven multi-party or dual-party or non-party is a matter of modality and should clearly not occupy the centre stage in Africa.

I do not end my de-politickerization with just the *un-African* tyrants. I have also largely castigated us (*AITWs*), who have the privilege of being able to profit from two or more cultures and, therefore, to become better and exemplary citizens (of both host and home countries). But we rather prefer to stick to our deplorable attitudes, even becoming worse than when we had arrived in the host country (see Fossungu, 2013a). The present book picks up and continues from where *Africans in Canada* left off. Specifically using the CGAM's constitutional founding and objectives all through, this book shows that a lot of positive African communal values are not only maintained and fostered but also mixed with *modern* governance systems. This is a well-grounded structure through which the concerned *AITWs* were supposed to hone the leadership and other skills necessary for advancing the community, devoid of *biggytitlemania*. Chapters 3

---

supremacy, retreated ignominiously from the region. When Saddam Hussein tried to challenge us from within, we thrashed him in the Gulf War. Throughout the 1990s, we sent our economists, law professors and investment bankers to try to teach the Arabs globalization, which back then meant copying us. In a thousand ways, sometimes gently, sometimes brutally, we sent the message: We make the rules; you play by them" (Dabashi, 2012: 141). Commenting on this, Dabashi says 'they' never made the rules and thus 'others' did not play by them; adding that that has been a self-perpetuating, triumphalist, delusion, before concluding that it is more than a delusion which a Palestinian child with a stone in his hand could shatter at any time (*ibid*).

and 4 particularly thus question the actual practice and blending of the values and democratic administration of the community. A failing mark is accorded because of the failure to make hard choices, with high-sounding titles instead being pushed to the foreground, especially in the game with the banker.

Playing Hard Ball with Your Banker?

Unless the context makes it otherwise, therefore, I would avoid titles in this book for a number of other compelling *AITWsian* reasons. First, being one of the concerned *AITWs*, I will lead you into my loaded expibasketism and acquaint you with my very first '*shocking*' discovery or learning in Edmonton's University of Alberta. It is that my professors were always not at ease when I – who just could not help it then – always kept addressing them (for instance) as 'Professor Richard Bauman' or 'Professor Dr Bruce Elman' rather than just 'Richard' (the graduate coordinator) or 'Bruce' (my thesis supervisor). Most *AITWs* would agree with me here that, coming from an environment and culture where the real or *Datong* culture counts for zero and a great fuss is made about titles (especially academic and administrative ones), it was just not easy for me to make the switch. But I eventually got it right, right down my throat without the brutal globalization brushes; which brings us back to the brutal world of international politics.

My other key argument is that it is incumbent on the various global players to look ahead (like China has very interestingly done and cautiously devise cushions to appropriately absorb the inevitable challenges and shocks. What I am saying here, using China's current 'Development Partner' posture in Africa (Edoho, 2011: 105-107), is that "[o]ur collective efforts should be focused on asking how Africa can derive maximum benefits from China's engagement in the region. Ultimately, Africa is the one to define the terms of its relationship with, and what it needs from, China. China cannot do this for Africa" (Edoho, 2011: 102). Quite apart from President Barack Obama's practical thesis that "It's pretty hard to have a tough negotiation when the Chinese are our bankers" (Drezner, 2009: 15[5]) and, consequently that you just have to try to "be *nice* to the countries that lend you money" (Drezner, 2009: 8[6]), Edoho's suggestion to Africa is now very hard (if not impossible) to materialize: viewing particularly the manner these African states have generally not done their homework, nor relevantly heed to timely relevant advice that chapter 6 of this book (in particular) is loaded with. Thus, to date, they largely remain what Ferguson (2006) has called "Pseudo-" Nation-States; and this largely because of bellytics and biggytitlemania. This title issue is so rampant 'On the Other Side of Fifty and Rays of Lamentation'[7] that some Africans would even be blindly contented that they be discussed as youngsters even at their golden anniversary!

Discussing You at 16 as You at 50?

I must not be taken as here preaching that having your well-earned titles attached to your name is not a useful exercise. I am simply noting that sometimes those titles (especially when we push them too much to the foreground) make some of the people we are dealing with very uncomfortable. This then often inhibits fruitful reciprocal interactions and exchanges on African unity, for instance. My advice, in other words, is: Just let the accomplishments that those titles are evidencing better speak of the titles: through your exemplary putting of the achievements to the service of humanity. Imagine for a

---

[5] Quoting from David M. Dickson, "China's Economic 'Bargaining Chip'" *Washington Times* July 27, 2008.

[6] Quoting from James Fallows, "Be Nice to the Countries That Lend You Money" *Atlantic* December 2008, p. 65.

[7] See http://www.langaa-rpcig.net/On-the-Other-Side-of-Fifty-and.html.

moment the great (although, unfortunately transitory) mentality transformations that took place in Burkina Faso with Sankara at the helm. Tell me what part you think was played in catapulting those changes by the fact that 'a whole President Captain Sankara' was also riding a bicycle or self-driving a Renault 4 in the streets of 'Waga' like any ordinary Burkinabe or African. Or in South African reconciliation, peace and progress by the fact that Nelson Mandela who had been wronged that much could forgive and embrace his wrongdoers. By the way, I want those *AITWs* that know the so many people (where they now are) that sit in the back seat of their own cars with someone else driving them all over the place, to come to the front and tell us.

Closely linked to the foregoing factors for eschewing biggytitlemania is also the fact that, at its inception only two of the thirteen CGAM members were doctors, although you could have hardly known that, being a visitor to or newcomer in the CGAM Assembly. But the CGAM has since been positively evolving in many domains, a fact that is rightly and easily captured in its second president's "Giant Strides in the Community."[8] CGAMers have been quickly climbing higher

---

[8] In the president's popular *'Giant Strides in the Community'* communication of April 17, 2006, he wrote:

> Fellow Goodwillers: I am pleased to announce some giant strides being made by fellow Goodwillers who are making their mark in their various organizations. Three members of the community have recently been promoted to various positions, all of which entail greater responsibilities (and more bucks too!!!):
>
> 1. One of our out-of-town members, Dr James Tambong of Gatineau, has been appointed to the position of Research Scientist (bacterial taxonomist) at Agriculture and AfriFood Canada. He beat out three other candidates for the coveted position. He is expected to assume his new position in July.

and higher in the rungs of their host/new society, so much so that you would be clearly and ably unable to correctly count all the doctors in the CGAM today.[9] It is nevertheless true to say that most of us were not doctors when most of the events being examined in this book took place. Basically, I do not think that I would consider you as doing any justice to me by discussing the things I did as a high school student (for example) as if I did them while already being a university

---

    2.   Hans Najeme has been appointed to the position of Assistant Branch Manager at the Royal Bank branch in Lachine. He is expected to assume his new position immediately, following a brief period of training.

    3.   Denis Ako-Arrey has been appointed to the position of Personal Financial Services Rep. at the Royal Bank branch in Place Vertu. He assumes his new position immediately, following a brief period of training. To all the above, I would like to extend my hearty congratulations on behalf of all Goodwillers.

Are you moving up in your organization? Keep us informed so that we can all share the good news.

On another note, Pius Etube is one of the happiest Goodwillers today. His prayers were answered last week with the arrival of his wife and three children from Cameroon. On behalf of all Goodwillers, I would like to extend a warm welcome to them all. To Pius, my advice is... take it easy until madam fully recovers from her jet lag. My warm welcome also goes to Ngwa Fru Felexce who just returned from Cameroon after a one-month stay to take care of some family business.

[9] I can quickly give you a list of those CGAMers who have graduated into this academic class, as announced on the association's forum: Walter Tita Ndonkeu (October 23, 2008), Michel Ntemgwa (December 22, 2008), Eugene Lekeawung Asahchop (December 12, 2012), Macalister Usongo (March 13, 2013), Fidelis Folefac (March 27, 2013).

graduate.[10] Let those who think otherwise here raise their hands. I can see no hands. Is it that I am now blind, or is it instead the hands that are invisible? Could our titles (that are not even parts of our bodies) not then emulate our hands? That is, why don't we just let our titles shine from under?

The issue of titles has been discussed at length but I have already said that these titles are not very important if they are not reflected in what they evidence. The point I was merely making on posing the fossungupalogistic question (to Ajong) relates well to my using everyone's title (big sounding or not), if I decide to put in these titles. I am avoiding that too here as much as I can because (in trying to put in everyone's title), I might put in a 'Mr.' where it is actually a 'Miss/Mrs'. This fatal mistake is a real possibility in view of our African *nosexonomy* (that is, officially gender-neutral names). The title discussion here was essential though to acquaint you with tree-top politics, another name for midnightism, which will soon be fast piloting the midnight-train to visionlessness and constitutional adhocism. We often confuse *politickerization* and politics, the latter which some experts find to be a *necessity*. But I am trusting that this misperception would no longer be the case after you have gone through all the chapters of this book because my (true) friends, of course, would clearly know that I am better than a politickerizer. Otherwise, you would not be reading this book that many of the said politickerizers would

---

[10] Which could also justify my also quickly giving you a list of those who were already in the doctor class when they got into the CGAM, with their CGAM admission dates in brackets: James Tambong (July 2003), Peter Ateh-Afac Fossungu (July 2003), Aloysius Ibeagha (July 2005), Eveline Awemu Ibeagha (July 2005), Magnus Ajong (July 2007), Levis Cheussom (October 2007). This particular list cannot be exhaustive since I have since 2010 not been very regular (physically present) to sessions as I have often been away from Montreal. Thus, many more doctors must surely have joined the CGAM that I am not personally aware of.

doubtlessly describe as 'outrageous'. But who cares if the truth hurts them? And wouldn't African disunity and consequent misery normally be hurting authentic and savvy Africans?

Chapter 2

Uniting The Un-United Parts Of Africa: Is The *Grand Frère* Of Theories From Cameroon From One To Many Or From Many To One?

Some people are born to be dreamers; others are there to convert these dreams into reality. Yet others dream and [they] themselves try to realize the dreams. I truly don't yet know where some of us belong. Only history can tell. But all I now know for certain is that I have a dream for Africa's children. And that what is important for them in particular would be the realization of the dream, not who dreamt or realized it [Fossungu, 1998b].

People often wonder to me how we can unite Africans when there is no unity within the various African communities. For this thesis, they cite easily the fact that a Burkinabe in Aménagement MYR Inc. (hereinafter MYR), for instance, would extend a hand of help to a non-Burkinabe African, but not to another Burkinabe. My response to them is usually: "Does your thesis itself not make nonsense of your thesis?" They would then ask how and I explain that "African unity depends not on Burkinabe unity but on African unity. Does Cameroon unity mean that every Bangwa person would be loved by all Bangwa people?" We just need to be careful about some of these well-packaged 'justificatory' concepts that are mere tools of imperialism, especially as could be seen in the pre-Arab Spring employment of the so-called Islam-as-being-incompatible with democracy narrative to justify the persistence and prevalence of authoritarianism in the Arab world – what Edward Said (2001) regards as the direct results of "The Clash of Ignorance". But when the young Arab people rise against these dictators, the same advocates of 'democracy' move in to help crush the uprisings that are seeking to establish democracy. From time to time I will be talking a little bit more on the nonsense regarding this issue (especially as concerns the Arab world, part of which is African). But how could the experts explain the comportment alluded to in their 'un-united parts' thesis? I will assist you to find that out through studying two main topics: (1) the *grands coupeurs* of MYR: from Canada to little Burundi/Rwanda?, and (2) the *grand frère* theory from Cameroon to Africa.

The *Grands Coupeurs* of MYR: From Canada to Small Rwanda-Burundi?

On my first arrival in MYR in May 2010, the one phrase that quickly caught my attention was *"grands coupeurs"*. By this phrase, the environment was designating those *débroussailleurs* (tree cutters or what Cameroonians popularly call *Bush-Fallers*) that have so many hectares of cut patches or *térrains* to their names every two-week pay period. It did not take up to a month for me to challenge and redefine a *grand coupeur*, a new categorization that clearly excluded many of the so-called *grands coupeurs*. A *grand coupeur*, I told them, is someone who not only cuts a lot of patches, but also aids others (especially the *nouveaux* or newcomers) to advance in the field or domain. In short a *grand coupeur* facilitates the creation or formation of other/new *grands coupeurs*. Therefore, I concluded, on top of the very short list of persons worthy of the description is a Burkinabe called Salihou Dabre.

When you are new to any *métier*, there are basic things that you do not initially know until someone shows you. I remember working between Cameroonians. One day my cutter could not start no matter how many attempts I made. None of my two Bamileke neighbours would even want to stop for a second and see what was wrong. One of them that I approached categorically declared, without at all touching the machine, that "*le carburateur est noyé. Il faut l'amener au camp*" (Take it to the camp for reparation because the carburettor is flooded). I took the machine out of the patch and spent several hours on the road before a *contremaître* passed by. He heard of the starting problem, took out a pair of pliers from his toolbox and pulled out the choke button behind the engine that I must have mistakenly and unknowingly pressed in. On one attempt, I heard my saw running. I thanked him and returned to my patch to complete the few hours of the day still remaining. *Sans commentaire*!

A week or so later I was working between another Cameroonian and a Burkinabe. The Burkinabe (Salihou Dabre) must have observed me for a while when he beckoned for me to come along with my machine. He took about thirty minutes plus to carry out some maintenance on the apparatus, showing me at the same time what he was doing and why. When I started the cutter after the Salihou touch, it was like someone else's thing, not mine that I had just been using. It was quite clear that water had been entering into the fuel tank and the fuel filter was jammed with lots of it, and thus not functioning properly. The air filter too was overwhelmed by dirt, etc. My Cameroonian neighbours would never stop to do a thing like the Burkinabe did; preferring instead to come around from time to time just to sucker me. One of them (Bami-X) even told the *contremaître* that he had cut 0.3 hectare of my patch and got paid for it. Another called Bami-Y played *mercenary* and got a hundred dollars with no real effort. A mercenary, in the language of *bush-fallers*, is someone that *aids* you on an agreed sum to get you out of the patch so that you do not return there the next day or so, when everyone else has left the zone. This guy clearly knew I was still going to finish my patch on that day, with or without his help. But he played his pranks on a *nouveau* all the same.

The 'go for back for before' business or the Eko-Roosevelt Dance (of the feminists and homosexuals) is outside the scope of this book; but some Africans also attempt to confuse me (like the feminists and homosexuals) with their transforming Canada into Little Burundi/Rwanda. I can just tell you here that the critiques against the feminists (see Randall, 2010: 114-135; Brooks, 1996: 325-356; and Ferguson, 2010) also apply to these groups of Africans. Concretely, I will concisely demonstrate how their so-called 'unity' works against African unity, using the left-in-forest meeting, which also questions whether we have moved from English-French to Kirundi as official language(s) of Canada. The *grands coupeurs* section would employ the Congo-Issa Story as a case of learning the hard way being the best way of learning, including the Diallo Brothers and the Sense of Entitlement.

Language and Communication Politics: The Left-in-Forest Nightly Meeting

I must point out right away that language has always been a very sensitive issue to politics; especially in communities like Canada that have with more than one language group (for more detailed discussion, see Fossungu, 2013b: chapter 4). It is also important to note that the January 2006 CGAM Assembly is a milestone in CGAM history for a host of reasons, one of which relates to language politics. Until that date, English and French were "the official languages of Goodwill [with deliberations being]... done in the language of the majority of members" (Article 2). That first Assembly of 2006 four-eyesismatically changed the language dynamics. A proposal was tabled by then executive bureau (the Paulayahist administration) and received by the House: that English be made the only language of the association.[11] The move to

---

[11] As the CGAM 2nd president even-handedly explained, English should be maintained as the main language of the association because it is an "Anglophone Association". A lot of members were just talking for the sake of talking; not grasping what they were making noises about. Totally giving more bullets to the change was Peter Mungwa's four-eyesism on the last

change was somewhat successful, but not without a valiant fight from those who saw it as discrimination that was not good for what they called 'national unity'. That particular CGAM General Assembly's debates were emotional and long. But Fossungu would already have told you in 2013 that national unity to the English-speaking of Cameroon seems to be equated with 'pleasing the French-speaking' 2/15 majority.[12] I would not want to over immerse you into that

---

portion of Article 2; clearly pointing out that it was not smart for the association to maintain French and English as its official languages as found in said Article. He went on to explain that the future might bring more French members to the association and consequently the adoption (by majority vote) of French as the main language of deliberations. He therefore supported the president's view that the main language of deliberations of Goodwill be English. Many who had been letting their emotions take the better part of them could then see what (dangers?) they had not been visualizing because of what some critics have condemned as the fear of politics. The then Secretary General (Aloysius Ibeagha) suggested a modification to the modification to the effect that, while English be maintained as the official language of the association, French speaking members be free to voice their opinions in French as the case may be. The Assembly then voted 23 to 4 to make English the official language of the association, with the Ibeagha-addition. I will here leave it to your imagination to figure out what the entire language (and even membership) situation would have been like, with a 'reversed' CGAM here, while I continue with circumscribing other aspects of the language question to you, notably its contribution to African unity.

[12] "Imagine being in a gathering of, say, fifteen – thirteen Anglophones and two Francophones – and finding almost all thirteen talking almost exclusively in 'bad' French. You then ask them why they cannot talk in the English language they are more comfortable in or with, and here is the response: "We want the majority to understand what is being said." You can see then that they are not here, as elsewhere, looking at 13/15 as the majority but themselves as Anglophones, the minority in Cameroon that can never count in any circumstance in the country; not even with a half Francophone in the midst of 800,000 of them. And do not think the attitude is limited only to being inside Cameroon because I have had to deal with this same Cameroon-Anglophone frame of mind even while studying/living in Montreal, Canada. Who is ever going to give you your language rights if you cannot stand tall and defend or impose them in glaring situations like these?" [Fossungu, 2013b : 24-25]

funny majority here where I rather need to talk mostly about (1) the regular majority's language in MYR and (2) the irregular minority language in Canada.

From English-French to Kirundi?

The language of Burundians/Rwandans is called Kirundi, and seems to have become the sole language spoken in the MYR camp. That is not the huge problem since they constitute the majority of the workers there. I do myself try, as usual, to grasp some basics of the language because, like Momany's siblings of the household, 'I don't want to be sold in my own presence' (see Fossungu, 2013a: 30-31). The real gigantic problem I do find with the attitude of these Burundians/Rwandans is its noted inhibition to African unity. I used to envy African countries with a single national language like Congo and Zaire (Lingala), Burundi and Rwanda (Kirundi), Kenya, Tanzania, (Swahili), etc. But after my experience with the Kirundi speakers in the MYR camp especially, I think I would rather have the "Cameroon Gift" of over three hundred local languages, with none overshadowing the others.

I often ask myself a lot of questions when interacting with some of these Africans. Because you find your sense of correctness often abused to an extent that you begin to wonder if associating with some of these people is worth the pains. As an African-loving African, you get easily alienated by Zairians and Burundians/Rwandans. You are sitting there with them and are completely ignored as they keep on talking only in their language that you do not understand. Worse still, on several occasions I have heard these same guys from Burundi/Rwanda aggressively telling West Africans who happen to be conversing in Bambara that these West Africans should speak in French (so that they too can know what the others are talking about)! Seeing the fleck in another's eyes with the colossal log in your eyes does not even begin to accurately describe it. It is simply ridiculous and I am sure I would have totally kept away from these blinkered Burundians/Rwandans but for the fact that I needed you to read what I have discovered being with them, as graphically concretized by the left-in-forest night show – I for once in my life was a midnighter! Thank you Burundi!

The Left-in-the-Forest Nightly Meeting: There are several workers that have often been abandoned in the forest. Most of the time it has been because they do not come out of their patches on time, combined with the fact that some *contremaîtres* are so careless and do not take the time to cross-check the list that is usually created in the bus each day. This was particularly the case in September 2014 in regard of a Burundian/Rwandan called Come (the Bakossi in Cameroon would quickly alter the C to K and claim him as one of theirs). Come was lucky to have had his cell phone with him and also that it was in Senneterre (a town in northern Quebec) where it was possible to call 911. The Senneterre Police came to the restaurant (Resto Centre-Ville on 630, 10e Avenue) where we used to eat and informed the *contremaître* concerned, who then made the two-hour drive into the forest for him. In 2012 one Burkinabe worker called Nazare actually spent the entire night in the forest, being met there only the following morning. He did not come out on time and had also not written his name on the list and, worse still, he (like Come too) was not sharing the *roulotte* or dormitory with anyone else. It was hard for anyone then to have realized that he had not returned to camp.

On August 29, 2014 it was a whole different kind of being left in the forest. 2014 in MYR has had its own uniqueness with vehicle breakdowns and the consequent late returns to camp. And it makes some of these Africans' day that a cutter-blade that costs just twenty-five dollars is handed over to each of them when they reached the camp after such unwarranted incidents! The bus broke down on 29 August and no one came for the four of us that were in a different area from the others. One hour after the normal time that the pick-up truck was to have picked us up, I told the other three

Burundians/Rwandans (including Come!) that we had better be walking to somewhere rather than just sitting there and waiting. That is what I call self-help or the 'do something about it' spirit. It was not easy for them to see the utility of what I was proposing, but one of them later sided with me and the other two (Come included) reluctantly followed us, still complaining all along as to where the fruitless trekking was to take us: considering that it is a two-hour bus drive from the camp.

We had trudged for about twenty kilometres, it would seem, when we noticed fire at some distance ahead. We arrived there to join five other workers who narrated the events to us. Following the problems with the bus, every worker had scrambled for a hand-on position on the only operational pick-up truck (the other had broken down in the forest a few days before and was still immobilized there). What a way to travel about two hundred kilometres! The five workers we (the completely forgotten four) joined had out rightly refused making the journey in that gruesome manner and position and were thus there waiting for Bruno Lavoie to return to pick them up. And you would not want to believe that Bruno came back at about 9 PM with just the pick-up since he knew only of the five persons who had refused to hang-on! What would have been our lot then had we stayed in our area waiting to be picked up? Spend the entire night in the forest, of course.

Surprised to find nine instead of five persons, Bruno asked us to hop on, openly lying that another pick-up was following him and would take those in the baggage compartment when we meet it. You can easily divine that only people who care much about their dignity and security would act as the five people that the Forgotten-Four stumbled on: Alexis, Alphonse, Celestin Niyo, Celestin Singa, and Michel Ndikumana. Prompted by me, the nine of us had made it clear (even before Bruno's arrival) that no one was leaving without everyone at the same time and in the cabin of the pick-up truck(s). Bruno started driving away slowly but realized that none of the nine gave up the stance. He stopped the engine and began communicating with his white colleagues in the camp who work as *'autonomes'* with their private vehicles. Two of them came along two hours later with two other vehicles. In the meantime, the eight Burundians/Rwandans had been in constant conversation in their language. At the end they told me how I had been chosen as one of the two people (Come being the other) to take our case to Mario, the owner of MYR, with Come trying to then recap their discussion. I was very blank when I told them that there was no need for any summary because I should have been part of the conversation from the start. "As I was not, I will not now enter into it." The whole thing thus fell apart because none of the other seven guys was willing to join Come as representatives or *porte-paroles*. So, where is African unity going to get to with people like these? Are the two official languages of Canada not English and French? Or did I hear someone saying I should rather be saying 'English and Amerench'? I am talking about the world of North American language *copy-mixing*.

Amerench and the French Speakers' Agony in Quebec

I was then sitting among the Burundians/Rwandans in the Nightly Forest Meeting turning in my mind the enormous agony of the French speaker in Quebec and the havoc that not understanding one another can unnecessarily cause. I had perceptibly mistaken Quebecers for great four-eyesismatic people, just like oversimplification does in the Middle East. Byman regards the Middle East problem as being tied to oversimplification, the result of the dichotomy between reality and perception. He argues that to understand the region, it is not just enough to know the history; recognizing how the history is perceived is also vital (Byman, 2012: viii). For example, while the religious fervour of Islam has died down since the 1979 Islamic revolution in Iran, Byman explains, elsewhere in the Middle East, political Islam has grown in importance. He pins this development to the discrediting of Arab nationalism after the Arab states' abysmal performance in the 1967 war with Israel, and years of repression and economic dysfunction which steadily sucked the life out of the once-vibrant and –dominant Arab nationalist movement. Political Islam, as Daniel Byman sees it, filled this void, with Islamists of various hues playing an important political role today in Egypt, Iran, Iraq, Kuwait, Lebanon, Qatar, Saudi Arabia, Tunisia, and Yemen; such Islamism being far from monolithic, either in doctrine or in political practice (Byman, 2012: ix). Is such French as exists in North America not also far from being French, as it pertains either in Europe or in Africa?

Amerenching Four-Eyesism: On my arrival here in 1995 I had some documents to establish, like SIN (social insurance number), medical or health card, etc. In short, I made trips to several offices. Do I still need to mention that, coming from Cameroon where you have to first serve the civil servants in order to be grudgingly served by them, I was impressed by the quality of public service in my new environment? Every time I was very exquisitely served, I said *Merci beaucoup*! (Thank you very much!). Every time the response was *Bienvenu*! Wow! How come these people are that smart to all know that I have just arrived in Canada! I cannot count how many times I was in front of the mirror whenever I got back home. Just to see if there was anything, anything at all, *sur mon visage* that was giving me away so easily. At the airport the *Bienvenu au Canada* was only normal. The plane that had just brought me in was still there and I was myself at the port of entry. But how do all these people, weeks after my landing at Mirabel International Airport, still know that I have just arrived in Canada? I was so doubly impressed until the surprising discovery that their *bienvenu* assumes a different Americanized French (*Amerench*) connotation than the one I know from my study of the French's French. Briefly, it is a whole Middle-East tragedy for a

French French-speaker arriving in Quebec to comprehend what is actually going on.

The Innocent and Mistaken 'Cat-Using Gay' and Middle-Eastern War Machines: It was ten years later, precisely in September 2005, that an employment agency (called Thomson Tremblay Inc.) assigned me to work at a can recycling industry somewhere on the Montreal-Ottawa road (Highway 40). This white guy walked up to me and, after *Salut!*, added: *"Tu as un char."* (Remember, it is spoken, not written as here.) I don't know whether it was a question or what. But I am like 'What a minute!' Where is he driving to? Short, I was stunned that this guy does not even know where I live and yet can be so confidently telling me that I have a cat? I retorted: *"Non. Je n'aime pas les animaux dans la maison."* (I don't like living with animals). Perhaps it is my French that is low-levelled, I don't quite know, knowing though that we do not often pronounce the last letter in the language. But the guy kept insisting that I have *un char*. I quickly walked away, thinking to myself that the guy must be a gay who is trying to try something funny. I have witnessed these white people several times (especially at day-cares) using animals that they call pets to log and lock the other in. So, in my mind I was telling the 'cat-using gay': "Nice try, but not good enough and with the wrong person. Adieu!" The guy apparently could just not believe my rudeness because, as I have come to realize (too late for him), he had been out, perhaps, to simply request for a ride after work to any Metro Station on my route. He was talking of my having a car while I understood him as saying I have a cat! Where the hell did Quebecers get their *char* for vehicle/car from? Certainly not from the French that I know, which would refer to it as *une voiture, un auto, un véhicule*. Or, should I have properly divined that this guy was talking battlefield matters (*char* in French French) with me in the can-recycling factory? What the hell would I be doing with a war-machine in there? Was I really in Canada or in the Middle East?

As the meticulous study of the Middle East by some of the experts has shown, a portion of the Islamist community, small but deadly, supports a radical religious interpretation and the use of violence. Their actions, according to Wiltorowicz and Kaltenthaler (2012: 109), have long puzzled scholars and the public alike who just cannot understand: "Why do Islamist radicals engage in high-cost/risk activism that exposes them to arrest, repression, and even death?... Why not free-ride off the efforts of others rather than jeopardize personal self-interest?" The matter could be simple indeed, as I see it. Isn't Naomi Chaza of Hebrew University of Jerusalem well known for saying "Religion is about having faith because we doubt"? In other words, shouldn't those of us imbued with and/or brainwashed by selfish capitalism (see Serwer and Sloan, 2008; Lakoff, 2012; Eagleton, 2011) wonder why individuals would kill themselves or otherwise engage in extreme activity that, from rational-choice theory's self-interest point of view (see Hindmore, 2010), seems so irrational? Could this be one of those many things that an Indonesian intellectual is talking about, by condemning some Western 'democratic' freedoms for being inconsistent with Muslim principles?

The debate about democracy and democratisation in Muslim societies, though of older vintage, Hamid Ansari writes, has acquired an edge in recent years. One line of argument, Ansari carries on, is typified by Francis Fukuyama and his judgement that 'there does seem to be something about Islam, or at least the fundamentalist versions of Islam that have been dominant in recent years, that makes Muslim societies particularly resistant to modernity', with democracy being an important ingredient of the latter (Ansari, 2007: 7). The other argument, equally strident (according to Ansari), is articulated – amongst others – by the Indonesian Islamist intellectual Mohammad Shiddiq Al-Jawi. This intellectual posits that the 'Muslim community will evaluate democracy from the perspective of the Islamic faith' and will find that 'democratic freedoms are in sharp conflict with the freedoms found in Islam'. The convergence in rejection, in Ansari's estimation, is noteworthy because neither side makes allowance for revisiting the texts for evolving perceptions or for varied patterns of behaviour amongst Muslims as groups in societies living in space and time in different lands (Ansari, 2007: 7).

Who should rightly be the judge of what is incompatible with what here? Two or so answers are given here, first by a well-known Cameroonian human rights writer called Tatah Mentan and then by Wiltorowicz and Kalterthaler who brought up the puzzle. Mentan (2013b) sees democracy as the faith in the process of experience being more important than any special result attained (see the quotation opening this book). Appleby (2010) supports it too when he indicates that "Many Americans and Europeans are taken aback, to say the least, by our suggestion that collaborating with religious groups on matters of shared concern is a necessary element of advancing democratisation and prosperity in many parts of the world." Quintan Wiltorowicz and Karl Kalterthaler would also answer by contending that religious conviction matters for many radicals and makes their activities rational by their own lights: they take the ideas seriously and believe their sacrifices will advance their individual salvation as well as group agendas (Byman, 2012: ix). Wouldn't Japanese 'Kamikaze' wholly agree with them here?

While the radical agenda is behind much of the terrorism in the Middle East and can shape the politics of the countries in question, Raymond Baker and others have contended that Islamists have effectively adapted to modernity and the globalized world, reinventing their faith even as they adhere to its core principles (see Baker, 2012; Embong, 2007; Göymen, 2007). Baker specifically points out that it is the Islamic mainstream that will have the biggest impact shaping the future of Islam and the societies in the Arab world. Indeed, Byman concludes, Baker has contended that allowing the religious mainstream to assert itself more effectively without Western interference is the best way to counter radicalism (Byman, 2012: ix-x) because "in these times of unprecedented material vulnerability, Islam of the Awakening has emerged as a powerful wave of world-historic change that is sweeping through communities of Muslims around the world" (Baker, 2012: 197). So, are the concerns about Islam standing in the way of democracy founded, as presented? Are the claims of French being spoken in Quebec also convincing or confusing?

Amerenching Génévière: Just hear 'original' Quebecers again calling their Ford F150 or Honda CR-V *mon camion* and I am still waiting to see the "camion" that is actually going to completely move my 'prospective' and jonetobarring lover that never was into my *jamai-vu* 101/2 apartment on July 1.[13] Yes, if Généviève had the intention of becoming my next wife or lover, my not understanding Amerench stiffly stood on the way. I am talking about this lady I worked with in Polinex Plastics Inc. (on 2850 Botham, Saint-Laurent). The company was full of Indians and Pakistanis and other English-only speakers from the Caribbean. She must then have felt really good having someone supposedly also speaking Amerench there working the nightshift at the same work-station with her. Of course, we had already exchanged phone numbers at her prompting. One Friday night breaking Saturday (end of our week), as we were working, Généviève said: *"Il faut me caller."* No doubt, I am talking about a very attractive white woman here; one that I was beginning to like getting to know better. But why, I am thinking, does she want me to stand so close to her at work? What kind of lady is she? Is hold-tight part of our work ethics here or what? She wasn't sure I heard her well and

---

[13] *"Jonetobarism* is the love and understanding philosophical terminology that describes the effects and consequences of Joan's New Togetherness Bar; the lady herself also being a generally acclaimed *mami wata*" (Fossungu, 2014: 106, emphasis is original).

repeated, this time with an "O.K?" ending. I then said: "*Je vais voir.*"

Monday night (when our shift usually begins the week) was simply Madness Night. My colleague had simply become another Josephine, Momany's sister, who "(like many of his virgins) might actually have fallen so deeply in love with him at first sight and subsequently became Momany's greatest nightmare when, because of his ignorance of the real facts [resulting here from Amerench], he was not reciprocating her love in like manner" (Fossungu, 2014: 94). "What do you take me for?" Géneviève angrily inquired; further wanting to know if I thought she had nothing else to do than wait endlessly for my calls that have never come since I had her phone number. (Are you wondering here like me why she herself didn't call?) The worst part was that she even specifically asked me to call her (*me caller*) and I proudly did not, even after having agreed to do so. As you can see, Géneviève wanted me to *me caller* while I was thinking of her inviting me to *me coller* like in Compagnie Créole's very danceable *Collé-Collé*; *un morceau qui a belle et bien chauffé à un moment et qui continue à chauffer jusqu'à l'heure*. Where did the French *appeler* disappear to in Quebec?

Many French-speaking Africans (*nouveaux* especially) confuse the MYR white *contremaîtres* and cooks when they keep talking of *mon 'essence'* or '*carburant*' and *donnez-moi le haricot*' instead of *mon 'gas'* and '*donnez-moi le beans*'. That is also why, at first, I myself could hardly comprehend the *contremaître* in MYR who asked: "*Peut-tu chauffer le camion?*" and I am wondering why his pick-up needs *warming up* in plain summer. That was not what the man meant at all. Since in American English that they are directly Frenchifying, a driver drives a car, *un chauffeur donc chauffe* [rather than *conduire*] *la voiture*. So why have a *permis de conduire* rather than a *permis de chauffage*? This question could be extended and asked concerning our troublesome *saucisse* (hot dog). Why didn't Quebecers go straight for *chien chaud* or *chaud chien*? Most probably because of the stupidity of saying 'Give me two *chiens chauds de poulet*? Shouldn't I just leave us Quebecers alone with our *Zoa-Zoa*? After all, didn't the Boers rename their funny Dutch Afrikaans because they were speaking it in (South) Africa? Should Quebecers not also politely rename their confusing French, and instead call it Amerench so that some people don't come here assuming they already know and understand the language spoken in Quebec? Why do most MYR *grands coupeurs* also think that being *grands coupeurs* means that they have the right to dupe newcomers?

The Congo-Issa Story: Learning the Hard Way Is Learning the Best Way?

Most *nouveaux* have to learn some of these things the hard way. Seydou Congo and Issa Ibule are two Burkinabe guys who got to MYR the same 2010 season as I did. We shared the four-bed *roulotte* (container-like dormitory) together with a Burundian called Michel Ndikumana who was also a *nouveau*. Four *nouveaux* – two Central Africans and two West Africans; *match nul*, according to the French-speaking. Wait a minute! Isn't the correct mathematics here supposed to be: One-and-half Central Africans and two-and-half West Africans since "Preponderant evidence portrays Cameroon as properly fitting in both West and Central Africa" (Fossungu, 2013b: 32)?

Be that the case or not, I therefore had the privilege to know these three guys better than those I have mostly known only as patch neighbours or generally in the camp. The Burundian came into MYR through the Quebec Government training door, referred to as *Étudiants*. Could this be the reason for the School Bus in the forest? If so, are the yellow school buses meant for university/college students (*étudiants*)? Ndikumana has some question-responses: "Why all the foolish questions? Why don't you just know that working in the forest itself is a kind of university or college? How many people can successfully complete the forest-work programme?" Sorry Michel then for the query, but it was merely due to the fact that not everyone comes in there as *étudiant*. The remaining three of us were brought along by some *ancients* who were supposedly to provide our training.

The first few days (or even week) were not good at all for the two Burkinabe who worried much about not being shown anything by Salihou who had brought them to MYR. Perhaps they were lucky that we shared the same living quarters. I did my best to encourage these guys who were almost on the verge of giving up the Forest University programme, the more so as they were not even admitted as *étudiants*. "You see," I told them one evening, "although I have been working for a couple of days now with Alain, he has never really shown me anything. When we get into the patch, he has no time to waste and I am on my own side just doing what I can do." They were surprised because they had been thinking that they were the only in their situation. I made it clear that I was going to master the job whether or not anyone would show me anything because "the mere fact that someone brought me here is enough help from the person. Every other thing for success now depends principally on me." That was the last time we talked about the matter because thereafter I realized just how determined the Burkinabe were and how they had constituted a team of two that was to become one of the most dynamic and outstanding in the camp.

Not long ago, in September 2014, a Burundian called Jean-De-Dieu (JDD) who is known to behave as if he is competing with everyone,[14] was Congo's neighbour on the right. I was on his left. JDD was talking too much about finishing his patch

---

[14] "There are many known cases of workers who would not even stop their machines in order to eat a sandwich or an apple simply because they continuously hear the neighbour's machine going almost all-day. They thus behave as if they are in some sort of Tree-Cutting Olympic Game; or that the neighbour would have cut all the vast forest before they could complete their particular patch, if they took a break. And, most often, they end up taking more than just a few minutes break, and not in the forest but in hospital" (Fossungu, 2013a: 24).

before the Burkinabe. I merely let him know that the only one Congo competes with is his partner. And this is good because that is the sure way a serious partnership makes the money. "So, if you are thinking of a *terrain*-cutting competition with Congo (your neighbour)," I warned JDD, "be sure then to lose both legs and hands without still winning." Of course, Congo (as solo now) who even had a larger patch than each of the two of us flanking him finished two days before us – his *vagins* as another Burkinabe called Oussou is known to call *voisins*. Oussou actually surprised (flabbergasted is the right word) one of his neighbours when he started talking about their being his *vagins*. It was not until Oussou insistently explained how this guy's *tiren* (meaning *térrain*) was next to his that most of us got an idea of what the Burkinabe was talking about.

The Congo-Issa duo became that good because they felt no one was there for them, since, to them, Salihou did not work with them even for a day, as was habitual, to show them this and that. They thus became very focused on making it. I suspect I was not shown anything by my own *ancient* solely because of my *truth* fault. The first thing Alain Tchato told me as we got to his patch the first day was this. 'When people are crying about their patches being difficult, you must also do the same even if you are in a *crème*.' (*Crème* refers to a very easy-to-cut patch, deriving its name from the fact that even children that hate eating have a different attitude when it comes to ice-cream, for instance.) My response to the *crème* advice was: "Why must I cry when it is actually time to laugh and rejoice?" In short, I was questioning the fact that I have to lie just because everyone else is lying. That uncompromising stance most certainly had blocked any further 'advice' from my *ancient*; thus landing me in the same camp with the Burkinabe duo. I have had several occasions to be their *terrain* neighbour. When they *démarrent* their machines in the morning, they only stop when it is lunch time, and then closing time. You cannot even think they speak the same African language or work together on the same patch. Each person is on their own side of the patch doing just what they should be doing; no talking distraction as is the case with most of the team-workers (or *couples*, as they are popularly known).

Burundian/Rwandan *couples* most often spend the bulk of their precious working time conversing and the like. Rather than form a team with some of these people, it pays better to work even as a half person. You find a team that is full of what my late mother (Regina Akiefac Fossungu) liked to call *millingho*. That is Bangwa for 'things that make you laugh to breaking point'. One team member stops to drink water, the other follows suit; one urinating means the other too urinates; and so forth. You often hear one of them complaining behind the back of the other how the complainant does the bulk of the work while the other fools around and then later makes the same amount as he, etc. The question that one would be asking is: why then are they in a team? Just because of the fear of bears?[15] No surprise at all then that some of these pairs never lasted a couple of weeks, not even to mention a month. Congo and Issa certainly lasted for three solid seasons without a hitch, excelling and advancing because the competition between them was progressive or positive. This duo very quickly transformed themselves into unarguable *grands coupeurs*. I remember someone in September 2014 calling Congo a *grand coupeur* and his reaction being that "This is not an issue of *grand coupeur*; it is one of concentration!" I just listened to their conversation quietly, reassuring myself that only a real *grand coupeur* would be telling you what it takes to become a *grand coupeur*. Did Salihou's philosophy of 'teach a hungry man how to fish rather than giving him cooked food' not create *grands coupeurs*?

---

[15] "A lot of the *nouveaux*, because of the frightening [bear] stories from the *ancients*, are forced to take to working in pairs (which is usually also a big distraction as most of the day is spent talking to, or checking on, each other)" (Fossungu, 2013a: 23).

The Team of Rwandan Cousins

During the 2013 season the camp was 'shocked' to see Congo returning without Issa. Where was Issa? Congo explained that Issa moved to work instead in the West, precisely in forest-loaded 'Beautiful British Columbia'. Of course, the problem must certainly have been that of one person preferring to go around while the other favours the known hazards of MYR. It could also be immigration-related. But, as Funnyman jokes about it, on the breakdown of marriages that are that solid and long-lasting, the parties scarcely want to be near each other. Whether or not Funnyman's suspicion holds true, the breakup or absence of the Congo-Issa team leaves room to the only competing pair that came into being one year after theirs. I am talking about the Alphonse/Jean-Marie team that is made up of two Rwandan relations (cousins, I think). In terms of duration, I would venture to say that this Rwandan team is going to go places. This is because only a focused and positively competing duo can do some of the things I have witnessed from the team. I noticed, for instance, that in August 2014 Alphonse (a lawyer by training) went to work one day alone. It is not like Jean-Marie Vennes was away from the camp. He was present but not feeling well, needing to rest. Pairs without such cohesion would see both members sitting back when one cannot be on the patch even for a day. By next season, this team would have beaten the Congo-Issa pair by two years, if they continue to work together (which I am sure would be the case).

I cannot talk about the team's ability to perform on the patch like the Congo-Issa equip since I have hardly been their neighbour to observe their *térrain* comportment. The one time I had that chance in the 2014 season, they were unfortunately at the top of my patch. I could only then have observed them by the time I was nearing completion, at which time they would have been long gone, or at their own finishing point, far off. They even left about two days before I could reach the end. But I think they are really good by now, judging from my working with them in a multiple-person team when they were still *nouveaux*. We went to Chicoutimi (a town in Quebec) in 2011 to do what is called *Hydro*: that is, the clearing of Hydro Quebec electricity lines. Here, group-working is a must and each group is given a number of electricity poles to take care of. The *ancients* (one of whom I then was) would not want to have anything to do with the *nouveaux*. What are they to do then? I took up the challenge and composed a group of seven with some of them, including one Rwandan *ancient* of my batch called Celestin Niyo. Having had many occasions to be his neighbour, I can tell you that Niyo is one of the most honest, conscientious and assiduous workers who would now merit the *grand coupeur* description. This guy is simply superb, whether working alone in his personal patch or as a member of a team like we were in with the *nouveaux* – that included Alphonse, Desiré, Jean-Marie Vennes, and two others that have long left the job. Niyo gladly accepted to be part of the unusual team that I was then constructing, which included the family duo. Could the family factor have any role in their long-lasting working togetherness? Could the Diallo brothers help us with the answer?

The Diallo Brothers and the Sense of Entitlement

Family and business (or even self-help) would seem to have hardly moved appropriately with Africans for several reasons, one of them being this funny entitlement thing. For a start, take the simple case of parents that are operating an off-licence bar in Molyko, Buea in Debundschazone of Cameroon. This is how they are able to send their children to school. But every time during the weekend that a certain daughter, for instance, is asked to take her turn at the counter, she is thinking only of the *mblacaus* thing. She consequently serves drinks to her boyfriend and his many friends he often brings along without receiving payment. The *mbombo*-thinking sons are doing the same to their girlfriends. The business eventually falls apart and the children can no longer be sent to school. The children, including said daughter begin to point fingers at the parents for not doing this and that, feeling they are just entitled to be sent to school notwithstanding their contribution in ruining the family business. Thank you, therefore, Bamileke, for understanding that business is business: your '*Affaire Nkap*' maxim is well known; but don't you think it is being taken too far sometimes? We will find that out below in their money-harvesting methods, but not before we are through with the Guinean bothers.

Junior Diallo faced the same situation like Congo and Issa. But rather than stick it out, he went back to the factory in Montreal, complaining all the time about his senior brother not doing this and that. There can be no doubt that putting money over family was involved in this case. This is even explained by the fact that the senior brother brought the other in through the training or *étudiant* door. But let's give the bear-fighting man his credit that he deserves. As I made it clear to the Burkinabe duo above, someone who does not want your success would hardly even take you to MYR. After that considerate opening of the door, making it or not is your making, not anyone else's. Sitting on your ass and waiting for all to be done for you is not the ingredient of success. It is just like this *bobby*-interested or *woman-wrapper* brother of mine who thinks that the mere fact that I am in Canada entitles him to be there too. You just need to hear him telling women in bars how he is going to take them to Canada! Call that his clever cocklering strategy, if you like.[16] But just come to imagine that

---

[16] "Most often when Joe wanted to know anything from me at all it related to how to *cockler* a girl. *Cockler* was generally used in the community but I heard it for the first time from Joseph who had a nag for creating his own words or phrases and for giving people nicknames from nowhere. I remember asking him how he came about the word and he described it to

he would be doing so while soya-drinking the money meant to make his passport! You are surely wondering if people still can (like during the *known* slave trade) travel these days from Cameroon to Canada without passports. You are not wrong to conjecture. Take also a sister who will not do what it takes to obtain a student visa. Brief, she wants me to not only get her admission in a Canadian college and pay for her program but also kind of attend her visa interview in Yaoundé for her! Where did self-help disappear to? Does *grand frère* simply mean 'do all for me'?

The *Grand Frère* Theory from Cameroon to Africa

I was a quality inspector at Rossy Inc. (on 5555 Royalmont, Montreal) when this young man was sent by a "cashy" employment agency to work there. Just looking at him, I could tell that he had just arrived in Canada, certainly from one of those villages in the West Region of Cameroon. Yes, Bamboutouszone I salute you! Also evident to me was the fact that his highest level of education could not be above the BEPC (*Brévet*). "Grand frère", he approached me and greeted. Most people in Cameroon use this phrase (as well as "Mon frère", "grande soeur", "ma soeur") not because they actually consider you as such but mostly when they want to rip something off you. Not that this particular *petit frère* was out for that also. But you never know until you know. And since that knowledge may come too late, the better thing therefore is to quickly jump off at the approach of the 'mon frère' exploitative vehicle (see below).

Yes, *petit frère*, what can I do for you? I asked. "Are you from Cameroon?" he also asked. I said yes and he said he too was Cameroonian. I said I could tell he was Bamileke. He

---

me: You know how a cock does when it wants to mate? I got it right away because for the first time I saw *cock* in the word" (Fossungu, 2013a: 45).

confirmed. What brings you to Canada, I inquired. He said he had been around for quite a long time studying at the Université de Montréal. Like the silliest creation of victimhood in Canada, this was a very bad choice to *fey* on. *Fey man* normally means liar or crook but the Biya regime has turned everything upside-down so much so that today youngsters would proudly tell you how they are or want to be *fey men*. As to what *petit frère* was studying, he said philosophy. I was seeing a very stupid liar in this *petit frère*. I asked him the department or faculty that is next to his. He failed in that, not even knowing that I was a Université de Montréal graduate and knew the campus so well.

Petit frère must have learnt that I was a lawyer. He came one other day and started talking about this friend of his who has this and that problem, wanting to know what said friend should do. "Petit frère," I told him, "go and tell your friend that information is paid for in this country. It is not given for free." But, I added, if it were you, I could waive payment. About thirty minutes later *petit frère* came and confessed that he was the one in need of the information. You simply cannot get the right or helpful counsel if you present the counsellor with twisted facts. I decided nevertheless to help *petit frère* (like I have done for many others) because he had come down from the tree-top and became real; also realizing that he was not as smart as he had imagined himself to be. The fact remains though that had I not been from the same country as *petit frère*, he might easily have gotten away with his riding me like the horse he thought he had gratuitously found. That may in a way explicate why some people may not want to be close to those from the same country as them at the workplace here in Canada. Look at it this other Lockwood Manufacturing bragging way too.

The Lockwood Manufacturing Bragger and the Bamileke Money-Harvesters

Éric Desbiens is the name of the manager when I arrived in Lockwood Manufacturing Inc. on 8104 Montview in Ville Mont-Royal (Montreal). When I got to Lockwood there were no Africans working directly for the company. Those of them who could be found there came through the agency. It is always like that with most well-paying factories. Sometimes, it may also merely be because people do not go applying there directly. I got to Lockwood Manufacturing Inc. through the agency but quickly applied to be *titulaire*. There were Indians (from India, not Amerindians), Jamaicans, Haitians (almost the majority, if you include the agency workers), and whites at the administrative level – with one company mechanic called Adam Arsenault. This company is specialized in the washing and treatment of bakery pans of all sorts, with clients scattered all over North America. It therefore uses a lot of chemicals and its workers are no doubt exposed to these toxic materials, not to forget the heat. It paid comparatively well: compared to the standard of minimum wage of most factories at the time.

Éric Desbiens was moved to the company's headquarters on 360 Brook Street in Brantford, Ontario. Among the long-serving and very experienced lot of Indians, Jamaicans, and Haitians this company simply wants us to believe that it found none that could competently replace the transferred manager other than the white-skinned mechanic, Adam Arsenault? Was it an issue of competence or simply that of skin colour? Of course, it is the latter. And the new manager himself knew it and was therefore haunted by the fact, as clearly evident in his zealously-bossy attitude towards the workers that he kept in constant fear of this and that. It was truly a 'Wonders-Shall-Never-End' case. The contrast with the former boss needed no magnifying glasses for even the blind person to see.

The Scary-Doctor Animosity

By the departure of the first manager, I had already brought in three Cameroonians who had just arrived in town as landed immigrants from Belgium. They were Donatus Ayuk Ako-Arrey, Valentine Usongo and Walters Tita Ndonkeu. As soon as these Cameroonian *titulaires* started working there, my troubles began because Ndonkeu took upon himself to tell everyone there that I was a doctor. The same things that I used to do without a problem now became things that I do in order to *show* the rest of the staff that I was a holder of a doctoral degree in law. Concretely, after Ndonkeu's pompous announcement, when I stood up for my rights like I had been doing, the response was just that "He wants to show us that he is a doctor!" This is one of the reasons for Africans (this writer specifically) loving MYR. Everyone there knows I am a Ph.D. holder. But that does not scare anyone. Rather, they seem to admire it. That fact also provides good cover for me to observe and write about them without engendering the artificial comportment common with subjects that know they are under observation. My open taking of notes (especially during the 2014 season) for this particular book during long bus trips to and from the patches did not rouse suspicion since many of them (if not all) also knew that I was taking and dispensing courses at the University of Windsor. Not so at all with these other town-based factories, why?

The acrimony in Lockwood was just too much. It came from all angles, but especially from the mechanic-turned-manager. He wanted me gone from there at all costs. Thanks to the fearful Haitian supervisor, he got an occasion for his first Warning Letter of September 23, 2003.[17] What the

---

[17]*Monsieur Peter Fossungu,*

> *Le dimanche 14 septembre 2003 nous vous avons surprise a laver votre auto sur vos heures de travail, de plus nous avons remarqué que votre dossier accusait plusieurs retards.*

manager is talking about (the car-cleaning) is correct. He came in that Sunday evening and found me outside doing some cleaning of my car. That is what I usually did during breaks in order to stay away from the chemicals inside. That particular day the shift supervisor had extended our break because, as he justified it, *"il n'ya pas grandes choses qui restent à faire."* By the time Adam met me outside, the extended break was not yet over and it was the supervisor's place to have explained that to him. He chose not to, rather behaving otherwise, either because he was so scared of the manager or because it was all going according to their joint midnightistic plan. It was not even habitual for the manager to be there on Sundays. Whatever it was, I just did not want this Haitian man (who could be Adam's father, age-wise) to lose a job that apparently might have been his everything in life, knowing also that implicating him was not even going to be worth the trouble since I already understood where the unqualified and inexperienced newly appointed manager was heading to – his second Warning Letter of 21 October 2003[18] being good proof.

Chez les Industries Lockwood Ltée, les besoins de l'entreprise font en sorte que nous devons compter sur des employés qui puissent nous offrir une prestation de travail continue et régulière.

Nous nous attendons donc de votre part une amélioration très marquée de votre assiduité au travail.

Toute récidive de votre part pourrait entraîner des mesures disciplinaires plus sévères pouvant mener au congédiement.

[18]*Monsieur Peter Fossungu,*

Suite à l'examen de votre dossier, nous avons constaté que vous accumulé toujours des retards. Nous vous avons averti le 16 septembre 2003 verbalement ainsi que le 23 septembre 2003 par écrit. Je me vois donc dans l'ouligence de vous suspendre de vos fonctions pour une durée de trois jours.

Toute récidive de votre part pourrait entraîner des mesures disciplinaires plus sévères pouvant mener au congédiement.

There is no need to spend much time arguing the fabricated lateness crab here: except to point out that I couldn't have started being late there only when Adam Arsenault became manager. Neither did I begin working there only then. Someone with such a lateness record would hardly have enjoyed the cordial working relationship with the former manager, a connexion that must even have made it very easy for me to bring in the *three* Cameroonian at once. Perhaps Rossy Inc. could have some small amount of validity to make such accusations, not Lockwood Manufacturing that was nominally a night-weekend job (Thursday-Sunday) for me. I worked the 7 PM to 7 AM shift Thursday to Saturday, with an alternating schedule on Sunday. With the second letter, there was just one more to go to justify firing. The manager and his advisers (and I am sure he had lots of them) were even taking the pains to build up all these fabricated reasons just because of their knowledge of my knowing the law. Otherwise, I would have been shown the door long ago. I valiantly refused to give the manager that pleasure they often derive from saying "You are fired" by quickly slapping him with "I Quit!" That two-word phrase that the 'you are fired!'-loving employers hate to hear actually led me to Niki in Mega Bloks.

Asked why he had to do what he did, Ndonkeu responded: "*Massa, e beta sey dis pipple sabi weti yu dey.*" Of course, Ndonkeu is right about the fact that these fellows ought to know who they are dealing with. Eric Desbiens knew that, and that might be why I was able to easily get the trio in there. I also know another Cameroonian who has made that move and it paid off big time. A general hand in a Montreal factory, Bafut-man walked up to his supervisor one day and began conversation. He let the supervisor know that although he was there as a general labourer, he was holder of a Master of Sciences in the IT domain. Point well noted. Some months later, the company's IT specialist was going on vacation and the supervisor contacted Bafut-man to see if he could be a replacement until the return of the vacationing employee. No problem at all, said Bafut-man. But that was indeed a huge problem to the replaced because he never regained his post after the miracle performance from Bafut-man. In the course of a few weeks, the replacement superfluously outdid the complete achievement of the replaced person with the company. The brilliant Cameroonian (who normally would have been excluded by the no "Canadian Experience" bullshit) became the new and permanent IT specialist overnight, with an exciting and encouraging pay cheque.

Bafut-man would, no doubt, not be there if he had not let the supervisor know what he really was. Nevertheless, the point remains that Bafut-man did the telling himself, not a third-party; and just to the supervisor, not to the entire factory. Hence, if anyone had to brag in Lockwood about my being a Ph.D. holder, it was to be me, not Ndonkeu. I wonder why people just wouldn't mind their own business. As you can see, some people would want to keep some opportunities in their organizations out of the reach of others from the same country as them, not because they are not keen on helping their fellow country people, but solely to eschew situations like the Lockwood one here or like those of the Bamileke money-harvesters.

The Bamileke Money-Harvesters

Sometimes others avoid their country people where they work because they have built a personality for themselves there based on lies. They then know that a savvy countryman (unlike others) would be quick to dismantle the trick. A typical case in point is this Bamileke guy who is known in the MYR circle as *Commissaire*. This is a guy we kind of liberated from a sort of capagivist-enslaver in Longueil (Quebec).[19] He worked with us in Rossy Inc. for a while before going to MYR. He kept promising to take me along to MYR until the day he absconded from Canada (escaping from credit card problems), still promising to return and take me there! Why, you are eagerly looking forward to knowing? Because the questions a savvy Cameroonian in MYR would be posing include that of what on earth would a police commissioner be leaving Cameroon to come to Canada for? *No bi na dem withi Paul Biya get dat contree*? Wouldn't some of these Bamileke guys say and do just anything to make money?

Just hear Lazare Domo, for instance, calling a white *contremaître* 'grand frère' to be able to comprehend why Meiway (the popular West African singer) calls them *Juif Noir*. Domo has some repairs to be made to his machine. He gets to the garage and is told what the problem is. There is a part to be changed and he thinks it is too costly. He goes away and then returns with said part (used) that he must have 'stolen' from someone else's '*machine de spare*' lying under the *roulottes*. The *contremaître* then announces the cost of labour and Domo begins singing the 'grand frère' song, disrupting the flow of service to the others on the long waiting line. I then ask this 'villager' if he thinks he is still in Cameroon, adding: "You are truly a disgrace to some of us with the Cameroonian tag. Since when did your mother give birth to a white boy? My fault for asking though; since you wouldn't even know because your 'grand frère' was born before you! The man has told you what it is: take it or leave it! And stop belittling yourself!" As usual, Africans just laughed uselessly without getting anything into their heads. Why do we live here when we cannot understand that the white man does not generally haggle like we do in

---

[19] *Capagivism* is the strategy of 'giving Canadian papers' through marriage to someone else who is not a Canadian permanent resident or citizen (see Fossungu, 2014: 122-124).

Marché Central in downtown (or do I say uptown) Yaoundé? My brother left, my brother right; my brother up, my brother down! That is only when we want to exploit the so-called 'brother'.

When Bami-X came into my patch to dupe me, he came under cover of *'pour aider mon frère'*. He spent some minutes there with his "brother" but went telling the *contremaître* to pay for an exaggerated quantity of *térrain*, a fifth of which he could never have cut during the period spent with me. Bami-Z also had to travel together with Bami-Y and me from the camp to Montreal. Normally, in this case each of them contributes about $30.00 towards fuel. Between the camp and Dolbeau-Mistassini, the car developed an alternator problem. Strangers (white people) very splendidly aided by regularly boosting the battery to get us to town that Sunday. We booked accommodation in a motel because repairs could only be carried out the next day. Next morning Bami-Z abandoned us very unceremoniously, taking the bus (costing over $100.00) to Montreal while we were trying to resolve the problem. On the eve of our supposed return date, Bami-Z was on the phone asking: "My brother, we are leaving at what time tomorrow?" I simply told him to go to any hell nearby to think that I could ever travel again with him to anywhere. I asked in conclusion: "Are there no more buses plying the Montreal-Dolbeau road?"

Bami-X also calls Diallo from Guinea 'my brother' all the time. But he does not want Diallo to ever be able to drive his own car to and from Dolbeau. Diallo then had but a learner's permit and needed company to be able to drive. He already had bought his Toyota Tercel. Bami-X would instead want to be the only one to drive it, refusing to give the owner the wheel, justifying: "I cannot risk my life with Diallo on the wheel! His hand is not strong!" So, when would his hand ever get 'strong' until he starts driving regularly and long-distance? Is that even the real reason? No. If Diallo begins long-distance driving his own car to and from Dolbeau, Bami-X loses the free ride he enjoys when he is the one driving Diallo's car, with the owner as passenger. To cut a lengthy story short, Bami-X is just too *Japanese-brake-like* or penny-pinching. I first came across this Camtok expression when someone told me that it was the way people in the community in Montreal were describing my brother-in-law who lived for years with his sister's friend but never contributed a dime to the household expenses. In Njangawatok (see Fossungu, 2013b: 161-166), saying *your hand strong* means you are miserly. To then describe it with 'Japanese Brakes' (known for their effectiveness) takes your stinginess to after the superlative.

I recall the same Bami-X telling us (a group of Cameroonians) when I just reached MYR that he was certain that Diallo uses a talisman in cutting trees, which explains why the Guinean is a *grand coupeur*. I was very surprised at this because the two guys (Bami-X and Diallo) and two other Cameroonians had travelled (Montreal-Dolbeau) with me in my car. It was because of these same Cameroonians that I encountered Diallo prior to reaching the MYR camp. I thought they were friends. To then hear them saying and listening to such nonsense about the other who was absent was very repugnant to me. I had reacted immediately therefore, telling those Bamileke this:

You guys amaze me a lot. Why don't you just recognize that everyone has a domain or two in which they excel more than others? So, you also want me to simply believe everything that other Cameroonians say about Bamileke? That is, that you only make money through *famla*? Please, when you are with this *Anglo* and don't have any progressive thing to talk about then wait until I am gone before gossiping.

They were all fixated by the time I concluded and was leaving their company. Some of these people would easily give the entire group a bad name. Bamileke are very hardworking people and, following Bami-X's theory above, lazy and visionless Cameroonians are then entitled to attribute their resourcefulness to witchcraft (famla)? Of course, no one wants to deny the existence and use of famla by some of them. But just listen to the tale of a University of Yaounde (UNIYAO) Bamileke student. At the time I was studying there, we were accorded *bourse*. The comportment of a lot of us with this monthly stipend can be very appropriately aligned with that of Ferguson's (2008: 18-19) so-called "primitive peoples [who,] chanced upon each other, it seems, they were more likely to fight over scarce resources (food and fertile women) than to engage in commercial exchange. Hunter-gatherers do not trade. They raid. Nor do they save, consuming their food as and when they find it. They therefore have no need for money." Yes indeed. Yaoundé City always knew when *epsi* had been *touché* by the bulk of us.[20] We merely temporarily 'touched' this money before it speedily settled comfortably in the bank accounts of chicken-parlours, of night clubs, of expensive boutiques, of high-class *nkanés* or *ashawos*, of you-name-them.[21] Yes, *likehewasians* (see chapter 6), you can go ahead with the stereotypes.... But wait for a minute.

On the other hand, I know this Bamileke classmate who did not even have to wait till *epsi* was 'touched' before having his own bank account inflate itself with our free-to-spend cash.

---

[20] "Today, despite the fact that the purchasing power of the [American] dollar has declined appreciably over the past fifty years, we remain more or less content with paper money – not to mention coins that are literally made from junk. Stores of value these are not. Even more amazingly, we are happy with money we cannot even see. Today's electronic money can be moved from our employer, to our bank account, to our favourite retail outlet without ever physically materializing. It is this 'virtual' money that now dominates what economists call the money supply" (Ferguson, 2008: 28-29).

[21] "Is this leaving one for the other what made Anna and others... to describe girls of Joan's ethnic group as *ashawo*? Quite apart from this *epithetization* being like judging B from A's acts, would Momany's for-no-apparent-reason leaving of Christine for Joan not then also be similarly defined as harlotry or *ashawonism*?" (Fossungu, 2014: 110, omission supplied).

He was always coming to class in t-shirts and in two pairs of jeans trousers, at the most. Meanwhile some of us would be dressed up like the 'goats' that some anti-gays Ghanaians best describe it with: tie and suit under hot sun. During breaks we would be eating this and that in a campus cafeteria own and run by this same 'poorly-dressed' guy with us in class. While he and I are having lectures, his junior 'brothers' that he had brought from the village and trained would be taking care of the business. It is long and very interesting, especially if I give you all the details. But I would shorten it and let you just know that by the time we graduated in 1987 and Paul Biya had declared that *ngon chegh sweanteh-sweanteh* (as the Bangwa would put it) and many of us could not find a job, the T-shirt-wearing Bamileke was not looking for a job but for employees: to drive his taxis, to do this and that in his other food-catering businesses. Would some of us now be humble enough to go and work for him? *No one day ya*, of course.

You will then find some of us quickly jumping to tag him with *famla*. Yes, I agree with the musician who has theorized, singing, that the real *famla* is hard work. A Chinese guy I worked with in a factory in Montreal (Royal International Corporation on 430 Stinson in Saint-Laurent) understood this hard-work theory very well. You would find this guy all the time in the garbage bin collecting any returnable cans of coke and other soft drinks. His case was so notorious that no one dropped these cans anymore in the garbage, handing them directly to him as some sort of mockery.[22] But he was just as happy with every such 'gift', always *thanking* the donor in Chinese that none of us understood. Do not be surprised to enter into a *dépanneur* somewhere on the Island of Montreal and find the proprietor being our factory can-collector! And then

---

[22] Africans, on the other hand, would not even bother about recovering the money from their very own returnable bottles that themselves have paid out. See Fossungu, 2013a: 125-27.

people like Lazare Domo would get into his *dépanneur* and start haggling and calling him '*grand frère*' just to have him kind of give away his many years of sweat to them for practically free. I guess we have Chinese-Bamileke, just as there are African-Chinese like me? Just also listen to the debate about regular visitors in the CGAM to be able to comprehend that the *mon frère* thing (if actually invented or initiated by the Bamileke[23]) is now a national (and even continental?) trait. Don't therefore make the fatal error of not speedily jumping off the Exploitation Bus because it is an Anglophone Cameroonian using the "*my big brother*" exploitative cover.

CGAM Regular Visitors and Exploitation: A 99-Sensism Affair?

There is more on this association everywhere in this book but right now let us see what it has to offer to our great question of *mon frère* and exploitation. The issue of regular visitors (RVs) in the CGAM has always been one that has scared the hell out of those who cannot speak out their mind in front of their so-called friends. (Did the Japanese have this concept in mind when they designed the Honda Cameroon-Regular Visitors (C-RV)?) These RVs always know the just mentioned fact about their friends so well that they often take their exploitation to the outer limits of exploitation. They had certainly attained this height when on July 16, 2007 Peter Ateh-Afac Fossungu (also popularly known as the CGAM trouble-maker) applied the brakes to the fast down-slopping, out-of-control, "our brothers and sisters" exploitative Honda car. This came through a piece titled '*CGAM: An Open (Charitable) Soup Kitchen And Beer Parlour For Some?*' and read in its entirety:

---

[23] Don't you go around pinning the genesis of this theory on the 'Bamis': unless you want to expose your ignorance of the "Lessons in Brotherhood" from the Foumban actors (see Fossungu, 2013c: chapter 2). Or, would it be because Yes-No-My-Brother-Foumban is in Bamboutouszone that is dominated by the Bameleke?

Dear Goodwillers, I know that many of us are not going to like this. But I am not the type that would say things simply to please people. The truth, it is said, is bitter and scary to many. I would therefore advise those who cannot swallow the bitter pill to quickly get off the back of the Cameroon Goodwill Association of Montreal (CGAM). The issue is whether or not CGAM has transformed itself into a place for free food, drinks, and music for some people. I was going to raise this discussion at the next meeting but, because that would be one more session of free food and drinks and music for our notorious "regular" non-members, I have preferred that we talk about it now through this medium so as to put those concerned on guard.

I do not understand why I should contribute 15$ for entertainment (note that 15$ cannot even buy a pack of 12 of heineken) but make sure that I come along with one, two or more persons who are not themselves contributing anything. Is that being fair to other members, and especially to the host? We often hear members complaining (and these days it is becoming especially very frequent) that there was not enough drinks or/and food at this or that meeting. But I have been eagerly waiting to hear the same complainants tilt their complaints towards what I have categorized as "regular" non-members of Goodwill. It is understandable that my friend or relative comes to town and I come along with him or her to a Goodwill session while he or she is still in town. But I would certainly be abusing the intelligence of other Goodwillers by regularly coming along with my girlfriend or wife or adult child who is not a member. If my sister or brother loves attending Goodwill meetings and other events the way some of these "regular" non-members seem to do, what stops him or her from formally joining? The answer resides comfortably in Goodwillers themselves. These numerous non-members cannot always be there except through our timid indulgence and the almost uncontrollable desire of some of us to take others for a rough ride. We often see some of these stark irregularities but pretend not to have seen them simply because they emanate from some quarters that we have dared ourselves never to criticize or point a finger at. I was particularly amazed by the vast amount of non-members at the last meeting at Dr. & Dr. Mrs. Ibeagha's: especially so as only one out of the whole lot came there to formally join the group. Why were all the others there then and what for? And will they be there unless there are regular members giving them cover? We must put an end to this unbecoming practice of thinking that we can very conveniently and ruthlessly turn other Goodwillers into our horses. Tell me, for example, why these "regular" non-members were always absent during sessions at Caribbean Paradise [where each member is entitled to his/her two tickets for drinks from the bar]. Let us collectively and firmly say adieu to 'regular' non-membership and thus give CGAM the added strength for growth by making it an association that is almost exclusively for Goodwillers. Thank you for your time reading, for your reflexion on, and for your input into, this matter.

If you have not yet realized that 99-sensism is akin to the "my brother/sister" theory, then know that now. "Like most ethnic groups in Cameroon," Fossungu (2014: xi) writes, "the Bangwa's epithet is 99-Sense; with some explanatory attachment that they are so craftily clever that they would not sell you a hen (but only a cock) for fear that it would produce chicken for you, thus preventing your coming back to buy from them. I do not know how far or correct this epithetical thesis (as all the others) could expound the attitude of most of the Bangwa people." Perhaps the exploitation issue currently on the table could help? On that same day (July 17) Eugene Lekeawung Asahchop (a Bangwa-99 senser like the first speaker) stated:

Dear Goodwillers: In regards to Dr Fossungu's concern about notorious regular non-members who attend our meeting sessions because of food and drinks, I personally would not consider this to be true. I believe that they want fun and companionship among their Cameroon brothers and sisters. We cannot say there is any among these non-members who cannot afford for what he or she want[s] to eat or drink.

If we want to use the issue of food and drinks to send away visitors from goodwill, [w]hy that name goodwill[?]

Eugene Asahchop seems to answer affirmatively to the question in the title of Fossungu's contribution with his own concluding question that not only another Bangwa could conveniently answer and thus convince you that it is not just idle anti-99-sensism. Take the non-Bangwa answer first. On the same day Aloysius Ibeagha told Fellow Goodwillers:

Once more, I will like to seize this opportunity for and on behalf of my family to thank you all for the wonderful turn out and show of love for one another. Thanks to the cooking and transport committees for a marvel[l]ous job. It is my fervent wish that the Lord will continue to bless you abundantly as you grow from strength to strength in all your endeavours. This issue of regular visitors has come to the lime light again. When somebody attends our meeting more than once, he/she becomes a regular visitor. We are all culpable including m[e]. I propose the following:

1. That we create room for them to be sympathizers i.e. they are observing the group until they feel the desire to join the group (the assembly can decide a time frame);

2. Each meeting they attend, it is absolutely mandatory that they pay the normal $15 for entertainment;

3. Sixty percent of the sum raised should assist the host while forty percent goes to a sinking fund for social activities. I hope we can put this to law and respect it as such.

What Ibeagha proposes as law is already in place but no one cares about enforcing it, just like the late coming fines. Lateness has always been an insidious problem with *AITWs* generally (see Fossungu, 2013a: 165). It has even been a topic of discussion in several CGAM Assemblies. But I am not here going into all of that, being concerned mainly with enforcement of CGAM (lateness) laws. The rule in CGAM is clear. A late member pays a dollar fine and there is always a lateness basket or bowl at the entrance. The expectation is that when you are late, on entering the hall you drop the dollar in the bowl before taking a seat. A lot of members would often just walk in as if they were totally oblivious of this practice and, if you make the indication, you are then surprised at the reaction. Often, it is the other contradictory *'law-abiding'* members who would even be quickly and irresponsibly reprimanding you: *Massa yu no go even leaf man fess settle down?* Now you are the bad guy who is bugging people with respecting set down rules. Where is Africa heading to with this kind of big-title empty-heads holders?

Whatever you want to say in response could be good and very lengthy but let's stay on *regulavisitorism*. Denis Alem (then CGAM Vice-President) was the fourth and last contributor to the CGAMing-scary issue on the same July 17 when he wrote:

Many thanks to the Ibeagha's family for having us last week-end. As evidenced by the turnout, the distance to reach any Goodwill member is never long.

To brother Eugene, Goodwill has some history and for your info, some wise brothers and sisters of Goodwill had thought of this issue in the past. It was agreed that a repeated visitor (after showing up more than once had to pay 20 dollars (Canadian) for each appearance. There was even a limit to the number a host could have as his/her guests. This was implemented for some time. We relaxed and we seem to have returned to square one again. Just as we pay taxes to belong to an organized society (in this case Quebec/Canada) it is just normal that Goodwill should ask for some contribution from repeated visitors if I can put it this way.

This is not a practice only here. If I can use myself as an example, during my last visit to Cameroon I attended a meeting for the first time. As I am an out of station member, people knew my name but had not seen me. When I got into the meeting room, the person who was with me (also a meeting member) was immediately asked to pay 50.000 CFA (it is the fine for bringing in a non[-]member to the meeting). The fine was dropped only when they realized that I was a meeting member.

Now that the sum is 15 dollars, I suggest we have it at 15 dollars.

Chief-Whipping Lawlessness

Like Denis Alem rightly puts it, the law is always there but no one wants to enforce it: either because they are afraid of stepping on their so-called friend's toes, or they are just ignorant of the existence of the law (which is, of itself, no excuse), leading also to the question of whether or not the conditions for admissibility had been met, to begin with (see chapter 5). It is not surprising, in view of the conspicuous absence of a whip, that Lawlessness reigns supreme in the CGAM. The post of Chief Whip was formally introduced in the 2005 elections for the following year's bureau. It is the most important office for obvious reasons, but especially as it could be likened to a community's police force. We all know what a society becomes when its police force is ineffective and corrupt. The question that would be lingering on your mind then is: How was the CGAM operating till then (2006) without this policing agent? If I wanted to be really rude, I would simply have thrown back the question: Why and how has the CGAM been operating ever since 2008 without a chief whip? That, in any case, as you will understand, is not rudeness but merely to prepare you for the lawlessness that CGAMers love so much. Thus, it is a good question you have asked, which takes me back to my employment of 'formally introduced' in late 2005, as seen in Table 2.[24]

Since that 2005 formalization, only the pioneer Chief Whip has been able to live up to the task until the short-lived phenomenon known as *Stevasongalism* (below) after whom, as you can see from Table 2, the position has disappeared from the bureau. You will find that not a lot of people have even occupied the office and even those who have, have assumed functions only after, not at elections. It was the case in the 2007 bureau when Sylvanus Asonganyi only opted to occupy the position in late January or February that year. In several elections years the position (you tell me why) is completely ignored. So explain to me why there could ever be the kind of rigour and moralization (not the *Biyaist* empty-words type though) in the CGAM that were characteristic of the first four administrations (2003-2006). This era's discipline is attributed to the pioneer president who used to combine so many tasks, including that of policing to make sure that the regulations and practices were respected by whomsoever. Thus, even without

---

[24] Table 2 shows the chief whips of CGAM.

Table 2: Chief Whips of CGAM

Name	Year(s)	Name	Year(s)
Peter Ateh-Afac Fossungu	2006	None	2011
Sylvanus Asonganyi	2007	None	2012
Stephen Asong	2008	None	2013
None	2009	None	2014
None	2010		

its official introduction in the next administration, Peter Ateh-Afac Fossungu is well-known for having on countless occasions "embarrassed" both late coming CGAMers and so-called "regular visitors". Even as president, Fossungu kept battling almost alone to keep some order in place, and continued doing same during the Paulayahist first bureau (2005). It was therefore not surprising that the post was formally put in the list of positions for the 2006-bureau election agenda and that Fossungu was nominated and chosen.

Stevasongalism

A young man recently had everyone so "impressed" as the CGAM Chief Whip. You are asking how and why impressed is in quotations? To begin with, the campaign message of the candidate for chief whip for the December 2007 elections (he was unopposed, of course), was quite fascinatingly telling in regard of the issues being evoked. On November 21, 2007 this message came (I add square brackets since I have also altered paragraphing): "[A] Vote for Stephen ASONG [is one for] Changing the Whip[p]ing system in the Goodwill Community. [It is one for] Peace and tranquil[l]ity in any of the Goodwill Gatherings. Above all making Goodwill de[se]rve the name GOODWILL." And, believe me, it was not just an advert meant to just get elected. Stephen Asong meant business as seen after the very first meeting following his being victorious. The Chief Whip on January 14, 2008 communicated with CGAMers, without the usual politickerizing distinction as you can see.[25] Yes. *Stevasongalism* had skilfully found a unique way

---

[25] Good morning fellow Goodwillers: I will commence by thanking you all for the attendance at our January Thematic meeting and also for your constructive collaboration. I will not forget to thank you for your calmness.The meeting was scheduled for 8:00 pm prompt even though most of us were not present at the scheduled time. Any Goodwiller who turned up after 8:00 pm was considered a latecomer. Latcomers are entitled to a fine of $1.00 CAD per meeting. Below is the list of all latecomers for the General Assembly held on the 12th of January 2008: Etube [P]ius,

to embarrass the perpetual BMT out of so many of us in a way that few or none were expecting.[26] If only someone could have had the nerves to fearlessly continue Stevasongalistically doing the job after he soon thereafter relocated to Calgary! A lot of the perpetual *BMTimers* must have released a thunderous sigh of relief just learning of his departure. You can cement what I am saying about the Stevasongalist effect with Paul Ayah's "Way to go Mr Chief Whip!!" that followed the publication of the Stevasongalist list on the airwaves.

PT Ayah is very happy about what he sees because some of us had grown so weary arriving early to sit there wasting precious time waiting for the others that it simply became more profitable to start being late too. Steve Asong was therefore a kind of timely medication for the creeping ailment in early-goers. Attendance at the following Assembly spoke volumes to the effect that few or none wanted a repeat of their names on

---

Vincent Cheg, Usongo Macalister, Nsom Ignatius, Lysly Ayah, Tatuh Felicia, Sumboh Amos, Takang Edward, Taka[n]g Roseline, Egbe Maggi, Egbe Martha, Felexce Fru Ngwa, Ngum Evodia, Paul Ayah, Lewis Cheussom, Happi Gina, Bridget Fomenky, Kwenga Gabriel, Ntongho Chrisantus, Ndonkeu Walters, Ndonkeu Phyllis, Techoro Tah, Anung Wilson, Fai Ndofor, Asong Edward, Magnus Ajong, Peter Fossongu, Peter Mungwa, Nkengfack Nicolas, Achaleke Helen, Tebo Nixon, Akong Vivian, Berri Nsame, Denis Alem, Naya Ngalla, Ntemgwa Mitchel, Ntemgwa Alechia, Ngweyin Herverge, Nyambi Beltus, Georgia Kometa, Linda Kamga, Ashu Julius, Orock Baiyee, Hans Najeme, Caren Najeme, Valentine Usongo, Caren Ayah

Thanks for your co-operation and we hope our attendance in subsequent reunions will be timely, substantial and peaceful. Wishing you a very good week start, I remain Stephen Asong, your humble Chief Whip.

[26] BMT means 'Black Man time', a concept that has come under heavy fire because "I find it amazing that most (Black) Africans have decided to immigrate and live in 'the Whiteman's country' but always content themselves with this brainless BMT cover for their gross irresponsibility. Imagine being invited to a ceremony billed for 8 PM. You arrive at 7.55 PM and the hosts themselves are not even ready; and then the occasion ends up beginning at 11 PM, and when you are wondering if your wrist watch had three hours advance and all you get is that 8 PM in BMT is about midnight. What rubbish!" (Fossungu, 2013a: 165; 2014: 131 n.13).

that dreadful list. The mere fact that the post has been completely relegated since Steve tells you just how *impressed* CGAMers were with Stevasongalism, and as well just how much they love lawlessness. As already noted, lateness has not been the only battle for any dedicated chief whip; there was/is another more complicate one. It is complex in the sense of its being waged against the chief whip's order and discipline by non-CGAMers with CGAMers' cover or complicity – the Honda C-RVs. Quite apart from the constitutional and other irregularities, the important thing is that you can obviously see that the "brother/sister" cover for exploitation is a national affair in Cameroon. Why use the brother/sister thing when in actual fact something else is intended? Is it not also the case of politickerizing with clean and clear daytime rules?

Chapter 3

Fossungupaffectism And The Unknown Battle With Midnightism: The Revolutionization Of Elections In The CGAM

He fascinates by both his curiosity and his seriousness. In his scholarly life, he succeeded in researching and publishing about any problem that concerned him. He crossed disciplinary boundaries with the ease of a Balkan smuggler. He was consistent without being dogmatic and political without being partisan, and he succeeded in influencing both his academic colleagues and the general public [Krastev, 2013: 502].

Fossungupaffectism defines the Fossungu-Peter-Ateh-Afac-Effect. Variety has always been considered to be the spice of life. Thus, Ferguson (2010: 247) tells us that calls for change are unavoidable parts of politics. That is what political and other forms of competition are meant to bring about. For instance, when factories compete healthily, the consumer has a variety of goods and services from which to choose. When countries engage in this type of competition, the peoples of the world get to enjoy more and better amenities. When human beings in any grouping compete positively, it is the entire community that benefits. Collin Hay (as cited in Marsh, 2010: 224) thus sees "the question of change [a]s far from a complicating distraction – it is, in essence, the very *raison d'être* of political enquiry." One of the most pronounced methods for ensuring that change is called regular elections of officials. Elections are not elections if the rules do not ensure that only the best wins. *Dictelections* that African and other dictators employ to embellish their "for life" rule do not meet the definition of fair and free elections. There is an imbalance in this instance.

The CGAM President is no doubt the Chief Executive officer and: (a) ensures adequate management of the affairs of the Association; (b) presides over all meetings and special occasions or ceremonies; (c) represents the Association at third party functions; (d) signs all official documents of the Association: (e) appoints officials to the special organs of CGAM (CGAM Constitution, Article 9). Table 1 above is a list of the various presidents until 2014. A special thing to point out is that the CGAM president does not select or appoint members of the bureau s/he heads. Every bureau member is elected on his or her own. The issue of going the ACC-way (the president forming a list of bureau members with which to be voted into office) was brought up by Paul Takha Ayah during the Fossungu era. The idea was heatedly discussed and eventually discarded in preference of what has since been the CGAM unique formula (which I am sure most other mini-Cameroonian association are at home with). Paul's argument was aimed at avoiding some of the problems associated with the posts of Vice-President and Secretary-General (*viperizationism* and *resignationism*, terms that you will encounter later). But the better argument that prevailed was that independence of bureau members was to work better for the association.

The position of CGAM S-G has a chequered history, suffering from both relocations and resignations.[27] On such

---

[27] Table 3 here shows holders of this office.
Table 3: Secretaries-General of CGAM

Name	Year(s)	Name	Year(s)
Donatus Ayuk Ako-Arrey	2003-2004	Rita Ebude Ewane	2009

occurrences, the president is *silently* empowered to appoint a replacement and communicate same to the General Assembly that then ratifies the appointment. I say silently because (until late 2008) the constitution said nothing about it, and any charismatic and sensible president would astutely exercise the power. If it is not covered and not prohibited then it can be done, is the maxim, isn't it? Thus at the September Assembly in 2005 Denis Alem accepted his appointment as S-G by the Paulayahist presidency to complete the term of Emmanuel Ngwakongnwi who had relocated to Thunder Bay, Ontario, in August for further studies. Wilson Ajanoh Anung similarly took over as *interim* S-G in late 2007 when Jackson Acha Atam moved to Lome (Togo) for work-related reasons. The GA in September 2009 confirmed Yacubu Mohnkong as *acting* S-G for the remainder of the year when Rita Ebude Ewane relocated in October 2009 to Toronto, also work-related. Without these cases, bureau officials are all elected individually.

In the history of the CGAM's elections, many people would easily cite that which involved the choosing of the 2008 bureau as historic. After that election, Rosaline Tanyi Takang, for instance, wrote on December 9, 2007: "Hi all, I send here a congratulatory message for the successful, fair and peaceful election that was conducted under our four wise electoral

Emmanuel Ngwakongnwi	2005	Yacubu Mohnkong	2010
Denis Alem	2005	Patrick Tanyi	2011
Aloysius Ibeagha	2006	Ekwe Enongene	2012
Jackson Acha Atam	2007	Richmond Bassong	2013-2014
Wilson Ajanoh Anung	2008		

committee members: Mr. Paul Ayah, Auntie Berri [Nsame], Mr. Albert [Sekoh] and Mr. Fai [Ndofor]. I write to congratulate you on a job well done. You did so well!!" On November 15, 2007 Jules-Blaise Komguep had also written: "Hi Goodwillers! Thumbs up for the Electoral Committee for the job that the[y are] doing. Continue the same way."[28]

Yes, of course, that particular election was a milestone in a way. But the one that is the historic catalyst for that December 2007 history is the out-of-the-ordinary electoral practice that was inaugurated in December 2006 for electing the same 2007 bureau that was then being challenged like no other bureau had. What I am saying simply is that we cannot adequately glorify/debase the December 2007 events without a correct understanding of what *midnight* or *daylight* history is behind them. Many people in the CGAM are simply wallowing in the dark and do not comprehend the power dynamics at work. I am therefore here to four-eyesly break it down for those who never saw it the way it was/is. To help your comprehension, the first part of the chapter looks at the background to fossungupaffectism before the second focuses on the actual electoral practices (Lyslyakoyahism) resulting from the new fossungupaffectivist rules.

Back-Grounding The Elections Revisionism

Until 2007, the ELECOM was often created on the spot during the December Assembly and then given about thirty minutes during which to come up with elections modalities.

---

[28] Jules-Blaise is evidently French-speaking and often ends his Always-English write-ups with "Do not mind my poor [E]nglish." I must admit that his language is very far away from poor, coming from a French-speaking Cameroonian who joined the CGAM practically not even speaking the Queen's language, and comparing it also with the silent editing I am doing on some of the texts emanating from English-speaking CGAMers in this Forum. More grease to your elbows, J-B Komguep!

The practice was almost standard: nomination of a person for a post was usually acclaimed (most often even before the said person has had the opportunity to accept or reject) and the person was considered "elected". That was exactly what happened even at the pioneer Assembly with the 'acclamation-election' of Peter Ateh-Afac Fossungu as the first president. At that time, I think, it was normal and accepted. It is only normal to note that the first CGAM administration was quite small, consisting of just three members: President, Secretary-General, and Treasurer (Peter, Donatus, and Lysly). This smallness can be understood in a number of senses. First, the CGAM was still a young organization with a handful of members; second, these 13 members operated almost free of rock-etched formality, most of the tasks being voluntarily performed even without any specific title attached. Valentine Usongo would tell you more on the subject (in suggesting 'The Way Forward' to the Goodwill Football Club (GWFC) 'Constitutional Crisis') when, on Tuesday, August 6, 2013 at 12.50 PM he wrote to the GWFC Forum as follows:

I hope you all are having a great week. I have been keenly following the debates on this forum though I have never posted my views on this forum. I think the only way to solve problems is through dialogue. The name Goodwill speaks for itself for what it represents. It was not given by random [choice] but out of foresight to represent the vision that the trio of m[e] and my good friends Mr Ako-Arrey Donatus and Dr Peter Fossungu sacrificed time to put together ideas that culminated in the formation of this association. This spirit of Goodwill was equally manifested by its founders. Mr Ako-Arrey Donatus was available 24 hours a day to help pick -up and drop any member of the community wherever he or she was going with his car that we famously called "Nikoo" and Dr Fossungu equally did the same because at that time only few people in the community owned cars but believe me these guys were servants to the community. This is just to let you guys know that the main objectives behind the creation of this group was for us to come together as a community to foster love, harmony and solidarity which is also the case in [Goodwill] FC and which we must strive to preserve.

Biggytitlemania clearly had no place then. In short, there was that most noticeable willingness on the part of all then present to make the new baby not only crawl but walk and work exceptionally well. Newly 'independent' African states seem never to have gotten this simple message: that it would clearly be unacceptable to try feeding a new-born baby with hard cocoyam simply because every adult around is eating *macobo*. Of course, you wouldn't expect that same selfless comportment when the membership would begin to double, triple, quadruple, etc. But what is important right now is that at the end of the second year in office members were still proposing that Fossungu should continue as president. That is exactly how we create our dictators in Africa (Biya, Eyadema, Sengho, Bongo, Mobutu, Mugabe, you name them). We clap him/her on even if deep down we are not happy seeing him or her continue blocking our chances to also show what we are worth. But then are we really worth anything if we do this involuntary clapping?

There was nothing then in the CGAM Constitution that prevented Fossungu from continuing as wished. But he was firm in letting the others know that someone else needed to take over from him and bring their own style and talents to the show; suggesting at the same time that a limit of two consecutive one-year terms be inserted in the Constitution. The Assembly agreed with the out-going president and Paul Takha Ayah was elected as second CGAM president. As I have just said and need to reiterate it, even after the first two terms (actually 'one-and-half', viewing that CGAM was created in July 2003), members were still acclaiming Fossungu's continuation when he said 'Not so fast guys'. He had then insisted to them that there was need for some other person and ideas at the helm; that two consecutive terms were more than enough for any one person. That is precisely how the two consecutive-terms limit found itself into a body of rules that had no restrictions to the issue. PT Ayah too was then voted the same 'acclaiming' way. Even during Ayah's election for a second term I did not quite think this procedure that was initially okay and necessary with the formative years) was still a good one to continue with. But when you are a predecessor, you do well to avoid looking like (or actually being) an obstacle to your successor's freehand and *differentiational* success that comes with it. That is what a good pioneer does.

Qualities of a Good Pioneer and the Arrata-Poison Theory

Two subjects would aid your grasping of the matter here: (1) *nominutism* and *pioneewantism* and (2) the *arrata*-poison thesis. **Nominutism and pioneewantism:** An associated issue to successful leadership concerns relations with other members of the team that one is leading. Its lacking egoistic characteristics as noted earlier is not to say however that all was rosy with/for the pioneering bureau about which you would certainly not be hearing much 'big-book' citation, notwithstanding its being the peter or bedrock of the CGAM. This is because the pioneer Secretary-General (Donatus Ayuk Ako-Arrey) was often so lost in the fun that he never actually left the association with documented minutes of meetings and other events (call that *nominutism*), always reproducing record of matters of previous Assemblies off-head. In short, Ayuk was so good at memorizing the deliberations at the time that no one even saw the need to have him produce written minutes then. This is not to excuse the president (in the person of Fossungu) for not having correctly taken care of business by making sure that the S-G actually produced these records for the future. But, again, look at the other side: Would the pioneer president not have been accused of playing dictator, if he did so? The numerous S-G crises in the CGAM (some of which you will encounter from time to time) would seem to suggest a positive to the question and a very big negative to CGAM progress. No one but a perpetual politickerizer would frankly deny the plain fact that this pioneering bureau was very efficient and did a marvellous job. But this no-written-minutes issue called nominutism undeniably forms its soft underbelly.

I may not exactly have some exceptional leadership characteristics. But I know well what I have, and also perfectly know that I know how to use what I have to effectively help to create quality leaders and appropriate environments. I am not only good at shooting straight at rule-breakers. I am also a very good pioneer; these being necessarily tied to the objectives I have defined myself with. Using just the long-undermined female here (see Terretta, 2013; Fossungu, 2013b: 115-121, Konings, 2012; and Fonjong, 2012), I would define a good pioneer as someone that begins what she starts principally with the interests of others in mind, not just her own self-aggrandisement. As such, this type of pioneer not only creates but knows as well how and when to pass on the torch; appropriately creating opportunities for successors to excel and surpass her record. Briefly put then, a good pioneer's motto is 'Shine and Let Shine'; knowing that her job is to create a suitable and solid base upon which others can continue building or erecting skyscrapers rather than the bungalows she has been able to build. Her job is not to do everything to the end: except she wants to be the *bad* by being there forever or remaining the only one, a tyrant. Can we even really correctly talk of a pioneer X or Y until she has one or more successor(s)?

Africa suffers from the stack lack of good pioneers. I will classically call that suffering from the disease known as *pioneewantism*. You can then clearly visualize that President Ahidjo of Cameroon (like most of his same-time colleagues elsewhere on the continent) was not a good pioneer. (This does not in the least justify the fact that his hand-picked successor prefers that his corpse should remain in 'foreign' lands to date.) This characteristic of his largely explains Ahidjo's well-known *arrata*-like attempts to use the "docile Biya" (as he erroneously thought then) to perpetuate his iron-fisted rule even while he was 'in retirement' or 'had stepped down'. That is clearly the fear of progressive competition. Could that be the reason Biya is afraid of Ahidjo's ghost: that it will be around to do just the same thing that its human form wanted, if Ahidjo's remains are brought 'home'? Of course, do not think this is all my reasoning; it is just the logical conclusion from the Witch-Experts' Theory that witches/wizards are always not comfortable with other witches/wizards. Whatever it is that the witchcraft experts are telling you would not change much because my unbroken thesis is that neither of these Cameroonian presidents is justified in their anti-competitive behaviour of personalizing and emotionalizing official and collective matters. That is the kind of attitude I am out to also condemn and expose in this book; doing so like no one else "addresses questions too often thought of, but afraid to ask by so many" (Killough, 2009).

The Arrata-Poison Theory

They do not address the questions mostly because of the fear of being accused of taking sides. Such fears of politics are baseless, unless you are a politickerizer. I recall once telling a group of African students that if you are not a rat (*arrata* in Njangawatok) you will not be killed by rat poison. They were so puzzled by my statement, with one of them unbelievably bursting out: "Prof, until today, I never knew you were one of those who could fool someone into the grave. *How you go manage talk sey man no go die if e chop arrata poison?*" Well, I had to break it down for them; indicating that it just means that you would not be eating (poisoned) rat food if you are not a rat and refuse to play one. Politickerizers (especially the tree-topping ones) know this *politickerizality* (or politickerizer-mentality) well and this is where PT Ayah's especial problem lies, as you will more elaborately see in chapter 4. The Politickerizing Bus is like the *famla* that is tied to Bamileke wealth. When you venture into that Bus, it is often very difficult to thereafter get off it. Fidelis Folefac (henceforth also Fifolefac) tried doing just that when he realised it was not as rosy in that *Bus* as one would have thought.

I would be saying it over and over again that Folefac has some rare organizational and other leadership qualities which would be very useful to the community: if he could just learn to avoid politickerizing from the start. If he (or anyone else) sticks by/to this simple rule, there is never any reason to fear daytime politics. Otherwise, this fear takes hold of you all through, preventing your acting decisively when need be: since you would instead be too concerned with 'will your politickerizing colleagues be pointing fingers?' Politickerization and politics are clearly not synonyms. One of the greatest gifts in life is the ability to be able to stand up and say what you have to say, without fearing that someone would accuse you of taking sides. I think President Barack Obama could be credited with having this rare gift, not to even mention towering President Nelson Mandela (RIP). Like these two idols, I know I have that gift too. I know as well that I know that I must use it to ameliorate the lot of humanity. That explains, in a way, what happened in ELECOM in December 2006.

The ELECOM was independent once created and that was one important organ that had the power to reshape things away from the traditional stance operating till then. That opportunity presented itself in December 2006 when I was a member of ELECOM for the first time and its chair for that matter. Table 4 shows the various years and members of this important arm of CGAM democracy.[29] I was then in a privileged place to

---

[29] Table 4 here portrays the members of ELECOM.

move the CGAM forward and away from an electoral practice that "would appear to defeat the very concept of election" (Fossungu, 1999a: 347). This is because most experts think that "an election held in the humdrum of nomination and acclamation is bound to be a fake election as it does not indicate the real will of the people who are 'electing'" (Fossungu, 2010: 277). You can thus see that the CGAM was

Table 4: CGAM Electoral Committees (2005-2012)	
Year	Committee Members
2005	Hans Najeme (chair), Eveline Awemu Ibeagha, Jackson Acha Atam
2006	Peter Ateh-Afac Fossungu (chair), Berri Nsame, Wilson Ajanoh Anung
2007	Paul Takha Ayah (chair), Berri Nsame, Lysly Ako Ayah, Fai Ndofor, Albert Sekoh
2008	Edward Ayuk Takang (chair), Johnson Ngala, Margaret Enow, Berri Nsame, Paul Takha Ayah
2009	Felicia Tatuh Nzonji (chair), Rosaline Tanyi Ayuk-Takang
2010	Aloysius Ibeagha (chair), Ekwe Enongene, Roger Ekuh-Ngwese
2011	Micheline Acheah (Chair), Edward Ayuk Takang, Macalister Usongo
2012	Evaristus Ojah Ngoe (chair), Yvette Mbeh Fuh-Cham, Richmond Bassong

truly blessed that December when an elections specialist and critic would not only be an ELECOM member but also its chair. PT Ayah actually suggested Fossungu's name and chairmanship and the General Assembly (GA) happily ratified – obviously believing it was just going to be the same *bla-bla* show – with the other nominated members joining me thereafter.

The out-going president had barely been spared by the incessant adhocist attempts from the midnight gangsters to unconstitutionally overthrow him (see chapter 4). Was PT Ayah here truly four-eyesing the CGAM's future after his rocky second term by strategically managing the staffing of ELECOM? The question is apt, especially if you understand that it is those who draw up the agenda of a meeting that are the actual wielders of power, not those who put it into practice (Fossungu, 2010: 272-76; 1998a). Similarly, it is obvious that the status and influence of an institution like the Supreme Court (for instance) is largely tied to the status and vision of the Chief Justice – US Chief Justice John Marshall, England's Chief Justice Coke, and Canada's Chief Justice Bora Laskin clearly coming to mind. This is true since the Chief Justice can, inter alia, alter the course of a judgement through the power of scheduling cases (for more elaboration, see Fossungu, 1992). It is obviously the same with the chair of an organ like the ELECOM under discussion, an important arm of CGAM democracy. The question though is: How representative is this democracy?

A general discussion of democracy, with focus on Canada, can be found in Brooks (1996). There is a long-running debate in political science on democratization – how societies become democratic, and the conditions under which democratic regimes are likely to emerge; with the key controversy revolving around the relationship between economic development and democratic political institutions (Hopkins, 2010: 287; Najem, 2003; Schnabel, 2003; Posusney, 2004). Discussing 'Democracy and Political Culture' at pages 337-39 of his instructive study, Tessier (2002) came to the conclusion that "one of the leading sources of instability and political-economic distortion in the Arab world is the unchecked use of state power, combined with the state's whimsical ability to use the rule of law for its own political ends" (Tessier, 2002: 338). Such capricious use of rule of law invariably transforms the supreme organ into what can be called 'the most unsupreme in the system' (see Fossungu, 1998a; 2013c: chapter 3). Tessier outlines requirements for democratic transition and democratic consolidation, including accountability of rulers (2002: 338-39). All these things would not be possible when you are sitting in a CGAM General Assembly with a majority of whose members are *midnightistic demoncraz*. You can see from Table 4 that for the 2006 year in question ELECOM was a three-person committee – with Berri Nsame and Wilson Anung being the other two members that would seem 'scattered'.

Scattering the Wolf-Pack with "No-More-Acclamation"

We retired from the GA to determine the rules, as usual. But my ideas seemed totally out of place to the others who were completely taken aback and clearly disgusted by the "innovation". I did not quite comprehend their behaviour then until long afterwards. They must have been thinking to themselves: 'He is obviously involved in counter-conspiracy'. And, frankly, that is exactly what I was actually doing without myself actually knowing it then. When you are someone that deals with people openly and directly, you do not quite get to quickly comprehend schemers. **But** your *upfrontness* always dislodges their schemes before these get to fruition (see generally Fossungu, 2013a). That is exactly *why* and *how* it worked with the Ad Hoc Extraordinary Democrats' numerous after-midnight diabolical meetings at which they had planned and devised means to hijack democracy in the CGAM. They had formed their midnightistic cabinet that was to be unconstitutionally imposed upon the so-called founding members, as the story goes. What a folly!

The Founding Member Distinction Theories

You may think it is no folly as I say: until you realize that, for those who cannot speak out their minds, *Fifolefacism* can prove to be a very good brand of tree-topperism. Your understanding of the thesis would be enhanced with some facts on founding members. The issue of being a founding member or not has led to very heated and community-tearing discussions that have sought to distinguish between 'founding' (conceivers) and 'launching' (present at inauguration) members. There are many of such writings but the best exposition of the points would come from Hans Najeme's write-up of August 7, 2013 at 10.58 AM titled '*Walking Down Memory Lane of Goodwill Association*' in which the former president opened with "It is with mixed sentiments that I am compelled to tell my own story about the creation of Goodwill, who is who etc." He clearly indicates that he is not a founding father and not currently a CGAMer, "but as a former President of Goodwill, I believe my input will positively contribute to this debate." His story is in what he characterizes as 'two episodes'; with the first harping on the initiators of Goodwill which he firmly attributes to "those I will rightly call the Founders of Goodwill (M. Valentine Usongo, Dr. Peter Fosungo and M. Ako-Arrey Donatus)"; adding that Valentine Usongo had told him "that the ['Goodwill'] name was actually suggested by Dr. Peter Fosungo." In his second episode, Najeme agrees that "M. Paul Ayah's narrative is also correct, the first meeting as he rightly puts it with the members present is right, however, we will be doing a disservice to our great community, if we do not differentiate and clarify these two episodes and recognize them for what they are." In concluding his contribution to the debate, CGAM's third president stated: "My call on the

Community since we are still in the tenth anniversary year of Goodwill Association, is to recognize all those who have contributed to this Association and my special commendation to those who initiated and actually found Goodwill thus: Dr. Peter Fosungo, M. Valentine Usongo and M. Ako-Arrey Donatus."

The unnecessary wrangling about/against Founding Membership was clearly tearing the organization into pieces. They made it look like a lonely initiator is worth everything in the world! It was also to help 'put the right information out there' (as advocated for by President CO Ayah) therefore that, appreciating the audience "for wanting to know it as it is", Fossungu on August 9, 2013 at 11.45 PM first indicated that "I would have really liked to read Mr. Valentine Osongo's piece that most people are talking about and which, from the bits I can gather, sparked off the debate." Fossungu then proceeded to make some historical corrections; pointing out "On the issue of the name 'Goodwill' [that] it is President [PT] Ayah's version that is correct. Scholastica takes the credit for it, and it was during the first meeting as Paul says. I perfectly understand the confusion here because, then, Schola and Peter Fossungu were almost indistinguishable on the CGAM Question."

Turning to the issue of Who Initiated the Idea of Creating "Goodwill", the CGAM first president elaborately enlightened the audience as follows:

> I would like to say that this question is not a very important one in the sense that if you float an idea around and no one actually buys it no Association will be here today with us. But since a lot has been said and re-said about the question, I think I am better placed to clarify the controversy. There are actually two sides (and I would even say three sides) to this coin.

On the one side, there are those who say Dr. Peter Fossungu, Mr. Valentine Osongo, and Mr. Donatus Ayuk Ako-Arrey. They are not exactly correct as they are missing Mrs. Scholastica A. Fossungu (as she then was). The bachelors (as they then were) [that is, Donatus and Valentine] had just arrived [in] town and, as you already know from some of the write-ups, our door was always open. Schola cooks extremely well and these particular two single guys (with my encouragement) suggested that my wife be operating some kind of weekend restaurant where they could be coming for good home delicacies and drinks and fun. When Scholastica was not giving in to the restaurant idea, the question of having a formal association began as the four of us were discussing over a meal one evening at our Bishop Power residence.

On the other side, it was during Christmas 2002 that Dr. and Mrs. Tambong invited my family to dine with them. While there, I met Dr. Ndonkeu for the first time. He had just come to town from Belgium (I think) and had also been invited over by the Tambongs. While we were talking someone (I cannot remember if it was Dr. Tambong or Dr. Ndonkeu) wanted to know if there was any Cameroonian association in town. I informed them that the only I know from our own side of the Mungo River was called Njangi but that I was not a member of it. The reason being the third side of the coin, namely, that the first day someone (Moses Nkwenti) took me there [in October 1995] and introduced me as a newly arrived Cameroonian student the first question someone posed to me was: From North-West or South-West[?] I made it clear [to my questioners] that I would not want to belong to a group that looks at people only through their ethnic group or region of origin. The idea of forming an Association was also tossed around before the women called our attention to the dining table that was [set and] ready. While we were eating, Schola revived the talk on the formation of an association, even throwing in ideas on how to go about it (men bring drinks and women prepare food).

As you can therefore see, by the "the birth of their second child on April 1, 2003, [when] members of the community flocked to the Fossungu residence to pay their respects to their new born child" (I am quoting from President [PT] Ayah here), the idea of forming a formal association had been discussed within two sets of persons, with my family being the link to both groups. Therefore, if you want to be correct as to those who initiated the "Goodwill" Idea, then put down the names of all those in the two groups, with a bold on Scholastica. Alphabetically, then, you should say Mr. Ako-Arrey, Dr. Fossungu, Mrs. Fossungu (Scholastica), Dr. Ndonkeu, [Mr. Osongo,] Dr. Tambong, and Mrs. Tambong. I agree with President Najeme that "we will be doing a disservice to our great community, if we do not differentiate and clarify these two episodes and recognize them for what they are." I hope I have been of help to those who [Hans Najeme also says] want and deserve to "know the history of our community here in Montreal, and this history should be written and told as it is."

I do think that we often find it difficult telling it as it is solely because we are bent on creating 'illegitimate truths'.[30] To the spin that was being put on the simple omission, I can only say such reasoning could be tied mostly to cronies and the wait-and-see people who are hardly creators of history. They

---

[30] The falsifiers are all over the place looking for the slightest avenue to do their unholy midnight job. For example, the inadvertent omission of Valentine Usongo's name in the alphabetical listing between those of the two doctors was already being interpreted by some as being the handiwork of the instructor that I am yet to know who was behind Peter Ateh-Afac Fossungu's writing on Goodwill history. Valentine himself brought this to my attention during our phone conversation on 12 August 2013 and I was totally stupefied after re-reading the sent email and seeing that he was right. I was delighted though by his manner of handling the matter because it proved without a doubt that Valentine Usongo not only understood me but was also living with the 'Goodwill spirit' that he rightly says is behind the creation of the CGAM.

are most of the time wishers of history. History happened or happens before they could/can get on board and they then try to distort it in order to be even a remote part of it. Visonless people, midnighters, tree-toppers, etc., are what they *are* because they just don't have the guts to think for themselves. Just ask them why my "director" would want to even allow me to talk lengthily about and recognize Valentine Usongo as one of the initiators in the first place if this "director" wants Valentine's name to be left out in the alphabetical listing?

And you also clearly see such illegitimacy in the folly of the anti-founding-member theory. Fifolefac is alleged to have been the mastermind behind the so-called anti-*founding-members* midnight team. The league, paradoxically, included two notable founding members – Usongo and Ndonkeu! What a messy concept! The whole scheming muddle would again become very ridiculously midnightistic after the 2007 elections. The Najeme breakaway faction (called UNICAM) would be regarded by some simplistic minds as an *Amumba* or Northwest Affair. These weak-minded rumour spreaders would then get so confused when I would again confront them with these simple questions. Is Hans Najeme now from Savannazone (Northwest) with Walters Ndonkeu also now from Debundschazone (Southwest)? Ndonkeu oddly was Folefac's well-known chief strategist (Number One, as Folefac calls him) and yet was at the same time in the Najeme bureau! (Not too strange though since it is not a list system that CGAM uses.) Oh, this midnightism confusion in the CGAM! You can begin to see just how dangerous midnightism can be even to its practitioners, and therefore to the harmony of the CGAM. Anyway let's get the new election rules that would plunge us more profoundly into this CGAM midnight politics, a palpable case for *AITWsian* negative competition.

The New Rules and the Criminal Love Thesis

The rules that were introduced were simple enough to have still allowed the midnighters to carry out their scheme: but this time walking and working through the democratic process, call it progressive competition. But did they use it? Nay. Perhaps, as some experts do theorize, marijuana would no longer have the appeal it now has, if it were de-criminalized. Criminals obviously do not like non-criminal activities. It is just like this other popular Cameroonian saying that is regularly heard in several Canadian factories that *"Na anoda person e woman/massa dey sweet"* (it is only when they are committing adultery that they enjoy sex). African dictators seem to be enjoying living by this maxim. Remember always that this illicit sex is mostly carried out in the dark, even if in plain daylight. Recalling our attention to the young lad's question to his dad about politics, the quick question is: What is it with the night in African politics even in the sex domain? Better still, others would explain that when you are so blinded by your blinkeredness, you just don't see things the way they are, seeing only the one thing you want as the reality in this whole wide differentiated world. I can hear someone giving me the order to 'go ahead with the rules'.

For every position, I had made it exceedingly clear that the following "No-More-Acclamation" conditions must be satisfied: (1) there must be at least two candidates, (2) those nominated must have positively accepted their nomination, (3) members must actually cast their votes, (4) the exact number of votes received by each of the candidates must be shown in the electoral record, and (5) non-members (unregistered) had to leave the GA and stay upstairs until after elections were over. The rapporteur was Nsame while Anung was charged with collecting the ballot papers which all three of us then counted together on the table (our office corner) before the chair announced the results.

If the other two members of ELECOM had been perplexed, the GA was wholly dumbfounded with the announcement of these rules. I guess what must have totally *bouleversé* the midnight group was particularly the preface "No-More-Acclamation". CGAMers were witnessing this for the first time and (because pioneewantism is such a terrible disease with us) you could hear all sorts of *Dis one na reely come see for yasef*; *this man like for strick too mush*; *why e di bring too mush complication now noh*? I do not know what must have been going through the minds of the midnighters but I was not there to please or displease anyone, just to do things as they ought to be done. These new rules of positive competition scattered the midnight conspirators like the sudden appearance of a lion does to a herd of antelopes. But that is not all because the rules also provided an eye-opening opportunity for a daring hijacker to hijack his colleagues – thus dealing a demoralizing and exposing blow to midnightism. That is to say that the resistance to my new electoral rules crumbled when, after their nomination-rejection strategy was kind of working, someone (who must obviously not have been part of them) nominated Hans Najeme and he quickly accepted to contest for the presidency – the first position to be filled. The wolf-pack was at a loss because, as I said earlier, they were bent on just one thing – get it their way or no way. Otherwise, wasn't this the proper place to nominate one of their own to compete with and teach their blacklegging colleague (Najeme) the lesson that he needed to be taught?

Rather, they were counting on there being no other candidate and, therefore, no election as per the new model. You get this interpretation from the fact that no other person that people were randomly and jokingly throwing up, accepted their nomination – not even Denis Alem who later ended up as Najeme's Vice-President. The midnightistic plan seemed to be making a come-back, they thought. One little piece of the puzzle they forgot was the fact that not everyone in the GA was a midnighter, and that the jokers who were throwing up those names were a serious unknown force. We were clearly headed for a constitutional meltdown. But when you are on the right side of history there is often no reason to be panicky or capitulating simply to please. I stood firm against all suggestions from many so-called eminent members in the GA for a refashioning or slackening of the rules. (Most of these people *suggesting* were even tree-toppers that the others – myself included – in the GA could then not quite four-eyesly divine until many years later.) Unfortunately for them, I clearly reminded them that the ELECOM was independent from any pressures, whatever their origins, in performing its tasks. That it had already made the rules clear to the GA before the process commenced and, therefore, that the GA's duty was simply to fill those positions through the said rules by nominating at least a second candidate for the president to be elected. Usher in *Lyslyakoayahism*, please, says the drunkard.

Lyslyakoyahism And The Ahidjoist Agenda: Explaining Her Ousting

At this point, one of the aforementioned 'bottle-emptying' jokers threw up Lysly Ako Ayah's name for president. Why don't we Africans listen and reflect rather than just laugh? The general laughter that followed took quite a while to subside. Surprised as the former and constitutional-term-breaking treasurer was,[31] LA Ayah heartily thanked "whoever" it was

---

[31] 'Lysly Ako Ayah, CGAM Treasurer: 2003-2005, 2008'! What happened to the two-consecutive-term ban? The post of treasurer has been practically dominated by two names – Lysly Ako Ayah and Precilia Nkengasong Folefac. This speaks volume of them, as well as anyone who has occupied the post. CGAMers do not usually nominate and/or vote for just anyone when it comes to the guardian of their *nkap*. The competition, as I have said, remains between the two dominating personalities – Lysly and Precilia. They have both served in different administrations. They provide evidence too that the CGAM has what I call the *Poutine-Door* and in chapter 6 I would be advising some former presidents to instead use it to come back and serve rather than obstructing their successors by constantly violating the constitution. Constitutional violation or not, these two

that thought she could do the job, concluding that "it is a challenge that I must not shy away from. I therefore accept the nomination." From negative to positive competition, is what one can say here. Was this not history unfolding right before our eyes? Did the drunkard or *paplé* just lead us to where the key had been hiding, lost? (You will better grasp this by visiting 'The Theory of Drunklampostism' in chapter 6.) The relief on the image of the first nominee was palpably visible. In my position then I could not vote or do anything else to alter the results but I had then interpreted Najeme's relief solely on the basis of his satisfaction that the stalemate was over. But there was more to it than just that, as you will see soon.

I asked both candidates to make their election campaign speeches, each having ten minutes, beginning with the first

---

treasurers can already give more force to my thesis above that CGAMers would rather joke with their constitution (as they do all the time) than do same with who handles their finances. *Fossungupaffectism* would seem to question all this though. Table 5 shows all the treasurers so far.

Table 5: Treasurers of CGAM

Name	Year(s)	Name	Year(s)
Lysly Ako Ayah	2003-2005	Emmanuel Fokoua Tene	2009-2010
Precilia Nkengasong Folefac	2006	Julius Etaya Ashu	2011
Mirabel Fambo Lukong	2007	Precilia Nkengasong Folefac	2012-2013
Lysly Ako Ayah	2008	Yacubu Mohnkong	2014

nominee. I would tell you this one sure thing. If there were many in the GA that had until then been underestimating LA Ayah's capabilities, they all had a change of heart after her spontaneously passionate and eloquent appeal and dedication to continue serving the association in the capacity of president just as she had done till then as treasurer. It was a truly fixating moment because she was very believable too. If no one could see it then, I did realize that this lady had vision for the CGAM; otherwise, how else would anyone explain her resignation from the ELECOM in late 2007? On October 28, 2007 we all learned about the only progressive non-protesting resignation in CGAM history from the chair of that body which informed all CGAMers "that Lysly Ayah tendered her resignation yesterday from the Electoral Committee. Her resignation notice was as follows: 'After serious consideration, I have decided to resign from the electoral committee in order to better serve the goodwill community.' This means that during our November meeting, the Assembly may have to appoint someone else to fill the vacancy." In 2007, LA Ayah not only beat her incumbent opponent for the coveted treasurer position. She was also the elected official in those hotly contested elections with the highest percent (68%) of the votes cast, with Vice-President Aloysius Ibeagha following on her heels with 65%, Financial-Secretary Pius Etube with 62%[32] and President Folefac with 61%.

---

[32] The December 2007 election brought forth a financial secretary that would undoubtedly change the CGAM's *finsecism* (short form for the portfolio of the financial secretariat). A discussion on the pioneering of positive changes in the CGAM would clearly be artificial or incomplete without *Peetubecism* in the domain of Finsecism. This financial secretary post was introduced in 2005 for electing the following year's bureau because, with the exponential membership growth, it had become very clear that the treasurer alone (coupled with the S-G *breakages*) could no longer efficiently handle both the accounting books and the finances. In addition to the resignation of the pioneer Fin.Sec (as CGAMers love calling him/her), I cannot escape indicating that the one name that has revolutionized, professionalized and popularized this office is Pius Esambe Etube. His

As I have often indicated, when you are real, there is no need to struggle with your ideas. In December 2006 if CGAMers were actually out to preserve the bright future and foster what was already in place in their group, then LA Ayah clearly beat Hans Najeme hands down with just her presidential campaign appeal. She would evidently have been overwhelmingly elected by a well-to-do GA that would be interested in handing over to a leadership that had vision and zeal. I guess another important point I am raising here is that no one (not even this writer) would have discovered this woman's potentials had the old electoral procedure continued to be used. Her surprising leadership showings, clearly advantageous as they were/are, played wonderfully into the

---

successors have been equally innovative in their duties (their duration of term speaking to it) but they have all been building largely on the solid framework that was initiated by the award-winning 2008-2009 Fin.Sec. With the rise of *Peetubecism*, the treasurer became likened to the bank manager that you hardly see when you go banking, with the Fin.Sec becoming the teller or banking machine. Members have since Peetubecism forgotten about worrying about what their financial situation was at any time because these guys have just kept keeping them constantly fed with the information through the latest technology and software. Can I even be able to fully talk about the cordial and professional way they respond to any concerns addressed to their office? Table 6 gives you a list of all those who have handled the post.

Table 6: Financial Secretaries of CGAM

Name	Year(s)	Name	Year(s)
Mirabel Fambo	2006	Roger Ekuh-Ngwese	2011-2012
Nixon Tebo	2007	Fonderson Tataw Ashu	2013
Pius Esambe Etube	2008-2009	Henry Mesumbe	2014
Julius Etaya Ashu	2010		

hands of doubly-handicapped Najeme. The hijacking opportunistic hijacker now had all the fearful hijacked midnighters playing the popular Fru Ndi-Biya/France (and Ahidjo-Biya) *poligames* or politickerizing games. Don't they say two enemies would become real friends when they have a common enemy? How else can LA Ayah's ousting be explained? I will survey three possibilities with you: (1) not distinguishing individual from relations, (2) firstohocelectionism occasioning charalicism, and (3) dog-rule politics of exclusion or not ready for a woman as president?

Not Distinguishing Individuals from Relations?

LA Ayah lost to Najeme with a very large margin probably because, as it is also said, the devil you know is better than the angel you don't. But that does not seem to present the larger *midnighturism* (or midnight picture) until you understand why there was midnightism in the first place – boot 'founding member' PT Ayah out of office at all costs. As chapter 4 further shows, midnightism results from the numerous nocturnal secret meetings held by some ("teleguided") members who were bent on forcing the PT Ayah government out of office by whatever means, especially through mass resignations, following the failure of their constitutional adhocism (in the 2006 March-April Assemblies) to gain grounds and do the job through motions and voting or *motioncracy*. The whole scheme only came to the attention of non-midnighters like some of us when a heated argument broke out between them over the treasurer's (PN Folefac's) non-conformity with the mass bureau resignations as midnightly planned. There was then, it would appear, a high sense of black-legging within the black-legging group, and that would shortly replay itself in the 2006 December elections for the 2007 bureau, with an Ayah (and founding member too!) positively competing for the top post.

The mere thought of another Ayah taking over from PT Ayah was sort of very scary to people with very scary agendas. This scary agenda thing is such a 'religion' in midnight politics that it woefully inhibits a community's growth because it relates to not distinguishing an individual from their relations (parents, siblings, uncles/aunts, etc.). It is totally regressive and characteristic of Cameroon politics and has led Fossungu (1998c) to theorize that "A person is first and foremost an individual before being part of a society or group or family. That is the essence of individual liberty or freedoms." Therefore, Fossungu's argument goes on, "[u]ntil there is mentality change in those respects, it is advised [that] Cameroonians would simply not be able to decipher or detect the several volumes of half-truths and/or outright lies that have been clothed in similarities in sounds and appearances." Absent such mentality change, the critics like musician Prince Ndedy Eyango and the 8th CGAM President think that we would only be wasting precious time and energy talking about the building of a strong united community. Some experts have therefore posited that the attainment of 'our dreamland' of a democratic United Africa, with Cameroon as nucleus,

> would entail, among others, that we do learn, for instance, to judge one by one's own. By 'judge' here, I am not referring only to its negative connotation. That also must include the positive, e.g., judging if someone is fit for a certain post, etc. This should be an essential lesson if Cameroonians are really serious about the change they claim they are after. Do we seriously want a DRA [Democratic Republic of Africa] or not? Then the golden rule ought to be to only judge any individual citizen by his or her deeds and words (and not those of the parents, child, relatives or clansmen) [Fossungu, 1998c].

This is sane counsel because the silly way of reasoning in Cameroon (Africa's so-called torch bearer) largely explains why Africa is not making the progress that is rightly its own. We do not look at, and emphasize, the candidate's capabilities but rather things that have practically no connection with suitability for the job. All the lethal arms of midnightism were then to work against a very qualified woman. To begin with, the majority that LA Ayah needed to win had had their issue with the out-going president since March 2006 or even earlier. I really do not know why, except perhaps that the Vice-President first hotly contested election sparked off charalicism in the group's leaders. Did firstohocelectionisn actually beget Fifolefac's Charalicism?

Firstohocelectionisn Occasioning Charalicism?

Firstohocelectionism is a terminological shorthand in CGAM politics for 'the first ever hotly contested elections', being the handiwork of the V-P post that was introduced only on January 14, 2006 during that month's Assembly. The GA having duly adopted the executive creation of the V-P post, it had to be filled through elections. It was a historic election because, first, at the same session a 'new' condition was introduced and adopted as to who was eligible for election to a post: It was unanimously agreed during said meeting that henceforth a member should be at least one year in the association before he/she is eligible to contest for a position (January 2006 Minutes). This was *not* a new rule to those of us who were there at inception because it was a rule that existed from inception but which, until that point, had politickerizingly been treated as a no-rule.[33] Thus, the V-P would just have

---

[33] For a quick example, take the S-G of the 2006 bureau (Aloysius Ibeagha). He was elected in December 2005, having joined the association in July that same year. Just five months as a member: when was the one-year membership condition for holding office scrapped? The written constitution at the time mandated (in Article 3) that new members be

been "elected" the same acclaiming way but for the fact that this time it was apparent that more than one person was eyeing the prestigious position whose creation had long been announced (that is, days before the meeting date). It thus presented almost the same scenario as the ICAO-Korea case discussed by Fossungu (1999a: 346-53). You could then easily see that said 'new' law on elections was clearly targeting some particular persons (the less-than-one-year-old members at that date). Another very important flaw that Fossungu raised here but which was politickerized away was for voting to be restricted only to those who had duly renewed their membership that January Assembly. The validity of such membership logic is something people who fear positive competition (the adhocists) would rarely appreciate, as was also the case when Fossungu again brought it up in January 2007.

Anyway, both nominated aspirants for the post of V-P here met the one-year condition, Fifolifac having been strategically nominated by Denis Ako-Arrey (another strategist of his), while JB Komguep by Caren Osong Ayah (These Ayahs!). The historic vote for V-P ended in a tie of 17-17 (34 votes cast out of 56 members in total: what happened to the rest?) and the election was postponed to the February meeting. There is obviously more time at hand for more lobbying and the like of political jockeying. Could this be the effective time the midnight legion got its birth? Komguep eventually won the race and became the first V-P of the CGAM, as seen in Table

---

handed a copy of this constitution on being admitted, with a further provision that they be sponsored by an existing member who must have instructed them fully on what CGAM is all about (see also chapter 5). You may be wondering why I say Article 3 *at the time*. Does it mean that the situation has since changed? Not really. I use the expression because these days you can never be very certain of the constitutional and other developments of the CGAM because of *constitutional adhocism*. This problem is also tied to the notorious "Yearly Review of Bylaws" that has been entrenched because of an incorrect reading of the amendment provision, what I would disdainfully call *blackletterism*. Just only wish that this blackletterism applied as well to respecting other provisions!

7.³⁴ Did this election bring about something in the nature of payback to the Ayah clan? Did Komguep defeat Fifolefac simply because CGAMers might not have wanted to see husband and wife in the same bureau? Why was this post created in the first place only in January and not before December 2005 to be included in that December's bureau elections? Was this another strategic master play by PT Ayah? Could the results of this particular 'by-election' be considered as the real killer pill for the CGAM? You might find some of these queries unimportant until you realize (from 'Separatist-Foolish Dramacracy' in chapter 4) that the new V-P also became the first and only V-P to taste first-hand what Carlson Anyangwe would describe in 2012 as the 'Unconstitutional Overthrow of Constitutional Order in

---

[34] Table 7 below gives you information on the personalities that have so far held this position

Table 7: Vice-Presidents of CGAM

Name	Year(s)	Name	Year(s)
Jules-Blaise Komguep	2006	Ignatius Nsom Mbeng	2011
Denis Alem	2007	Caren Osong Ayah	2012
Aloysius Ibeagha	2008	Delphine Afor Ndemanga	2013
Martha Tanyi Mbianyong	2009	Roger Ekuh-Ngwese	2014
Florence Ngayap Nankam	2010		

Africa'.[35] Firstohocelectionism must have been viewed by Folefac as his own *Charalicism*? Charalicism is defined by Fossungu (2014: 29) as "the art of venturing with irresistible risk, danger that directly leads you to surprisingly taste your first failure or first success (as the case may be) in any domain." Was it this *first election failure* that needed to be *tree-topperly* avenged through midnightism?

Whatever it is, midnightism lacks in its not making a distinction between persons as individuals, leading to regressive or negative competition. There is imperative need for change, otherwise, as some experts have further explained it, there should not be any need complaining about or condemning naked tribalism, nepotism, *c'est notre tour de bouffer*, and the like. For, how would a person then be able to hold any views or opinions that are different from the family or clan's member: knowing that, come what may, he or she would be condemned by those relations' views? Just how, for example, is Peter's unborn nephew not going to adopt and defend the somewhat 'stupid' (to him and his epoch) ideas that Peter could now be airing if, while even still in the womb, he could reliably learn that in Cameroon – where he is to become a citizen – he could be arrested in the maternity or taunted all around because an uncle of his (whom he even hardly knows) committed such "imbecility"? Would it not be fitting that this child be rather given the chance and time to grow up and freely choose his own proper opinions; and then judge him only for/by what he has freely chosen to be and is, and not for what the uncle or whomsoever of his was or is? Aren't these children entitled to

---

[35] See http://www.langaa-rpcig.net/Revolutionary-Overthrow-of.html. Another first with this vice-president post is *viperizationism* that is discussed in chapter 6.

be born first before they have to start worrying over changing their lot? [Fossungu, 1998c]

Dog-Rule Politics of Exclusion or Not Ready for a Woman as President?

Not making the suggested distinction between individuals is a midnightism 'religion' that obviously was the reasoning with PT Ayah's sister in the December 2006 elections (as it might have also been in January 2006 with the Folefac-Komguep contest?). Or was it the 'founding member' thing too? Furthermore, quite apart from the dull act of voting with their feet (not speaking out mind), CGAMers seem not to have been ready for a woman at the helm *who was democratically elected*, not just a blindfold. This thesis is buttressed by midnightism. The midnighters' pre-packaged government, it is said, had Eveline Awemu Ibeagha (EA Ibeagha) as president. This midnightistic tree-topping arrangement, it has been rumoured, was arrived at because the 'real president', her husband (Aloysius Ibeagha), would not easily sell to CGAMers since he is of Nigerian stock. Do you not see how those who have no intention of respecting the constitution cannot constitutionally use it? In other words, why should these midnight people be thinking this way when, by marriage alone to a Cameroonian, a person acquires full membership that the constitution has authorized to go with all the rights and obligations incident to it (as further seen in Chapter 5's 'The Rights Battles')? Exclusionist politics, as usual, isn't it? Cameroon inside Canada indeed!

The Folly of the Nigerian-Connexion Theory

In addition, tree-topperism apart, the Nigerian connexion theory is wholly unsustainable especially as the CGAM is not the only Cameroonian association that Ibeagha belongs to. He has been introduced in several quarters of the community as having become the president of *Njangi de Montréal* which is predominantly Cameroonian. For instance, on January 7, 2007 Hans Najeme in presidentially wishing CGAMers Happy New Year 2007 also noted "Another important development. It is my pleasure to announce to you that our own **Dr. Ibeagha Aloys is now the new President of Njangi de Montreal**, following a General Assembly meeting of the Njangi held on Jan 06, 2007. So fellow Goodwillers, our great association is putting a stamp on the map of Cameroon Associations in Montreal. Please join me in congratulating Dr. Ibeagha and wish him all the best in handling the affairs of the Njangi de Montreal" [bold is original].

Cameroonians seem to have been well-nourished with the stupid idea of one city 'breathing' and the rest of their country living that while out here in Canada they would create a small grouping in a quarter of Montreal and the next thing you hear is that it is X-Group Canada! What a folly that follows people along miles and miles of distances! I am a SOBAN (Sasse Old Boys Association member) and can very proudly tell you that SOBA-Montreal (which used to be SOBA-Canada) is what it is today largely thanks to the efforts of Ibeagha who, with his team of very able young men, picked up the old dying unrealistic 'Canada' and revamped and renamed it to 'realistic' Montreal. Ibeagha has been that SOBA's president in the last three or so years.[36] So, is the Nigerian *thing* then something else or what the chitchat says it is?

Dog-Rule Politics of Exclusion

This whole thing does look very much like another version of Kini-Yen Kinni Fongot's 'Bakassi Politics of Exclusion and Occupation' by which some unthinking midnighters "are bastardised, humiliated and scammed by unscrupulous

---

[36] I am just hoping it does not also degenerate into the SOBA-UK imbroglio, with a long-ruling president thinking it was his birth right to be there forever without anyone ever raising a finger.

opportunists who deliberately misidentify them with intentions of dispossessing them of their ancestral lands and natural resources."[37] This claim is justified by the other question (four-eyesly linked to the foregoing Bakassi theory) that one could ask. It relates to why any of the non-*non-Cameroonian* midnighters could not have taken the place? Could a possible answer be that none of them then had the big-title qualification or the natural resources? As seen above in chapter 1, only the two Ibeaghas were doctors among these midnighters. Oh! Africans and high-sounding big-small titles! Just see it too in Monsieur Paul Biya. He is feeling wanting even as a *pleins-pouvoirs* president solely because most of the ministers he single-handedly appoints have this **DR** (did someone just call it Dog-Rule?) thing uselessly hanging behind or in front of (?) their names. So Biya sneaks into the USA and buys his own doctor title from one of those backdoor American universities (Oh, these Americans and ill-gotten money! Is that not the whole idea behind the Military-Industrial-Complex?[38]). But the

---

[37] http://www.langaa-rpcig.net/Bakassi-Or-the-Politics-of.html

[38] A notorious manifestation of the MIC complex that a senator has recently called attention to is "the 'revolving door' that exists between the Pentagon and the defense industry" (McCain, 2011). Raymond (1964: 170-222) has also gone to great lengths describing this 'revolving door' phenomenon and how the Pentagon generally works. In 1969 (four years after Jack Raymond's *Power at the Pentagon*), McCain narrates, then-Senator William Proxmire said this about the revolving door in the context of defense procurement: "The easy movement of high-ranking military officers into jobs with major defense contractors and the reverse movement of top executives in major defense contractors into high Pentagon jobs is solid evidence of the military-industrial complex in operation. It is a real threat to the public interest because it increases the chances of abuse... How hard a bargain will officers involved in procurement planning or specifications drive when they are one or two years from retirement and have the example to look at over 2,000 fellow officers doing well on the outside after retirement?" (McCain, 2011) Duncan (2013: 51-56) sees this as "Rent-Seeking Replac[ing] Market Competition". Let's take another glaring pork-barrel example to buttress the Congressional 'Sacred Cows' and show just how corrupt the whole American system has become. From 1978 to 1998, the air force requested a total of five C-130s, but Congress voted funds for

president is very embarrassed that the local press had found out this even before his return to base. The newspaper headlines "DR BIYA EMERGES!!!!!!!!!" that greeted his return virtually stole much (if not all) of the show, to the extent that no one hears of the midnight title anymore.

Do not begin to think though that it is all about the negative. It is just that the highlighting of bad news is the helpful kind that helps to improve the ratio of good news to bad news (see Fossungu, 2013c: x-xii). Because of the notorious out-of-meetings meetings and negative-competition scheming, the December 2006 GA could not completely elect a full Najeme-led bureau. Four positions (treasurer, two social secretaries[39] and public relations officer[40]) had to be carried

---

256 of the aircraft. This is surely a record in the pork-barrel politics which would justify John McCain's complaint that "there were so many excess C-130s that we could afford to park one in 'every schoolyard in America'" (Hartung, 2001: 41-42). There was obviously an immediate response from the congressional friends of the military-industrial complex, coming from Democratic Senator Max Cleland of Georgia who "felt compelled to suggest that the excess C-130s were justified since America needed the capability to deploy our schoolyard anywhere in the world on short notice" (Hartung, 2001: 42). This talk of deploying military aircraft in schoolyards squarely leads us to the Military-Industrial-Academic (MIA) complex that has American universities in chains, thus also being responsible for the excessive stereotyping of Africa in America, as seen in chapter 6.

[39] The Social Secretary (*socio*, as they call themselves) is responsible for the organization of activities and ensuring the success of such events. The position was introduced in 2006. Later it was split into two positions – female and male – since the argument was that one person cannot appropriately handle it as during a social occasion men and women assume different obligational roles: bringing drinks and bringing prepared food. The post has been held by those shown in Table 8.

Table 8: Social Secretaries of CGAM

Name	Year(s)	Name	Year(s)
Emmanuel Fokoua Tene	2006	Caren Osong Ayah	2011
Prudence Ayuk (female), Walter Ndonkeu (male)	2007	(Vacant at election in November 2011)	2012
Prudence Ayuk Tabenyang (female), Alain Foko Kamga (male)	2008	Micheline Acheah	2013
Nathalie Nchotou (female), Ignatius Nsom Mbeng (male)	2009	Mispah Tegum	2014
Berri Nsame (female), Alain Foko Kamga (male)	2010		

[40] This office is normally one that carries a lot of weight because it can be compared to the US secretary of state, for instance. The PRO is the liaison officer between the Association and the external world; should be well versed with the Association's activities; speaks to the media on behalf of the Association and briefs the executive; and is the coordinator of the website. Why is the ambience with this post otherwise in the CGAM? As important as it is supposed to be, it does not seem to be the case and even elections to the office bear proof. Members who have occupied this post that was introduced in 2007 are in Table 9.

Table 9: Public Relations Officers of CGAM

Name	Year(s)	Name	Year(s)
Vincent Cheg Nche	2007	Hilary Fuh-Cham	2011
Emmanuel Fokoua Tene	2008	Rosaline Ayuk-Takang	2012
Alain Kamga Foko	2009	Laban Nkuh	2013
Patrick Tanyi	2010	Evaristus Ngoe Ojah	2014

over to the January 2007 Assembly that held at the elected president's residence in Laval (Quebec).

Chapter 4

Getting The Government You Deserve: From Quebec Separatism To CGAM April-Fool Democracy

The former [civil servants], in particular, refused to join the wagon of change arguing: *Mon salaire passe: où est mon problème...* because, at the time, Mother France was still willing to back Biya [against Fru Ndi] by paying the civil service. This could only mean that (1) as long as everything is fine with them here and now, why do they have to bother about their children? [A]nd (2) they would have joined in the struggle to effectively bring down the system only if their "privilege" (that is the way this bunch of contradictory uncivilized civil servants consider their salary) did not flow. The gathering storm was, consequently, not strong enough to do the job.

Now, what has happened to the passing and even to the thing that used to pass? The ball has changed court. It is now the turn of these civil servants. The first thing they salute you with these days is always *"mon salaire"* that has been slashed into ten... and even the tenth he or she cannot get at the end of the month. And they will even be announcing [this] to you, expecting sympathy on your part! [Fossungu, 1998e]

The January 2007 Assembly is notable for a number of reasons that touch directly on clear points that CGAMers refused to see; and this largely because of the midnight that was cast in broad daylight. Najeme and his cohorts must have realized by then that the Fossungu-chaired ELECOM was not going to let them have 'their way or no way'. Whether by design or mere coincidence Berri Nsame was absent from that meeting at which we normally had to complete our task and end our mandate. As soon as it was time for the voting exercise, Najeme declared that he was appointing (not even suggesting for the GA to do so) a new commission because the other one that conducted the elections in December was incompetent, the proof being in the incomplete bureau. Didn't I tell you earlier that opportunists just don't think of anything else? How do you think I knew from my first meeting this guy that he was/is what I say he is?

Well, I took the useless time to remind the CGAM president that he was forgetting the fact that he was not the president of the CGAM right then "because the incompetent ELECOM goes into the dustbin with all officials 'elected' under/through it. Not also leaving out the incompetent GA that elected/appointed the incompetent ELECOM." I am sure CGAMers would still be laughing uselessly at this very moment but for PT Ayah's interruption to indicate that a third member be elected to complete the committee in place to finish its work. Najeme still insisted on his right as president to appoint a new ELECOM. Was he here not deliberately confusing a special events committee (SEC) with heads of special organs – as seen in the CGAM constitution[41]? Such a reminder clearly has no place to those who are bent on 'having it my way or no way'. Mr. President then switched gears a little bit, still insisting

---

[41] Chapter II of the CGAM Constitution (Articles 7-16) covers issues of organs and governance structure, dotting the association with some main organs (1) the General Assembly, (2) the Executive Bureau, (3) Goodwill Advisory Council (GAC) and (4) Special Events Committees (SECs). There are three special organs of CGAM, namely, the Goodwill Women Forum (GWWF), Goodwill Children Diversity Program (GCDP) and Goodwill Football Club (GWFC). For further discussion of organizations' inter-organ politics, see Fossungu (1998a). ELECOM is one of the SECs. Governed by Article 10, the SECs consist of members, chosen by the General Assembly or appointed by the President and adopted by the General Assembly, to work on a particular project for the Association. With a mandate and scope to be defined by the General Assembly, their report is presented and submitted to the General Assembly directly for adoption. The head of each committee is responsible for the activities of the committee. On the other hand, appointing the heads of the special organs is the president's exclusive prerogative. See chapter 6 for more on this issue.

on putting the matter of his dismissing the committee to vote. That was not only clearly uncalled for and dictatorial, but it was also indicating in black and white the constitutional adhocism that was in the pipeline.

The message opening this chapter was written way long before the CGAM was ever formed but it is like it was written when the events of this chapter particularly had already occurred. If you are still asking about the democrats of the CGAM, I ask you to hold on until that sane message to the uncivilized civil servants begins to apply because right now it is Fossungu's personal problem with the president, they think. When the GA even took to voting on the matter (the vote went against the dissolution by a slight 2-vote margin), I made it clear they had to get two, not just one, additional members. Okay, one more, because, before I could even finish what I was saying, Ibeagha had already imposed himself as a member of said committee and was acclaimed by the hand-and-bottle-clapping beer-drinkers. If only I could find the inventor of this opium called beer, s/he would no doubt have a good taste of the pains of Jesus' cross!

I do not know exactly how they did it after my withdrawal, knowing this though: Mr. Opportunist got all his opportunities to siphon the huge sums of money that had been announced in December 2006 by the out-going bureau as being in the association's coffers. Can you then see why the hijacker quickly broke ranks with his mates to be at the helm? Can you also see why he wanted and got the kind of treasurer he was after?[42]

---

[42] The treasurer position is a very sensitive one and, with the backbiting/gossiping that is so rife in the community, has led to expressions of disgust like Mirabel Fambo Lukong's on December 12, 2007: "FELLOW GOODWILLERS, A word of caution to those who run their mouths. I have had and heard enough: 1- Take note, the Goodwill association has never contributed in paying my mortgage while hosting at my residence. Besides, 150 dollars cannot pay my hydro bills. 2- When we bought our house at the time, I was not part of the exco, thus stop soiling my name that

But that is not all. CGAMers got a real big time dose of their sleepy foot-voting behaviour, including in the large measure the midnighters themselves. Before I take you to the pepsoheineken 'fringe' midnighters' fight to regain the torch in December 2007, let us have some of the things Fossungu saw coming long ago that others only saw when it later hit hard.

The Value Of Balanced Critique

During my long stay in Montreal particularly and Canada generally, I have had the rare opportunity (especially through

---

I use[d] goodwill funds to buy our house. Thanks. Mirabel." The campaign message of LA Ayah for the December 2007 elections could aid in your comprehension of the power dynamics in respect of the position that she took over after said contest: "As treasurer of Goodwill:

> 1. I will re-instate confidence in handling the finances of this association as evident by my excellent performance as treasurer in 2004/2005.
> 2. Your money will be in the bank at all times to avoid embarrassing members with bounced cheques
> 3. Money will not be given out to whosoever without due approval in keeping with Goodwill policies
> 4. The names of those granted loans will be treated as confidential, unless in cases of non-respect of the terms of the loan.
> 5. You will have adequate access to information on Goodwill's finances through regular financial statements to individuals and the General Assembly (GA)
> 6. I am willing to be audited at any time and accept criticisms without bias.
> 7. Financial records shall be kept clean without any suspicious cancellations
> 8. Efficiency, accountability & transparency will be ensured by providing receipts for payments made to and by the association.
> 9. I will establish a good working relationship with all members of the executive, not just the president and will be answerable to the GA

I will listen to you and remain an active team player of this association."

the CGAM that I helped in creating) to *observe and discover* some very exceptional leadership qualities in some Cameroonians that I have this far had the chance to interact with. But remember always that no one is a bundle of only good things. I am therefore writing the things I write here (or *putting forward some empirical data from my keen observation or four-eyesism*) with the sole intention of aiding some of those unique people to work on their negatives and thus become even more exceptional leaders. That is the kind of leadership that Africa now badly needs. I can four-eyesismatically see great potentials and our brighter future in some of them. Who (without four-eyes) knows! Some of them might tomorrow be our *effective* prime ministers/presidents, etc. in the new Cameroon we are all clamouring for. Hasn't it been said that the salvation of the continent lies in Cameroon?

I have a dream. That sometime tomorrow the children of this continent would regard themselves as Africans before anything else. That the salvation of this continent lies right here in our midst in this Cameroon whose name would soon change to the Democratic Republic of Africa (DRA). That some wise leader is soon to come up in this country and will begin this metamorphosis. (Let some lovers of dictatorship not start thinking of killing all our young babies like the Egyptian king anyway. The dream did not say it is a new-born or an already ripe person.) [Fossungu, 1998b].

I do honestly think Cameroonians should be entitled to have a prior idea of who exactly some of these prospective leaders are before they actually ever get to assume those positions, if they do. Gone must surely be the days and times when people just accidentally stumbled into power in Africa and then they themselves (or through their cronies) 'creating' an undeserved rosy curriculum vitae for themselves. Such modus operandi could explain why our country or continent is being run down by externally-imposed rascals, rather than being governed. That also elucidates why we are so *cronynized*.

All of these are largely due to the stack absence of good pioneers, fortified *en plus* by our over-belief in big-sounding empty titles such as Dr President X or President Emeritus Dr Y or *Ancient-Nouveau Directeur-Général Monsieur Le Sous-Préfet Agrégé* Z, etc. What is it with us with titles and midnightism?

Additionally, could the midnighters (in the majority in the GA) have then similarly been seeing LA Ayah as PT Ayah's own *sister-version* of EA Ibeagha, perhaps? They must have; especially as their eyes don't see the tree-topper who is *shitting* like an invisible bird on their inside-empty heads. To them my stance in the ELECOM must have been interpreted as my playing a pro-Ayah family game. Small-mindedness, don't you think? And why don't they divine some of these very easy things? It is because they are "easy-way thinkers", of course, "who, oxymoronically, do not quite seem to see easy explanations" (Fossungu, 2014: 118). Answered as it is, the question is still good since it also necessitates my digging once more into my rich expibasketism for both your pleasure and the displeasure of the politickerizers in the CGAM. This will have to do with 'The Political Economy of Democracy, Deaths and Births in the CGAM' – the Goodwill taboo subjects that I always do my best to *untaboolize*.

Death Sociopackism: Confirming the Arrata-Poison Theory?

Sociopackism, again, means social packages on the trio (birth, death, and marriage). Most people within the community (including the well-known politickerizers) would agree with the description by Fossungu (2013a: 130-131) of PT Ayah's inimitable achievements as CGAM president. I would not even want to venture near talking much about Ayah's dwarfing accomplishments as the president of the ACC (Association of Cameroonians in Canada). It was not until Ayah's presidency that this body assumed nation-wide stature, positively touching the lives of Cameroonians in the country from coast to coast, especially through his trademark innovations like the bilingual

Mt. Cameroon Magazine, etc. Until then, successive Francophone ACC presidents had just been badly running a Montreal-centred organization and calling it Canada-wide, like the SOBANS. I remember bringing up this particular issue at the level of the ACC Permanent Council (consisting of the leaders of the various Cameroonian associations in Montreal) when I was the CGAM's president. Do I still need to say what the usual reaction was? "*Les Anglos aiment trop déranger les choses.*" As indicated, I cannot sufficiently catalogue PT Ayah's achievements with the ACC. *Res ipsa loquitur* is the way lawyers would want to swindle the *unlawyerly* folks rather than talking in plain terms by just saying 'the thing speaks for itself'. Who wants to argue with these Latin-loving lawyers? No one at this point in time would. But PT Ayah has just one little 'nice guy' issue that very quickly becomes a huge problem, especially in an environment that is heavily infested with politickerizers. *Sociopackism* will begin illustrating the point and the GWFC Crisis will close it.

At the July 2007 Assembly (always bear in mind that we are in the Najeme era), the relationship of brother/sister was removed from the death social package coverage. From the previous talk about constitutional adhocism, I would not need to specifically indicate here that the issue was never even on the agenda of said meeting. But it was done all the same because the loss of someone (Felicia Tatuh Nzonji) who was not liked was presented. That is thus the *adhocist* new *Law on Death Assistance*. Your sister or brother is not anything of importance to you like a stranger to you is. But that is quite another matter. The other problem relates to changing the law at will and in response to particular cases; and worse still, not even respecting that newly made law. There are so many things in the Much Ado Basket. Get it all uncensored from a piece titled *'Double-Talking Meilleurism in the CGAM'*[43] by Peter Ateh-Afac Fossungu who lengthily wrote on August 20, 2007:

Goodwillers, I do not know how you look at it but it seems to me that the Cameroon Goodwill Association of Montreal (CGAM) has become one of the best places for lessons in the infamous art of Double-Talking. Some of us may want to impress on people that this is not the time for talking about the issue because of the sad events in our larger Cameroon community. I will beg to disagree with that theory because, as I see it, the level of double-talking within the CGAM would be directly or indirectly responsible for making some of these misadventures as sad and complicated as some of them now are. When we starkly refuse to apply set-down rules without considering our specific emotions towards the particular person affected at hand, we often (if not always) end up where we find ourselves today. Double-talking may actually be the best tool in the hands of diplomats but, trust me, it is not at all healthy to a grouping like ours. At its inception we specifically and unanimously chose 'Goodwill' as its name because we were bent on launching a gathering whose members were expected to be very frank with one another.

If there is any one person in the CGAM that comes the closest to comprehending what the Mungwas are now going through, that person will be no other than this writer who has recently been there himself [having lost a brother in the United States in June 2007]. That does not mean though that I have to allow my emotion to sweep me away from the law of organizations/associations. On Saturday 14 July 2007, the General Assembly of the CGAM voted (despite strong suggestions from some of us that we wait until the end of the year to do so) to wipe off "Brothers and Sisters" from the category of relationship for which a CGAM member can

---

[43] See also Peter Ateh-Afac Fossungu, "Double-Talking *Meilleurism* in West-Central Africa" *The Herald* (Cameroon) (10-11 August 1998), 10.

receive financial support in case of death. In an association such as ours we go by majority decisions, whether or not we individually voted in that direction. I would be guilty of the CGAM's most popular sport (double-talking) if I say I didn't feel grossly insulted on 14 July 2007 when a cheque was handed to me for losing a brother at the same time as the decision to strip the provision of the 'brother/sister' relation. As I have just said, it was the majority decision and, personally insulted as I felt, some of us have been trained to detach emotions from the application of laid down rules.

On Saturday 18 August 2007 (barely a month later), at a CGAM "born-house" [at the Lukong family in Châteauguay], we heard the eloquent speeches all converting the tragedy at the Mungwas to the CGAM's primordial responsibility. Double-talkers, maybe you need to be reminded that on 14 July 2007 we collectively effaced any iota of financial responsibility that, as a group, we should have had toward Mrs. Mungwa today. But for our propensity to double-talk she would have been entitled to a thousand five hundred dollars from the CGAM. But because of the erratic decision of 14 July 2007, she (as anyone else in the same situation) is entitled to zero cent from the CGAM. Yet, from the speeches of 18 August 2007, we have been told that it is the CGAM's responsibility to raise in the neighbourhood of at least six thousand dollars to meet up with the expenses involved. I know that these days rules are altered and made in the CGAM at almost every meeting but I would like to be enlightened on when this particular new law or rule (regarding the 6000.00$) was adopted in the General Assembly of the CGAM. The only way some of us would be ready to welcome further insults from the CGAM may be through majority decisions, not from a handful of individuals who would always want to turn their personal feelings overnight into the CGAM legislation. I think in this particular case appealing for financial assistance from people as concerned Cameroonians would be the better channel to adopt. Trying to tie it to the CGAM as we are attempting to do can only be counter-productive as the president even alluded to in his speech during the 'born-house'.

This particular *qui-a-osé* write-up was surely ripping through the unease in the politickerizers like Peter Tosh's Stepping Razor. The follow-up writings tell the story better. We just needed another bold speaker to follow up to completely shut the door to politickerization. Not in the CGAM at all at this time. The next day (August 21) Paul Takha Ayah wrote:

Docta, I think you made your point eloquently and I understand where you are coming from. This is the first time we are confronted with such a problem and the way we handle it will help to define Goodwill going forward. Unfortunately, I wasn't present when the president made his appeal on Saturday since I was heavily involved with the other bereavement that we had in the community. However, my understanding is that it is an appeal, not an obligation. The president was appealing to Goodwillers' sense of civic responsibility to provide support to members of Goodwill who find themselves in a hellish situation. The amount we have to raise to solve the problem is huge, so the figure of $100 that was presented was merely an example to show us how the problem could be solved. If a member cannot afford $100 but gives, say, $80, it does not mean that that member is owing Goodwill the balance. On the other hand, if a member can afford $150, that will be welcome. Given the way that the Cameroonian community in Montreal is organized, we have no choice but to assume responsibility for the current situation. Goodwill represents the Anglophone community. The BINAM, Bassa and Beti communities have had to deal with similar deaths and they have risen up to the occasion and raised the required money to send the remains home. This time, it is the turn of Goodwill. We have only one option: to succeed. Having said this, I would like to link this to the point Dr Fossungu raised last month regarding visitors at Goodwill. If people arrive in the community, know about Goodwill and prefer not to become members (probably in order to avoid the financial responsibilities that go with it), but attend meetings, have fun with us and know that Goodwill will be there to assume responsibility for them if the unthinkable happens, what incentive will there be for anyone to join Goodwill? These are issues we will have to address at the right time. For now, we have our first test; let us put in all our efforts to make sure that we succeed. The analysis of the situation will come later.

PT Ayah was here certainly playing 'the nice guy' card; one that obviously emboldened the politickerizers because Ayah knows like I do that $100 is the amount every member is required by law to contribute in the case of the death of a CGAMer (the *Chrisantus-Ntongho* case proving the point, as well as even the BINAM, Beti and Bassa examples he conspicuously cites). So, how could the CGAM executive have been asking for that amount if the issue had not been equated to the death of a CGAMer? What amount, moreover, was ever asked for when both (former/relocated) CGAMers in the persons of Georges Neba and Vivian Beng died? The *Chrisantus-Ntongho* case too is thus a classic in the selective application of association policies, depending on the affinity of the concerned to whoever is at the helm. It contrasts vividly with the *Georges-Neba* and *Vivian-Beng* cases – all three occurring during the Folefac administration. Whatever the case, Fossungu's response to PT Ayah on the same day was: "Hi Paul, I think you have grasped my point very well. The essence of any write-up I put on this website is to 'help to define Goodwill moving forward.' Thank you also for making further clarifications. PAF"

On the same August 21, Adolf Achu Ammah wrote:

Hi Dr. Peter Fossungu,

I read your mail with keen interest and the contents were well understood. I want to believe that you missed the whole point concerning this issue as it concerns the death of Anna Mungwa's sister. If you had understood the meaning of FREE WILL DONATION, you wouldn't have written that mail. I am completely dismayed by your article knowing full [well] that you should be one of our respected Cameroonians. The president of Cameroon Goodwill Association Montreal (CGAM) was making an appeal for donations and not forcing people to donate towards assisting the Mungwa's at this time. You got it all wrong sir. The other associations have been contacted and free will donations have been suggested to them. Goodwill is by far the largest Anglophone community that is why we came up with the 6500.00 dollar (six thousand and five hundred dollars) amount. Even without the other associations and even if you heard a fellow country man passed away would you not support? **FREE WILL DONATION**, if you do not want to donate please keep quiet. Remember that it was the issue of double-talking that people were doubting your relationship with Joe Fossungu (RIP) who died in America. It was because of double-talking, that I raised this issue during the July meeting hosted by the Ibeagha's, that we should conduct a 'security check' before issuing out cheques to members who lost sibblings [sic]. Maybe that has never been brought to you [sic] attention. Another issue you are insisting on is the fact that you are **guilty** that a cheque was handed to you and the same day the sibbling [sic] issue was cancelled. I want to remind you that, in psychology and ordinary language, guilt is an affective state in which one experiences conflict at having done something one believes one should not have done (or, conversely, not having done something one believes one should have done). **It gives rise to a feeling that does not go away easily, driven by conscience**. Sigmund Freud described this as the result of a struggle between the ego and the superego parental imprinting. Guilt and its causes, merits, and also demerits is [sic] a common theme in **psychology and psychiatry**. It is often associated with **depression**. we donot [sic] want to see you depressed, **So kindly return that cheque back [sic] to the CGAM if you are guilty**. Might be this will open your mind of understanding and you can start thinking well. Your mind is not functioning well because of guilt. Anything shot [sic] of this will be recourse to your soul, mind and body.

From your letter dated 20-08-07, you claimed to comprehend what the Mungwas are going through but you maintained a double standard in your letter by closing your eyes to the event of the moment. You are indeed the double-talker. I figure out that you do not understand what is at stake and one bit [?] what the Mungwas are going through. When Joe (your brother?) died we supported him as individuals, as a group and as a family. We were ready to go with him to Cameroon so that he receives a beffitting [sic] burial. When you talk of law, where were you on the 14-07-07 when the law was abrogated[?] You simpy [sic] collected your cheque and folded your tail in between your legs, and now you say you are **'guilty'**. Remember that the guilty are always afraid. Thanks you said the speeches at the born house were eloquent which indeed they were. It came from well-seasoned gentlemen who have given their all to serve humanity. I want to make you know that respect is earned but not given. It is only the hand that gives that receives. I think you need to learn how to give now.

Doctor, also remember that Individuals from Togo, Nigeria, Gabon, Congo who heard the call and understood the situation on ground had already donated $100 and more. I will still remind you that the president was appealing for financial assistance from people as concerned Cameroonians. The president did not put the sole responsibility on Goodwill, but Goodwill is a group of concerned Cameroonians.

Dr Ibeagha said it is a personal sacrifice and gave his total commitment financially, morally and otherwise. If this article is your own support, it will not deter those who want to give to stop giving. It will make us stronger and resolve to even give the more. So Goodwill and Cameroonian community ignore Dr. Fossungu and give your all. I am very sure that if the deceased had the opportunity to talk for one minute and was brought to that [S]uturday meeting, she would have gone down on her knees and say [sic] 'please, help me'. Let us help her. Lastly, I thought that at the end of your mail you will advice [sic] that [sic] Mungwa's with what to do with the corpse doctor. I strongly recommend that you retract you [sic] article. A word to a wise is enough.

In Goodwill we trust [bold is original].

I would have been very surprised if anyone that is so blinded with emotions actually understood Fossungu's write-up. On the same day (August 21) Fossungu wrote:

Hello Mr. Ammah,
I do not shy away from airing my views on any issue. I will therefore be the last person to tell anyone not to air his or hers. You are entitled to say whatever you want to say on the issue but don't you try to think for me or to put words into my mouth. Otherwise, why do you want the article retracted? The article is there to stay, sir. People are entitled to read all the articles, but especially yours and mine, and make up their own minds as to who (if any) is guilty of what, and as to who has missed what points or concepts. That's the beauty of these kinds of exchanges.

I was not aware, until now, of the doubt being cast on my relationship with late Joseph Njumo Fossungu. Thank you very much for having brought that to my attention. It now explains a lot of things.

Is the reader not here truly wondering where all the CGAM Democrats have now gone to, as far as the problem Fossungu has *untaboolizedly* put on the table goes? The tree-tops and under-basements are certainly chock-full at this time, don't you think? The fourth and last contribution to this issue came from Sumboh Amos Nzonji who wrote his '*S.O.S.*' on August 22, 2007:

Dear Goodwillers,

Given the situation at hand and the circumstances surrounding it, I feel this is a time for action and not one for near-insolent exchanges. I wish to echo Mr Ayah's opinion by saying that Doctor Fossongu's point was eloquent, objective and a reasonable food for thought to our noble association. Emotions or personal attachments should not dampen our sense of objectivity. Just as Mr Ammah has said, no mail nor [sic] opinion should deter our good intentions towards this humanitarian call to conscience and each person should act according to his or her conscience. However, for the future health of our association, and to avoid sowing seeds of discord, our humanitarian yardstick needs to be more neutral and even. This way, we will be adding God's Will to Goodwill. To all, stay blessed.

Cancellationism Exposes the Politickerizers

Let us listen to those who talk constitution and 'voluntary donation' from three sides of their unstable mouths to understand *adhocist* and *personal-driven* democracy. You will better understand if you peruse this with the same proponents' persistent efforts to overthrow the PT Ayah administration in 2006 on the basis that he changed or postponed a meeting date – better known as *postponementolodrama* that led to simultaneous S-G and financial secretary resignations. At the August 2006 Assembly Aloysius Ibeagha (who had first 'unsuccessfully played games' with his resignation during the April Session – see 'Separatist-Foolish Dramacracy' below) read out his letter of resignation whereby he highlighted lack of idealism, misinterpretation and disrespect of the Association's bylaws as reasons for his resignation as secretary general of Goodwill. He, however, avowed his commitment to the association and willingness to serve in whatever capacity in the future. Ibeagha was not alone because the financial secretary was on the same midnightistic *resignationism* page with him. On her part, Mirabel Fambo Lukong intimated that her exclusion from the loan granting process and the fact that she was not a signatory to the association's account made it difficult for her to produce financial statements, hence her decision to resign from her position as financial secretary.

In his reply to this double-and-simultaneous quitting from his bureau, the president appreciated the duty-consciousness of these individuals but said he had no option but to regretfully accept their resignations as they had a democratic right to their decisions. He said Ibeagha had already submitted his file but Fambo's file was still pending, proposing that a committee of two be formed to carry out an audit of the financial secretary's file. Hans Najeme and Precelia Folifac (then treasurer, and who was supposed to be resigning too) were nominated and accepted to serve on the committee. With Aloysius Ibeagha's resignation, no permanent replacement was made, probably because the president did not find someone willing to assume the responsibility, the then messy midnightly 'who-is-who' atmosphere obviously playing a big role. But let's hear from the postponementolodramatist now to comprehend Heineken Democracy.

On August 28, 2007 Fidelis Folefac (the most eloquent constitutional postponementolodramatist who had quickly moved for a motion to dismiss the Ayah government in August 2006 – exactly one year before) wrote: "Folks, All protocol observed and respected. Considering the active concern and involvement of Goodwill and goodwillers in, the events leading to and subsequently, the wake keeping of our fallen sister,

Granted that the September meeting is not a thematic meeting, Given the season, it is likely that many goodwillers may already have other activities planned for September 15. In this light, is it not possible for our leaders to consider putting off the September meeting? I am just thinking aloud!!! Lord! let your will be done. Nkem [paragraphing altered]" Democracy as and when I want it, isn't it? So, was Secretary-General Wilson Ajanoh Anung actually right in his reasons for resigning from the Folefac bureau?

We all must know by now that what goes around always ends up coming around. A much trickier and more openly-personal situation was presented by the Anung resignation-membership suspension. I have really racked my *dictionaristic* brains trying to find a single nice terminology that could capture 'resignation-membership suspension' (*resignaspension*?). S-G Anung's unique resignation came on June 21, 2008 because of reasons that included the bad "habit of this executive to claim that the General Assembly mandates them for decisions they have been taking. We all know that this so-called mandate is always done by motion which doesn't reflect the general will of the assembly. In a true democracy, motions are meant to be debated and voted upon for them to be binding. I for one will not stand by and see the executive disregard the constitution and only apply certain parts they perceive will suit their objectives or personal interests." What then is really going on with the CGAM S-G post? Is it that people just can't handle the S-G-Heat? Please, do well to just save all your further questions until after the famous *freewill-donation* talker has talked freewill cancellation to sleepy goodwillers.

Here then comes Adolf Achu Ammah on Folefac's heels (August 28, 2007 at 06:05:29) with the following (that I leave entirely unedited):

Hi Monsieur le Doyen (Nkem),

Welcome back from home and do accept our sincere condolence for the loss of your grandfather. We shall continue to thank God for granting you journey mercies and his never ending love towards you and your entire family.

Mon Doyen, Concerning postponing that September meeting, I want to think aloud in same direction with you. Considering the fact that many goodwillers are exercising goodwill by donating for the funeral arrangements of our fallen sister and will not be good for them to contribute again for a meeting, and also considering that fact that there will be a wake keeping probably on the 8th of September, it is also my view that September the meeting be cancelled. This is my opinion and my views.

I wish you all and happy life.

Paul Ayah who likes to play in-between rather than take a clear position would now find out, too late, that this strategy doesn't help when he followed up at 10:24:54 AM on same day (August 28) with:

Hi everyone,

I am not in favour of cancelling the September meeting. Granted, we are heavily involved in making sure that our fallen sister is returned home to her final resting place; however, I don't think Goodwill has to cease its activities because of that. As serious as the situation is, we have to keep emotions aside when making such decisions. Given that our fallen sister was not a member of Goodwill, it makes no sense to cancel our meeting in this situation. Such a move should only be reserved for a Goodwiller. If the date proposed by the executive is not convenient for many, we can maintain our meeting on the 8th, but keep it brief and toned-down, and use the rest of the evening as a wakekeeping for our fallen sister. I think this formula will ensure maximum turnout.

Peace!

Paul Takha Ayah (of all CGAMers) must know that one cannot have real peace without having valiantly fought a war against violence or disorder (or no-peace situations). It is this same ex-president's '*Highlights from Executive Meeting Held Last Week*' that made known on May 7, 2006 that "6. **Bereavement** Following the bereavement of our member Anna Mungwa, the Mungwa family has decided to keep the event low key, hence there will be no 'cry die' the way we have been used to. Goodwill will simply honour its financial commitment to the member during the next meeting [bold is original]." So, why was that "cry die" so private but not this one? As I have said elsewhere, rights are defended from the very first moment they are threatened, not after a long period of having given them up for some momentary convenience (Fossungu, 2014: 140). This theory perfectly accounts for what follows, despite PT Ayah's belated call for peace. The CGAM president (Najeme) had by then, it would seem, switched the best tree-topperism position with someone. This time I was just watching and feeling the 'I don't know what' as the politickerizers out-played each other in their domain because non-members simply were not tolerated on that pitch.

The same day (August 28, 2007) Fifolefac told PT Ayah: "Presi, I find your argument very convincing and logical. My suggestion was far from advocating for a halt in Goodwill activities [Since when did cancellation cease from being a halt to cancelled activities?]. That the executive saw the need to move the meeting in respect of our fallen sister, who was yet to be a Goodwill member, and if we were to truly keep emotions aside and reserve some moves for Goodwillers only, it is therefore equally important, in my view, to consider Goodwill and goodwillers in the face of this decision. Going by the above, your proposed formula of a twin event on the 8th carries plenty of wisdom as usual. Thanks for the insight. Fide." That was the real fine art of *doublesidism* which, I guess, was less of a surprise to PT Ayah (or was it?). You easily grasp what I am saying, knowing that on September 1, 2007 another well-known postponementolodramatist, in the person of Secretary-General Jackson Acha Atam, sent out this dictum, titled *'Goodwill September meeting cancelled'*: "Dear Goodwillers, Hope you are doing fine in health and other activities. This mail is to inform you all that the September meeting has been cancelled. This is because of the challenges and societal demands on our community at the present moment. We wish you all the best in coping with this trying moment[]. May God guide us all through safely. Remain blessed, office of the S.G." Was there any objection noted? Not even a quarter of one. I must indicate to you that postponementolodrama was about *changing a meeting date*, not *cancelling it altogether*. So, what is happening here when people keep saying that the CGAM bureau in the famous born-house in Châteauguay made that death a voluntary participation of members and not CGAM's obligation? And what about the football team crisis too?

In the so-called GWFC crisis (See 'Carenayahism Crumbling' in chapter 6), my friend, PT Ayah, has played politickerization with the politickerizers so much that he knew what was going on in 2013 (during his wife's presidency) was not right but he could not determinedly join me in resolutely standing up for CO Ayah and for the constitution solely for fear of the politickerizers accusing him for/of doing "politics" with the issue because it is his wife that is concerned. Again, is this not a gross failure to distinguish individuals from their relations? All these things I am telling you now about midnightism only came to my attention after that 2006 December election exercise because I hardly go around nosing for information about people. But, as I have noted several times, perpetual schemers always think everyone else is actively plotting against them. The fear of positive competition in December 2006 thus brought forth a bureau whose logo is pepper soup and Heineken.

The Pepper Soup and Heineken Government

As Example Number One here of Najeme's unconstitutional comportment, see the $500.00 cheque he signed to GWFC as a gift without authorization (see GA Minutes, October 2007, 'Matters Arising'). If you think money matters are just the problem, then you also need to consider this *'CHECKS FOR SAVINGS NOW AVAILABLE'* that was sent out by his Interim S-G Wilson Anung on December 10, 2007:

Accept my warm greetings! Every member of Goodwill who made some savings for this year is requested to pick up his/her check at either the residence of the Financial Secretary, Mr. Nixon Tebo or during the children Christmas party that will be taking place on Sunday Dec 16, 2007. Again these checks have been issued out and are now pending pickup by those concern[ed]. It's not the **RESPONSIBILITY** of the Financial Secretary or any other member of the executive board to drop these checks at your various homes, so people are cautioned not to turn around and blame others for nothing. Let's be responsible and act responsibly!

On a separate note, members who still owe loans to Goodwill are requested to pay back these loans with immediacy. Remember these loans are Goodwill members' savings and these savings need to be paid out.

Have a good one! [bold and capitals are original]

What is wrong with that, you are asking? Well, let Felicia Tatuh Nzonji tell you on the same day: "Hi Mr Interim Sec. Gen. I don't understand the context of this mail. Isn't it the RESPONSI[BI]LITY of exco to make these checks available on the last meeting of the year? Please let's respect one another and mind our DICTION." I think it is accurate to say that the S-G post is really a *Hot Seat for Level-Headedness*. This is certainly something CGAMers need to consider when they are voting. Hear, for instance, what a qualified person in this office does.

On February 2, 2012 Eugene L. Asahchop was not amused when he confronted "Dear Exco members" with this:

Is there any reason why the hosting Calendar was prepared and archived without sending it to members[?] The President informed me today at 6.00 PM that I will be hosting Goodwill [] next week. Although the hosting calendar was distributed to members during the January meeting this does not stop the exco from sending out the hosting calendar. I was not present during the last meeting, the electronic version of the calendar was not send out, I was not inform[ed] immediately after the meeting. Nine days is not enough to plan for a schedule to host Goodwill. The new resolution from the GA recommends that a cheque should be issued on a meeting prior to hosting to avoid members from running behind the exco to sign cheques. I don't know if this has been done. This is a very busy society and activities need to [be] plan[ned] well ahead of time. Thanks. Eugene [paragraphing altered].

Unlike the 2007 bureau's response to legitimate concerns, Ekwe Enongene proved himself to be up to the task when on February 3, 2012 he states-manly stepped forward and responded:

Dear Mr Asahchop,
As Secretary General of Goodwill, I want to personally apologize for this untimely information transfer. The goodwill forum is for sure our repository of documents for reference. So you are right to point out that the hosting/meeting schedule was not posted therein in time. For this, the Secretariat takes the blame and apologizes.
I must however remind you that Goodwill has many a time emphasized its position as a participatory association rather than a membership association. [It is n]eedless remarking that

this warrants members' physical presence in GA meetings (though with cognizance of situations beyond our control which may force us to be absent sometimes). It is in such meetings that the cheque you mentioned is handed out a month in advance and designates must be physically present to receive it. Even though you never knew before this meeting that you were to host the following month, the Exco believes that all members certainly recognize the importance of attending the first meeting of the year [Good point, Mr. S-G, but how did his name get on the hosting schedule without his having renewed his membership in January?].

The Exco also recognizes that your hosting partner is currently bereaved and this might likely add on the complications surrounding this situation. We are working on taking care of the food aspects of the hosting. Thus, even though nine days as of yesterday might not be enough for planning and delivery of a befitting GA meeting hosting, the fact that you will be taking care of the drinks aspects only might help and prove more realistic within eight days from today.

Permit me use this opportunity to remind members that the next meeting (February 11th) is the deadline for registration of old members in 2012. [Readers can here, at least, see with the points Fossungu has often been making regarding voting on the constitution in January by non-registered 'members'?] This meeting shall hold at the same venue as last month and shall start at 7:00 pm. Goodwill has been authorized to use the hall between 7:00 - 10:30 pm. Let's be early.

Best regards, Enongene Ekwe SG [paragraphing for this line altered].

After these fruitful exchanges, Fossungu on February 3, 2012 told Goodwillers that "I think I like when people openly express or speak out their concerns like Eugene did and get genuine, constructive and helpful responses like the SG has just tendered. That is the spirit of Goodwill and I would like to encourage all of us to emulate these examples. That is one of the ways through we can move the Association forward. Thank you." There are several other ways, I truly think, of making things right other than resigning from an elected position, and worse still doing so while calling people names.

Having said that the question becomes that of knowing why the Najeme bureau should even be singing about the cheques on the airwaves unless something was really amiss? Let the communication between the Financial Secretary and a cheque-picker also do the job for you. On Friday, December 21, 2007 PN Folefac wrote to the financial desk:

Hi Mr financial sec,
Here attached with is the check you issued me at the children's Xmas party last [S]unday as per my annual savings. I went to the RBC bank at maxi and the main branch on Angrignon, unfortunately I was told that I could not catch [sic] the check, after insisting as to why? I was told there were insufficient funds in that account. So Mr financial sec what should I do now because I need that money, SMALL AMOUNT THOUGH!

Financial Secretary Nixon Tebo was obviously perturbed that pepper-soup-and-Heineken has gone away from him because of this woman's husband when he wrote back on same day: "Dear Mrs. Government, Sorry for the calamity. I have just confirmed with the bank that the deposit made almost a week ago through Over Night Deposit has been processed. There is thus sufficient fund[] to ease your financial difficulties. Also ask your campaign managers who still owe loans and contributions to send in their money. The list of debtors shall be published by or before December 31, 2007. Members still owing Goodwill should endeavour to make their payments within this period. Savings checks are still available for collections. My office is opened 24/7. Best Christmas and New

Year Wishes, Fin. Sec." What is it in the *night* to these people? What a foolish question! What else do you expect from midnighters? Do CGAMers then recall Hans Najeme in the January 2007 GA threatening to make savings compulsory? And this guy is a banker, for those who do not know, with a conspicuous MBA attachment. CGAMers are obviously suffering from biggytitlemania? I do not need to have that flashy tag 'banker' or 'financial analyst' to theorize *correctly* on savings and other issues of finance as I have often done (see Fossungu, 2013a: 124-30).

These guys don't do night business only with the banks. Even CGAM committees that are created in broad daylight in the GA are *nightfully* dissolved. If they could do it with the Fossungu-ELECOM, which other dissolution is again impossible? The dissolution takes place, with CGAMers, including fringe midnighters, looking on perplexed, afraid. Those who were voting for the Fossungu-ELECOM to be dissolved by Najeme just hadn't seen anything yet. Just let the chair of a midnightistically dissolved committee, RT Takang, school you in it with her write-up of November 27, 2007:

Fellow Goodwillers,

My understanding of Mr. Anung Wilson's email, Quote

"In consultation with the President of Goodwill, Mr. Hans Najeme, and to make life much easier since time is playing negatively on us, we concluded that this information be forwarded directly [to] the leaders of this committee, i.e. Dr. Mrs. Evelyn Ibeagha and/or Ms. Karen Najeme." is that the committee created by the general assembly during the October meeting, of which I am one of the leaders, has been dissolved by the executive.

For courtesy sake, I think it would have been right for the executive to contact the leaders of this dissolved committee before sending such an email. However, we remain open to the new committee for any information, or should they want to know how far we went before our committee was the [victim of] dissolution [in favour] of the[ir] committee. Mme T.

And here comes the very one who had very over-nightly nominated and imposed himself into the Fossungu-ELECOM in order to quickly hand over whatever opportunities that were being sought by the *Mighty-nighter*. A midnighter has obviously been de-midnightenized, for sure? On the same day as 'Mme T', Aloysius Ibeagha stated either in awe or confusion: "Fellow Goodwillers, I think there is a mistake somewhere here. The General Assembly unanimously agreed that Mrs Rosaline Mpeh Tanyi Takang, Mrs Prescilia Follifac and Mrs Felicia Tatuh should handle the [Children] Christmas Party this year. There has not been any dissolution to the best of my knowledge and Dr. Mrs Eveline Ibeagha is on maternity leave and has not been contacted on this issue. I think this is a mistake and I call on the authorities concerned to correct it as soon as possible or inform us otherwise. Thank you very much. Sincerely, Aloy." The question is to know the kind of knowledge that the *fringe* can have of the *centre*, or that the de-*midnightenized* can have of midnight business. Those who help dictators to become themselves are usually those who are preoccupied with only now, never looking down the road. They are often the very first to feel the created dictator's pinch and weight. In short, they are the first to feel slighted and used. Some of them then simply accept the crony role and keep *Dimabola-ly* marching on and very loudly singing the dictator's praises, in spite of themselves; while some others venture to fight back.

The Battles For, And To Recapture, Midnight Power: The 2007 CGAM Elections

That the war between midnighters was raging on savagely, was clear from the fact that non-midnighters like some of us even got to know about their going-on. That it was being now shifted towards the same 'daytime' ballot box that they despised so much (reason for loving the night), could be seen in the October 2007 Assembly Minutes. It was suggested there "that the Goodwill Advisory Committee (GAC) [then composed of just four persons – PT Ayah, Fossungu, Usongo, and Ndonkeu] should take care of electoral issues, like organizing the elections and proclaiming the results. One speaker said this was going contrary to what was discussed at the extra-ordinary meeting [of what organ?] and suggested the creation of an independent electoral commission. A second speaker complemented the comments of the previous speaker by saying that going by the by-laws an independent electoral commission has to be put in place to organize, monitor and proclaim the results of the elections. The third speaker said the constitution [must] be amended before appointing members of the electoral commission."

Frankly, I am really wondering why Interim S-G Anung decided to write these minutes this time without specifics on the names of the speakers, as he usually does. But I can feel and sense the arguments of the grand tree-topper here. You will also realize that midnighters wanted a sort of level-ground between the fringe and centre; explaining why the 2007 five-member ELECOM (in Table 4 above) almost had practically no conspicuous person from either side in it. Let the outsiders referee the *poligame*, is the idea. Who said devils don't trust the angels they fought the heavenly war against to be fair at the gear-changing? To better understand what happened in this recapturing struggle, it is essential to grasp the earlier battle for midnightism against *daytime* or constitutional democracy whose rules the dramacrats hate and were trying to foolishly separate selves from.

Separatist-Foolish Dramacracy

Talking of the hating of rules cannot fail to drag in our separatists in Quebec who also want to eat their cake and have it too. Hear Pauline Marois, for instance, telling us that we will separate from Canada but continue to use the Canadian dollar just as if nothing happened. Perhaps General Charles De Gaulle of Old France also confused these people with "'*Vivre le Québec libre*' *dans l'association avec le Canada!*' just like he did with the weak-minded Africans in the 1960s? President Sékou Touré of Guinea would be laughing very loudly even in his grave at these separatists. Hear Jacques Parizeau also blaming his not pioneering the founding of an independent 'New France' on the very rules of democracy, this time tree-topperly shitting on the Rich and Jewish *plus* common non-separating voters like this writer: "*Nous avons été battu par quoi?*" he thinks aloud to his followers. "*Par l'argent et le vote ethnique!*" It is as if all these blamed factors were never there until a minute or so to the proclamation of the results! That just tells you what must have been in store for the Rich, Jewish, and those inside 'Vote Ethnique'. As I have just said, while the late Guinean president would be mocking them in his tomb, Fidelis Folefac would be applauding the separatists for being just as confusing as Folefac was in April 2006 with his suspended-and-yet-applying constitution.

The Power of the Video-Camera and the Minutes-Taking Fiasco

The April 2006 CGAM Assembly is well remembered by those who attended it, not so much because of the memorable 'Services Offered' presentation of the Cameroon Ottawa High Commissioner's representative in the person of Joseph Ayafor. The entire session ended at just the agenda point of 'Matters arising from last meeting's minutes'. To cut matters short, it was *adhocist-extraordinary* dramacracy at its worst, to best say the least. It is like this writer had had a vision beforehand when he came prepared to videotape the session in accordance with his earlier suggestion to the March 2006 Assembly. God alone knows why all of that had happened, otherwise, you won't be getting the facts as they occurred since the April Minutes do not actually reflect the reality. Folefac himself recognized this fact during the May Assembly when he pointed out that the April minutes failed to indicate how the S-G had attempted to resign.

That makes the case of the 'power-of-the-video-camera' thesis that Fossungu is noted for advancing. This author would fondly recall what the first president once said to CGAMers, although the first president's advice has never been taken for its worth, especially by the successive administrations. It was on December 2, 2006 when (the pioneer president of CGAM who was the) then out-going Chief Whip-cum-cameraman had announced:

Good Day Goodwillers!

I have the singular pleasure to inform you that all our meeting sessions (from April to November 2006) are now on DVD. At our next meeting on December 9, 2006, these will be formally handed to the General Secretariat. The VP (and Webmaster), Jules [Komguep], made it known to me that it was not feasible to have these on our website as previously thought. They are too large for the website. I even tried sending them [to you] as email attachments but the same message of size inappropriateness kept standing in the way. I initially volunteered to be videotaping these sessions principally for documentation purposes. But it is highly recommended here that Goodwillers take the time to take a look at these sessions. There are a lot of great lessons to be gleaned from watching – in the cool and calm corners of your room – how people (including the watcher) deliberate over issues, very sensitive as some of these issues have obviously been. But, as these sessions cannot be put on the website, how do members get to view them if they want to? Here are some proposals in answer.

1. PRESERVE ORIGINAL & RAISE FUNDS FOR A DVD BURNER

This is what we can do. A member who needs a copy can pay an amount (say $20 for all 9 sessions or $5 per session) to the SG who will transmit the requests to me. It takes a lot of time to have a copy ready but I will very gladly make the copies available: personalizing each member's copy or copies. The money from all this will remain that of Goodwill Montreal, the only thing I require is to be provided with very high quality empty DVDs like those that I am now using. I will keep records of all requests from the SG and of all DVDs received and used and make a copy of the same available to the Treasurer for purposes of financial control and transparency. Any members who have obtained their copies or a copy through the above procedure would, if they care about the progress of Goodwill Montreal, refuse other members burning from their copy or copies. Why should a Goodwiller who has paid some money into Goodwill Montreal's treasury not be entitled to insist that his or her Goodwiller friends also follow the same ownership and possession path to obtain theirs? Goodwillers, we have to be very straightforward with each other in order to succeed in our collective endeavours. If a member however decides to permit the burning of copies from his or her copy, there is nothing we can do about that except that all copies burned from his or her copy would bear his or her personalization. That would be indicative of the fact that we are not yet ready to make sacrifices toward our collective betterment. If I am not asking for any part of the money that CGAM stands to make following these proposals, it is not because I do not like making money for myself. It is simply because I would very much like us all to help this Association to better help us as a dynamic community.

2. BUY A DVD BURNER UPFRONT FROM MEMBERS' CONTRIBUTION

Goodwill Montreal can buy a good DVD Burner and divide the amount spent between its members. Thereafter, materials like these sessions on DVDs could be reproduced and given to members (as a matter of course) at just the price of the empty DVDs plus a small maintenance cost. These are just suggestions that may be adopted or discarded. Enjoy the weekend while also seriously thinking about what is happening to our brothers and sisters in UB [University of Buea].

You would not want to believe that none of those recorded meetings and other CGAM events have ever been shown to especially newcomers or anyone else, not even on CGAM occasions like the 5th and 10th anniversaries. How then are most of these newcomers to have an idea of what the association is all about until they can know its proper history? This is an important point that has been expounded upon by Fossungu (2013b: chapter 4). Of course, this knowledge of history and development does not work hand-in-hand with midnightism and tree-topping politics.

The April 2006 Minutes-Taking Fiasco is hardly surprising then. Those minutes are wanting since the official charged with that function was clearly a *partie-prise* in the meeting-out-of-meeting meetings that had midnightistically decided the overthrow of the PT Ayah government by whatever means: just like the separatists are bent on destroying Canada by crooked means. I will therefore bring the relevant portion of *April Dram*acracy to your attention directly from my viewing of the videotaped session, which took off so well until the foregone dispute on the disputed point arising.

The meeting was hosted by the president at 142 Colpron in Chateauguay. It started at 8.45 PM with an opening prayer from Josephine Ammah. Vice President Komgeup chaired the meeting because the President was not feeling too well. The agenda of the meeting was adopted by Emmanuel Tene and

Neba Georges; the minutes of the last meeting being read out by the S-G (Aloysius Ibeagha) and adopted by both Michel Ntemgwa and Emmanuel Tene. On matters arising, EA Ibeagha reiterated on the issue in the bylaws on bereavement that had been raised in the March meeting by Fifolifac. She harped on the fact that the $400.00 package to a bereaved member was too small, considering the fact that deaths are unplanned events that come with a heavy financial burden. In effect, Eveline Ibeagha went back to the March Assembly vexed issue of suspending the constitution, as had there been suggested by Folefac, in order to change and increase the $400.00 amount for death sociopackism. This 'matter-arising' issue brought forth a lot of emotions and clarion calls for the point to be put to vote because its advocates saw it as an extraordinary issue. EXTRAORDINARY extraordinarily dominated the meeting.

The President who had appeared on the scene by this time closed the issue then by saying that it was not an extraordinary issue to warrant suspension of the constitution under Article 5. The insistent argument of EA Ibeagha *et al* was: What is more extraordinary than death? That it is the GA that can tell us what is or is not 'extraordinary' through putting the issue to vote. The president's counter point was that it is not everything that a member suggests that goes to the floor for voting because the issue in question is clearly stipulated and covered by a constitution that this same Assembly had adopted just a few months back and which was good for a year's duration. S-G Ibeagha then asked the president to define what an extraordinary issue is. The latter described it as any event or situation that, if not resolved, the association cannot function; giving as example a scenario where the entire bureau resigns. In such a case, he explained, the GA can then extraordinarily vote a new bureau. (Can you now see the basis of some of the *bureaucratic resignations* noted here and there?) But the other side was not pacified and Ndonkeu and Najeme both argued that the issue of death is an extraordinary issue and that the president was obstructing members from exercising their constitutional rights since these members wanted to vote on it and the president was not putting it to the floor. The president then stressed that it is not just because someone has suggested a thing that a vote has to be taken on it, pointedly asking: "If a member here says for instance that we should kill one of us here, are we just going to put that to a vote?" (It is at this point that S-G Ibeagha became so furious and dramatized with his resignation.) Contributions to the issue that stood in the same line as the president's came from the vice president, Emmanuel Fokoua Tene, Peter Ateh-Afac Fossungu, Neba Georges, Vivian Beng, and Emmanuel Ngwakongnwi (an out-of-town member who had come all the way from Thunder Bay, Ontario).

The adhocist extraordinary *dramacrazists* were just trying to hide behind the death sociopackism to attain other goals and you could clearly see this in their inconsistencies even on the floor of debates. For instance, take the *three constitutionalists* of the very first CGAM BRC (Bylaws Revision Committee[44]) –

---

[44] The various members of this committee are shown in Table 10 (I am missing two years, 2007 and 2013; 2014 not having been formed at moment of writing).

Table 10: CGAM Bylaws Revision Committees	
Year	Committee Members
2005	Hans Najeme (chair) Denis Alem, Fidelis Folefac, Walter Tita Ndonkeu
2006	Jules Komguep (chair), Alain Foko, Berri Nsame, Eveline Awemu Ibeagha, Fidelis Folefac , Peter Ateh-Afac Fossungu, Prudence Ayuk
2008	Peter Ateh-Afac Fossungu (chair), Aloysius Ibeagha, Edward Ayuk Takang
2009	Magnus Ajong (chair) Felexce Fru Ngwa
2010	Fidelis Folefac (chair), Pius Etube, Walter Tita Ndonkeu
2011	Magnus Ajong (chair), Precilia Nkengasong Folefac, Rosaline Ayuk-Takang
2012	Walter Tita Ndonkeu (chair), Delphine Ndemanga Afor, Yacubu Mohnkong

Folefac, Najeme, and Ndonkeu. Ndonkeu insisted that he was amongst those who drew up the constitution and he thought of an extraordinary issue as any matter of importance to the general assembly. He further advised that death is a very important issue to the assembly and that in order not to cause further controversy the house should immediately vote on the issue. On his part, Najeme (Chairman of the defunct bylaws committee for 2005, whose adopted constitutional revision was now being questioned by they themselves), said some issues in the bylaws, including the matter under discussion have to be looked into. That in such a situation the onus and decision lies with the GA which has the supreme authority above all members and organs of the association.[45] Folifac reiterated that the constitution should be the yardstick for the executive. That if the House feels an issue of importance to them needs revisiting, Article 5 of the constitution should be applied in solving the matter. He even theorized that the constitution be suspended there and then and a panel of a few "dedicated" individuals work on a new and robust document to address certain issues that needed to be readjusted. When Fossungu (from behind his camera) asked him about what happens to deaths during the time of suspension, he said "It is not really that there is then no constitution because it [the suspended constitution] is provisional at that time and still applies to any death until a new one is adopted." Fossungu then asked again if a member who has suspended his/her membership is still a

---

[45] Composed of all registered members, the General Assembly of the CGAM is unlike that of the ICAO (see Fossungu, 1998a) because it is the supreme authority of the Association and it exerts the following powers and duties: (a) examines, amends and adopts the Constitution and Bylaws of the Association; (b) ratifies resolutions adopted by the executive bureau; (c) elects members of the executive bureau; (d) ratifies appointees to committees; and (e) examines and approves reports and policy proposals (CGAM Constitution, Article 7).

member during the suspension period. At this point Folefac said: "Well, maybe suspension is not really the right word", and he was still searching for that right word when his questioner interrupted and added: "You cannot suspend a thing and still have it applying. I think this your 'extraordinary issue thing' would very soon extraordinarily kill this association." And did it?

My counsel to Canada is that it must similarly unpolitickerizingly stand up to the Quebec separation drive now; otherwise, the separation thing will only end when the country is split into pieces. You can certainly visualize that the theories of the April-Fool dramacrats are very similar in tone and incomprehensibility to those of the Quebec separatists. If other Canadians are afraid to say it, let me help them. We Quebecers cannot be allowed indefinitely to eat our cake and have it. When we send Bloc deputies to Ottawa in accordance with the very Constitution we (through the Blocist and Péquists) then turn around and claim not to be part of, when other issues are brought up, what are we thinking (if we do even think at all)? *Je me souviens alors de quoi*? *La Nouvelle France* that the Plains of Abraham (Lincoln) ended (Slavery in the South)? Please, just don't give me the usual bullshit by telling me that the *Blocists* are people of the opposite pole to the other Ottawa politicians because I wouldn't hesitate to fire back to know if opposite poles no longer attract but repel instead? Are like poles (midnighters) not here repelling as evidenced by the 2007 elections?

In that famous election Folefac trounced Najeme for the presidency for a couple of reasons. The Electoral Commission (the CGAM uses the term interchangeably with Committee) kept informing and educating electors and candidates regularly throughout the election fever that caught CGAMers like never before midnightism openly appeared. As mentioned elsewhere, Folefac (a Bangwa 99-senser) was clearly bent on booting Najeme (Bakweri) out and had been strategically recruiting a lot of the *99-senser*s into CGAM (see chapter 5 for the tactic), while Mr. Opportunist was too engrossed in other pepsoheinekenistic things and counting on opportunities from nowhere (see Fossungu, 2013a: 131-132). The Bangwa man is just as opportunistic as the Bakwerian, but he is different in not being visionless, and in working for or planning his opportunities. In this sense, he leaves the opportunity class and becomes a good strategist (see chapter 6 for illustration). His only major problem has to do with his *underground* and tree-top politics – which then makes him very destructive to his community or organization, especially one which lacks a sizable number of *fossungupalogists* or trunk-cutters or straight-talkers. Fifolefac would be a perfect leader if he should just learn (which is very difficult to do if you are already enjoying undisturbed tree-topperism and *sous-marinnism*[46]) to do level-ground or daytime politics – positive competition. Here, of course, Folefac would still succeed because of his admirable strategic planning and organizational skills, and succeeding even better since his success would then not depend on the destruction of the harmony or cohesion of the group that he is leading: As we have seen in chapter 3, he had this opportunity to have very positively challenged Najeme in December 2006 through the set down rules: But why didn't he? Was he afraid of losing an election a second time, playing solely by the rules? Playing by set-down rules never destroys but strengthens a society. Otherwise, it does – the election under review strongly attesting. More of CGAM midnight politics will be seen in the next two chapters, beginning with the CGAMing of MYR's *AITWsian* reinforcements of the stereotypes about Africa.

---

[46] For extensive discussion of the sous-marin strategy, see Fossungu (2013b: 130-137).

Chapter 5

CGAMing MYR'S *AITWsian* Reinforcement Of The Stereotypes About Africa: From The MIC-Media-Dollarocracy To Onafridism?

Human rights are human rights, irrespective of where on the globe one happens to be situated – a thesis that is buttressed by the plain fact that there is the well-known *Universal Declaration of Human Rights* (signed on 10 December 1948) and not a 'First and Second World' Declaration of Human Rights. Most, if not all, independent African States that are Members of the United Nations, have affirmed their attachment to that *Universal Declaration* [Fossungu, 2013b: 240, original emphasis].

Onafridism stands for the 'One Africa' Stereotyping Disease. The perennial question has been that of how to address Africa: from one to all or from all to one? Good question. I am thrilled that someone is sapient enough to have asked it because it obviously better serves my "interest in the discipline and sense of ownership of ... [my] learning process" (Leston-Bandeira, 2013: 207). It is a timely question as well and would reflect James Ferguson's similar concerns: What kind of place is Africa? This question, on the face of it, Ferguson himself admits, is an improbable one. "Africa" is a huge continent, covering one fifth of the world's land surface, where over 800 million people live an extraordinary variety of lives. Is there any meaningful sense in which we can speak of this as a "place"? (Ferguson, 2006:1) My uncomplicated answer to Ferguson's improbable question here is *yes*. If Africans unite and federalize as has been variously suggested (see Fossungu, 2013b; 2013c; 1999a): how different would that be from referring to the USA or India or Canada or Australia as a "place"? Does that response also take care of Emmanuel Fru Doh's stereotyping issue? Is the Military-Industrial-Complex (MIC) not behind it?

The Military-Industrial-Complex and Offspring

If I properly catch the gist of it, the reader also wants to know if I am not *inversely* suffering, inter alia, from *Onafridism* being condemned by Emmanuel Fru Doh who "deals with an interesting but also painful topic: the stereotyping of Africa in the West, notably in the United States of America" (Konings, 2009). Ah! This ignorant US of America! You see what the Military-Industrial-Complex (MIC) and its other derivatives are doing to these people, and the world at large? On January 17, 1961, only four days before John Fitzgerald Kennedy's inaugural, Dwight David Eisenhower bid farewell to the Nation as the 34th President of the United States. At the heart of the farewell address was a warning that was keenly insightful in its sense of how, in a way new to the American experience, an immense military establishment and a large arms industry had developed in the 20th Century post-war period (Hartung, 2001: 39). While acknowledging the need for a strong national defence, President Eisenhower called for the American People to understand the grave implications of this new aggregation of political and industrial power. He particularly warned that "[i]n the councils of government, we must guard against the acquisition of unwarranted influence, whether sought or unsought, by the military-industrial complex. The potential for the disastrous rise of misplaced power exists and will persist. We must never let the weight of this combination endanger our liberties or democratic processes. We should take nothing for granted" (Hartung, 2001: 39; Duncan, 2013: 30 & 28; McCain, 2011; Oliver, 2009: 2; Derian, 2009: xxiv; Raymond, 1964: 18).

Press accounts at the time and the remembrances of those on the scene, according to William D. Hartung, suggest that Eisenhower's surprising attack on the military lobby initially had only a modest ripple effect because many might have viewed it as just a rhetorical throwaway meant to steal the thunder of the incoming Kennedy administration. But that is not exactly so because "it was deeply felt, grounded in his own bitter experiences" and today it is "surely fitting to look afresh at Eisenhower's warning, and to appraise the present and future of the military-industrial complex" (Hartung, 2001: 39). Dollarocracy is an inevitable off-shot of the MIC. The American media (caught in the Military-Industrial-Media-Entertainment (MIME) complex) is now only good at easily turning local incidents into global tragedies. That is, as Debrix (1998: 840) puts it, in "making good use of newly discovered victims by turning them into newspaper headlines and television video bytes." What François Debrix means is that the *Médicins Sans Frontières'* (MSF's) new re-appropriation or re-categorization of 'space of global victimhood' also provides lots of opportunities to non-humanitarian actors, notably the captive media. The decline in the amount and quality of independent journalism in the United States has been punctuated by "a parallel rise in the influence of Big Money in our politics" (Nichols and McChesney, 2013: ix), leading to what Senator Sanders of Vermont castigates as "the replacement of democracy with what they [Nichols and McChesney] describe as Dollarocracy" (Nichols and McChesney, 2013: x).

Yes, William Hartung and the others might well be right because to describe the American capital as "war-maddened Washington" as Raymond (1964: 4) does, is quite understandable to anyone who knows how the MIC has long been an economic and political factor in the United States economy. As Thomas K. Duncan puts it, the amount of resources fed into the American war machine is staggering because since World War II, the United States has continuously spent vast sums on the military, creating what has been termed a permanent war economy. Even in times of peace, the critic pursues, the armed forces are kept in a state of readiness under the auspices of foreign threats or the need to protect the industrial base (Duncan, 2013: ix). This continued preparedness, the critics have submitted, begs two central questions: (1) what is the proper size and scope of the military and (2) what is the institutional arrangement under which we can be assured of achieving that proper size and scope? (Duncan, 2013: ix).

I can write a whole book of its own answering that question. But concretely, other analysts would want to know if, after more than fifty years since President Eisenhower's address, Americans have heeded his admonition. Regrettably and categorically, Arizona's federal Senator John McCain says that the answer is negative. In fact, the senator says that the MIC has become much worse than President Eisenhower originally envisioned: it has evolved to capture Congress and several other institutions such as universities and media. So, the phenomenon should now rightly be called, the "military-industrial-congressional" complex or MICC (McCain, 2011); the "military-industrial-academic" or MIA complex (Martino-Taylor, 2008; Giroux, 2007); the "military-industrial-media-entertainment" or MIME complex (Derian, 2009; Nichols and McChesney, 2013); the "green-industrial-complex" (O'Neil, 2009). That is how the Complexes have complicated the US People's thinking, as you will see from time to time. The stereotypes from them about Africa ought to be understood in that light.

But perhaps I should audaciously theorize instead that Africa is being largely and successfully stereotyped in the West with the sufficient contribution of *AITWs*. This is done not only through their practice of midnightism as already seen in the previous chapters, but also in the sense that (1) they do not only reinforce the stigmas (as in this chapter) but as well (2) do not quite know how to aid in effectively de-stigmatizing the stereotypes and using them positively for the sake of uniting the so-called un-united parts of Africa (as discussed in the next chapter). This chapter's issue will be studied under two major heads: (1) finding out whether MYR is beyond Canadian jurisdiction with its moutonization/Africanization policies and (2) whether *AITWs* are western but un-westernized.

IS MYR The Hub Of *Africanization* And Out Of Canada?

The MYR Camp is said to be situated on PK 82 Chemin Bowater. But when I drive on that road, my GPS (Geo-positional Satellite) tells me that I am "Driving on Chemin Alliance." So, what is going on there in the forest? It is the hub of Voluntary Slavery where the Ignorance Theory applies with such force. This thesis could sufficiently elucidate why some of the *voluntary* African *slaves* ignorantly reinforce the stereotypes, with some excellent cases being (1) the Zairian Hang-On Rule and (2) the Guinean *Wata-Rain* and *Nouveaux* Theses.

The Zairian Hang-On Rule

That working and other conditions in MYR are deplorable no one doubts or questions. The important issue becomes that of why Africans are still working there and sort of loving it too? As I have said earlier, no one is a bundle of only good or bad things. Transportation is obviously one of the appeals of MYR. In many other tree-cutting companies, the workers are not only responsible for transporting themselves to and from work, but also for garage or repair services in regard of their machines. They most often also feed themselves. MYR offers (although not for free parts) most of these things that a lot of Africans would hardly afford or even want to burden themselves with. This explains why most of them that have left the company have always ended up returning to the known hazards of MYR. Some have even tried being *transport-autonomes* in order to gain time and one or two *tankés (*as they would say). A *tanké* is probably one of those Amerench terms for the machine's fuel tank. To say, for instance, that 'I will give you a *tanké*, means that I will help in cutting on your patch until my full tank is dry, usually after an hour. A lot of workers estimate their work day through the number of *tankés*. Some of us just cleverly look at the quantity of patch that is cut, not the number of times we fill up. But the *tankés*-chasers have always returned to the Forest School Bus because of the fuel expenses related to the long drives to the patches, most of which are often impassable.

It is generally said or gibed that anyone who is working in MYR would be a sure *grand coupeur* (experienced tree-cutter) in any forest-based company in North America (and perhaps Europe too?). Impassable *térrains* means especially that we either have to walk the several kilometres to the patches from where the bus can no longer continue or use the pick-up trucks with 4WD from there on. Hear about one of the Eastern Europeans. Most MYR workers would assume they are all Russians, but I am not going to fall for that. He arrived in MYR during the 2014 season with his Jeep Liberty. He was evidently hoping to drive everyday all the way to his patch. After the first two days, he vanished because he couldn't cope with the trekking from the point where his Liberty could no longer give him the liberty from the hard marching up and down and across *beaucoup de renversés* to the patches, a *jamais-vu* trailing that Africans seem to care less about. Just as they do with their dignity and safety, the hang-on Zairian rule commencing the cementing of the show

There was a day during the 2011 season that a Zairian insisted on breaking the law by travelling in the baggage compartment of the pick-up truck, boldly and happily justifying that "In Africa we travel in parts of vehicles worse than this." Wow! Funnyman was completely flabbergasted when he immediately retorted that "*Ton Afrique là c'est ne pas l'Afrique que je connais!*" ('That Africa of yours is not the Africa I am used to!') Nevertheless, the inhabitants of the 'different Africa' were all scrambling for a hang-on position in the passenger-prohibited section of the vehicle that is solely meant for the machines and flammable fuel, etc. Why? First, they want to start working early to make the money, according to them. Come to think about how much they are even paid for the dangerous job! Second, now that Zaire has short-sightedly made the dangerous rule, even those who do not care so much about early start (or the many *tankés*) still have to climb on. If you don't, just know that no one is then coming back for you as was the case before. It is now also habitual for the machines and fuel to be transported in the Forest School Bus because there is no 'camion' available. It is the Africans themselves justifying here too. What they do not see is how they are, for example, putting both (a) their safety on the line and (b) more money into the pocket of the MYR owner.

Safety on Line with Encounters with Bears

You would be told sometimes by Funnyman to go figure out what to come out as, being a Black who entered a company like Encore Automotive which is in town. But here you are deep into Quebec's vast forests where you may not even come out, whatever the colour of your skin that went in. Remember that just as bears don't distinguish *nouveaux* from *ancients* (see Fossungu, 2013a: 22), they wouldn't also make that difference between black and white. This Forest must certainly be where Michael Jackson did his university program! I mean to say: What a beautiful world it would be, with all of us being bears!

It was thus one of those rainy days in July of the 2012 tree-cutting season. I had completed my patch that day and took some time to change my wet clothing before leaving the plot of land. Most workers do this only in the bus. I put on some warm clothes that had spent the day in a garbage bag. This clothes-changing exercise took a bit of time and by the time I reached the road I was almost the last person walking to where the pick-up truck (to take us to the bus) was parked. The fact that I had finished my *térrain* was quite pleasing. But that also meant getting out every damn thing of mine from the patch to the camp, pending another placement the next day (that is, if I do not decide to take a short break before continuing). I had to attach so much to my backpack so that I could carry the machine on one shoulder while the other hand tugged along with the half-way full *gas* (or better, fuel) container.

Because of the attachments to my bag that were dangling and singing *Come-Along*, it was hard to hear any footsteps, especially behind me. But at a point I had this sixth-sense feeling and turned around to look. There it was, just about two meters away, walking very stealthily, certainly to snatch my bag that had sandwiches and other food items that I had not eaten. (We are instructed never to leave these left-overs in the patches.) Just having changed clothing, my whistle was not hanging on my neck but in the bag. There was just no time for procrastinating or for getting the bag off me. (We are also drilled to always leave the bag and run.) I shrieked to an extent that the surprised bear got into the bushes. I was running for my dear life with everything on and with me, not believing later how fast I vanished with the complete load. I don't even know how I went through the very swampy part of the *4-roues* (all-terrain transportation mechanism) road around a hunters' watch-out cabin. I think it could just be summarized by saying that if death had to be seen coming, even the lame and *footless* would get up and escape from its no-release grip.

The bear obviously wanted my bag and its getting into the bushes was not because of fright. It was rather its clever strategy to easily get me because, as I was making it up to the cabin, it was there again, also climbing up. I shiver always at the thought of what would have happened next but for the approach of the *contremaître* on his *4-roues*. Hearing the noise from Bruno Lavoie's *4-roues*, the bear decided to descend and hide in the bushes under and behind the glass cabin. Bruno eventually reached the cabin. I told him to be careful because there was a hungry bear hiding behind the cabin. He surprised me by quickly jumping off his *4-roues* and going after the bear with nothing but his bare hands. This Bruno guy is a real *teng-teng* (as Francophone Cameroonians would put it). The bear ran out of its hide-out as Bruno was charging on, and walked further off. But, as Bruno retreated, it also came back, finding a way to meet me up there, always trying to do something smart. It was purely a hide-and-seek the two were playing down there while I watched, stupefied, from the comfort and safety of the cabin. Thank you very much to the hunters that helped save me from another hunter.

From the Bruno-bear game, I learnt that these animals only have an upper hand when you prove to them that you are afraid. From that day, I made it a rule never to walk in the forest for long without looking behind at every five or so steps. It also became traditional, whenever I walk alone in the forest to always carry a good baton in hand, ready to defend myself from any bear that shows up. The risk is very real and you cannot avoid walking alone sometimes. For instance, you may complete your patch before closing time. If you had not informed the *contremaître* to come for you at this or that time for another placement, you would prefer to walk the kilometres to the bus to wait there rather than remain on your patch.

Being alone though is not just what makes the danger. Days before my harrowing encounter, and in the same zone, three Burundians were ferociously visited by a determined and hungry bear. Noticing its approach, they started their machines, thinking that was to scare the beast off. No success. The bear came on straight, kind of asking if they did not have anything better to show off. They threw off their saws and took to their heels, with the animal not pursuing them further after it got the bag of one of them. That is what it is after since these bears now know something to eat is in there. That is why it advisable not to abandon left-overs in the patches. It is said that bears would stay long in a place where they have eaten something so deliciously new, like the cheese and sandwiches that constitute our *térrain* food. But left on the patches or not the bears already know the taste and smell of these sandwiches, etc. Some of the bears steal the bag while you are busy working; others come aggressively asking for it, taking no for no answer. There is the story of a Guinean *grand coupeur* (one of the best patch-sellers in the MYR camp[47]) who actually staged a fearless fight with a bear that had grabbed his bag and was going with it. The bear lost in the struggle. Bravo Diallo Ngiandho! But I wonder what treasure was in that bag to merit confronting a beast like that for it. Just wish that all MYR workers were as brave as Diallo face-a-face the MYR management and MYR would be in Canada, not in an African village.

Listen again to the same Diallo in the matter of dangerous patches pricing. In 2011 we were assigned to a sector with patches that were very tough to do. The $500.00/hectare price was not good enough and a brave Cameroonian called Jules-Raymond led the fight for a better price of $700.00/hectare. The ensuing sit-in was something the MYR management could not easily play off. The owner (through his father who was permanently in the camp) accepted the new price. Guys were back into working and working with joy. But that success of the group as a whole was not something Diallo could live with. He therefore secretly contacted the owner's father and gave the management ideas on how to play down the $700.00 price on the basis that the father had no authority from the son when he asked us to do the job at that price, with the original price of

---

[47] Patch-selling is another appeal of MYR. It would hardly be found elsewhere. This is what it means. I cut the patch allotted to me and then privately *sell* it to another person who is in need of it: the seller notifying the *contremaître* who then enters the patch in the record in the buyer's name. The *contremaître*/MYR is obviously not part of the sale but merely do the original patch owner's bidding. The availability of this kind of transaction would largely explicate why these *ancients/grands coupeurs* would go to all lengths to do what some of them do in disrupting group solidarity. It is thus a sort of win-win (or '*scratch-my-back-I-scratch-yours*') situation for both MYR and the so-called *grands coupeurs*.

$500.00 being what Mario Richard ended up paying![48] It was only after another malaise that took hold of the camp that the secret patch-selling plot was divulged. During the argument that arose, with fingers being pointed at the old man, Mario's father publicly made known how it was Diallo who had engineered the reneging of the $700.00 agreement because paying the $700.00/hectare would not have facilitated his selling of many patches to *nouveaux* especially. Africans and egoism, when are we ever going to stop this? Yet, we go around singing white exploitation of the black! Who was actually exploiting who here?

Whites Getting Richer and Richer while Blacks Poorer and Poorer?

This issue has been largely covered in the next chapter (under 'Paradoxical Self-Made Victim?') but let us still exemplify it briefly here with the hang-on rule. Before the Zairian Hang-on Rule, the pick-up had to make about four 'to-and-fro' trips which have now been reduced to one one-way trip. Leaving out wear-and-tear, etc., the cost of fuel (or *gas* as it is known in North America) alone for the other three abolished round trips would stay in the white owner's pocket. The situation is also reminiscent of the scenario in the CGAM where we are ready to see non-members profit from the association but not its members. For example, just hear Emmanuel Fokoua Tene using the 'national unity' and 'brothers-and-sisters' covers to *successfully* argue in the GA against my suggestion that people (most of them Francophone) who come to the CGAM only to advertise their businesses should pay some token amount. Yet, as soon as some CGAMers – like Aloysius Ibeagha (Meni Bea Printing &

---

[48] Since I am not writing a law textbook here, I will simply leave the legal and other experts to wonder if the parties here even know of binding oral contracts and the rules of agency and of vicarious liability.

Service Centre) and Roger Ekuh-Ngwese (Bloom Talent Inc.) – start running their own businesses, the same GA quickly votes and passes Advertising Laws in the CGAM.

And the CGAM often uses the offices of Ngwese's Bloom Talent Inc. all the time without compensating the man with even a dime. But they would speedily and expensively rent same services from a complete stranger. What does all that mean? Are we just entitled to blindly go about accusing the white guys for getting richer and richer while we the black people get poorer and poorer? Do I also need to elaborate on the stereotypes that said Zairian rule and the Guinean *wata-rain* one below create about Africa? Why then wouldn't any of the all-white *contremaîtres* always get an African to handle his pick-up (while any of them is driving the Forest School Bus) *only* when there is no non-African around? And just come and see how said Africans unthinkingly jump at the request, in the same way as Diallo also jumped at preventing a response to my sensible drinking water concerns!

The Guinean *Wata-Rain* and *Nouveaux* Theses

Of course, there are many Diallos from Guinea in MYR; but my use of this name in this book would be referring to the bear-fighting guy, unless the context says otherwise. *Africanization* or *moutonization* (to use Funnyman's popular term for it) is the rule in MYR. The majority of MYR's *débroussailleurs* are from Burundi and Rwanda. They are always together and speaking mostly their Kirundi that is now almost the official language in the MYR Camp. When I first set foot in MYR in May 2010, this group was still the largest but less visible. It has since become the only and dominant. Why? Most of the members of the non-conformist or heady groups or individuals (like some Cameroonians) have been systematically phased out over the years by the MYR management to realize the goal of *moutonization*. This signifies that those who stand up especially for group rights have no place here, and by now you shouldn't be surprised to learn that these African themselves actively work to spur that management to reach the objective as also shown in both the drinking water tale and the rights battles.

I very quickly realized, on first encounter, that fighting for general and collective rights in MYR was not worth my time and effort. Is there any need for any general to lead a war knowing full well that the supposed soldiers are the ones to shoot him/her from behind? That is exactly what happened to Bertrand-Raymond Mabo, a Cameroonian and accounting student at the Université de Montréal at the time. This was the 2013 season. It was again the issue of under-paying a very difficult sector. After spending the first day in it, Bertrand decided he was not continuing working on the patch at the price. Many others followed in taking his stance and, before you know it, that same evening Mario had been duly briefed by his "spies" who reported to him that Bertrand was the one instigating others not to work. Mario immediately had the police into the camp in the night to shovel him out. It was very demeaning (if you permit my using demeaning to describe what was already so demeaning) and you would naturally expect that the others were to stand in solidarity with the guy. Big Mistake! Lazare Domo was brought to MYR in 2012 by Bertrand. Lazare calls him 'my brother' all over the place. But it was Domo who was the first person in the bus the next morning, despite some midnight suggestions that we were to stay away from work for the day as a show of our disapproval for the way a colleague had been treated. With Domo's comportment, how could the others then stay away from going to work? Cameroonians and backstabbing! Make it AFRICANS, please!

The Drinking Water Tale and the *Tetom-Claude Affair*

During the first meeting with the management in 2010, I complained about our drinking water. It was really what Anglophone Cameroonians call *wata-rain* (running water in gutters from rainfall). Before the MYR proprietor could respond, the bear-audacious *grand coupeur* from Guinea advised him not to worry about these *nouveaux* who complain too much, adding that "This water is a lot safer than the one we have in Africa and some of us [the *ancients*, that is] have been drinking this water for over six years and it has not killed us." Diallo means in effect that if I and others like me cannot drink the mess in the forest, we should take off to town. Until that particular day, I often held Guineans in very high esteem (despite the religious gaffe that is not only Guinean) from the mere fact that Ahmed Sékou Touré was a well-known '*qui-a-osé*' defender of human dignity. I have since learnt to evaluate every Guinean on their particular merit since it is now apparent that Touré fought in vain. His legacy in Guinea is a sham, judging from comportment as Diallo's here. How can a group succeed without unity or cohesion?

Talking of crooks working against group solidarity and sense of purpose also brings to mind this vexing membership issue in the CGAM that is seen in the *Tetom-Claude Affair*. That case is tied to what the CGAM calls 'associate members'. This concept is what can be considered as another *chameleon*, like globalization. Associate membership is restricted to children of existing members, between the ages of 16 and less than 18 years, upon application. That is what the constitution says now but it may be helpful to know that this is not the original attribution to the category. Associate Membership received a lot of attention during the famous first Assembly of 2006. It was then that the nomenclature of 'associate membership' was supposedly introduced. It describes in effect a member on some sort of probation, an idea that was surely provoked by some people who (1) come into the CGAM just to take advantage of the "social packages" and disappear and/or (2) hide behind the 'regular visitor' category forever. Remember that initially all sponsored members had a probation period to undergo before the enjoyment of full membership rights could clock in. It is due to the general side-stepping of the rules that CGAMers got the typical African-unity case following.

This typical example is a Rwandan member called Claude Tetom. When had the Cameroonian-clause even been repealed in the CGAM? I am obviously for African unity and for Cameroon fostering it.[49] But that should not mean African unity without laid down rules because that will simply be anarchy, the *Tetom* case itself testifying. Shortly after joining us in July 2005, Tetom talked of having had a baby girl. The CGAM arrived for the *born-house* with his social package. CGAMers saw neither baby nor mother who, according to the crook of a new father, were at his uncle's and such other *bla-bla*. Members of the CGAM did what they are used to doing at a born-house. I well remember that the very first CGAM born-house social package went to Ndonkeu whose daughter (Ginette) was born in Cameroon, not in Montreal. No one

---

[49] As far back as 1998, the dreamer for the children of Africa told us that:

> The Constitution of the DRA would be drawn up by this country's [Cameroon's] constitutional and political experts from all angles (and not as we have so far known it to be forced on us by the guy up there). It will be published in all the papers and debated especially by the academics and other professionals and the entire population will have to vote for it in an unprecedented free and fair referendum before its adoption. Of capital importance is the fact that the document will have an important clause making it possible for the DRA to be voluntarily enlarged by current African states into a Union of what could then become the United Republics of Africa (URA).
>
> But all that subsequent voluntary development will depend largely on how the DRA becomes attractive and exemplary (good governance through the rule of law). Therefore, that wise leadership of the DRA will have to realize certain basic things, especially as concerns the management of its two cultural groups. For that is what will very much matter in any union of the present states of this continent. Uniformization of any sort could clearly not be among the ground rules [Fossungu, 1998b].

until then had seen the child nor mother (Phyllis). But there was all the goodwill on members' part and it was truly a "come and see" born-house in Cartierville (Ville Saint-Laurent) where Ndonkeu was then residing – with Bah himself (as Ndonkeu is popularly known) providing the impeccable DJ service.

Tetom's case was therefore not like the first without sight of mother and child: except that the host did not spend even a dime in welcoming the CGAM, and also that, thereafter, no CGAMer ever heard again from Monsieur Claude Tetom, the duper. CGAMers had learnt the lesson the hard way from 'The Thief in the White Collar' (Jaspan and Black, 1960). It was therefore not surprising that CGAMers then re-brought in the associate member who they defined as someone who pays the entertainment fee, attends meetings, and is paid a social visit without financial obligations by the association in case of birth or death for an interim period before he/she finally becomes a full member of the group. (Weren't the founders then visionary enough, as seen in 'The Rights Battles' below?) Being new to town and without the background I have just given you, Georgia Kometa had asked to know why membership to the association could not be immediate (*automatic* is the word she actually used). The response she got was that the association deemed it necessary that there be a waiting period between admissions of new members for acclimatization and easy management. Nobody was here actually calling the spade what it was; a strategy that is not appropriate when we talk rights that some Guineans are happy to squash.

The Rights Battles: Vetopowerism and Mespoutomatism

The struggle for rights here would be exemplified with two main issues: (1) newness and rights and (2) vetopowerism, mespoutomatism and other admission criteria. *Newness and Rights:* Guineans are not the only problem in MYR because another conspicuous *ancient* from Cameroon (call him Bami-X) seconded Diallo's water-theory by asking to know when *nouveaux* like me even had the right to talk in a meeting. Yeah! Francophone Africa and this over belief in *ancienité* or longevity of *unservice* in public service! In short, empty titles! So, where would the pioneers ever come from? They make it look as if an *ancient* was never a *nouveau* in all of his/her useless life! This idea also has some resemblance to the CGAM's *vetopowerism* and *mespoutomatism* in its membership politics.

Goodwill membership is governed by Article 6 and has seen spectacular growth in the first four or so years. Membership entails obligations such as contributing towards the growth of Goodwill and the achievement of its goals and objectives; abiding by the provisions of the Constitution, bylaws and any other decision arrived at by the General Assembly; and fulfilling all financial obligations, etc. Thus, with the exception of out-of-town members, members are required to attend monthly meetings on every second Saturday of the month and pay monthly entertainment fee as stipulated in the Bylaws. In all cases of absence, the member must ensure that his/her required monthly contribution reaches the treasurer on or before the said meeting date. Members are also required to be of good financial standing. The Association does not honour any obligation (sociopackism) towards a member who is not financially up-to-date. To be in good financial standing, the member must not owe any contributions to the association for three consecutive months. For the purpose of reminder, the Association maintains a monthly list of all outstanding debtors, a list that is supposed to be read and published during the subsequent quarterly meeting.

Rights obviously go with obligations, making all members to have the right to vote and to be voted for. We have seen in chapter 2 that things have obviously not been like this at inception though. All members have the right to information of the day to day operations of the Association, with every new member having the right to be handed a hard copy of the constitution and bylaws in force, upon approval of his/her membership application. These obligations and rights depend also on the three membership categories: full membership, associate membership and out-of-town membership. The first category is open to Cameroonians and their spouses residing in the Montreal metropolitan area; and to other Cameroonians not residing within the jurisdiction stated above who (aged at least 18 years) may apply. In case of approval, the General Assembly defines and attaches conditions to their membership. The *Ngwafusi File* is a clear example here. Resident in Ottawa, Godlove Ngwafusi was admitted in one of the Gatineau sessions but the attached conditions included notably this one which made it known that he cannot expect to host a meeting in Ottawa, a privileged reserved then only to the *outstationists* (out-of-town members). In short, that he was not admitted as an out-of-town member a privilege reserved only to members who relocate out of Montreal and wish to continue being members. To retain membership, existing members have to renew their membership on or before the February meeting every year as stipulated in the Bylaws. Does the CGAM year begin in February or in January then? Perhaps vetopowerism and mespoutomatism could help.

Vetopowerism, Mespoutomatism, and other Admission Conditions: The foregoing is what is in the law right now but history is essential to understanding and development (see Fossungu, 2013b: 142-149). I would bet that most CGAMers today do not know how some of the rules that they have to just walk in nowadays and ask for their on-the-spot alteration, developed. For example, an argument on membership growth (but even stronger than what is currently in place) was brought up at the first meeting that each *original* member should be able to exercise a veto over new admissions (vetopowerism). That is, that if any existing or founding member does not feel comfortable with the admission of any new member(s), it was to be the end of the story. I remember this debate so well because this was clearly the overwhelming majority's position. Because the minority of 'Four Strongmen' (Donatus Ayuk Ako-Arrey, James Tambong, Peter Ateh-Afac Fossungu and Valentine Usongo) passionately argued against having individual veto power over admissions, a two-third majority was settled for, *plus* the requirement of sponsorship by an existing member. The passion for restricting the association to just a few 'other' members was so great then.

As I look back today, I guess the majority then (8/13) was more visionary, especially if you consider a similar suggestion in 2005. In the July 2005 GA the idea of putting a Cap on Membership was another proposition (which seemed also to be tied to the *Tetom-Claude Affair*). It advocated for Goodwill membership to be limited to 50, with new members only to be admitted when one or more of the already existing 50 would have left the group. Whoever it was that was pushing this proposal (the minutes do not say who) must have been four-eyesly seeing the future that most of us were yet to come to. I say this because at this moment of writing (2014) fifty is the number, and has been almost so for the past couple of years. The monumental fall in membership was accelerated by the Fifolefacist government's scrapping of birth and marriage social packages. That membership-capping proposal never saw the light of day, with people speaking from both sides of their mouths all the time. The membership door thus remained wide open to just anyone, without any cap or limiting condition whatsoever, because there was an outburst in the House and this proposal was strongly rejected by many. Stephen Ajab Asong (who had just entered into CGAM that same day[50])

---

[50] Table 11 gives you some of the admissions that I have been able to track since the July 2005 membership:

even went on to counter-call for an increment in the number of admissions opportunities per year (from then two – January and July). This idea quickly was strongly supported by EA

Table 11: Some CGAM Membership Growth or Admissions (since July 2005)

Year	Month	Admitted Members	Total
2005	July	Aloysius Ibeagha; Eveline Wemu Ibeagha; Alain Kamga Foko; Marlyse Guemgne; Stephen Ajabenyang Asong; Macalister Usongo; Caude Tetom	07
2006	Jan	16 new members (no names in the minutes), Belta Anung	16
2006	April	Edward Asong Asongu; Itambi Patricia	02
2006	July	Godlove Ngwafusi, Martin Atemnkeng	02
2006	Oct	Maggie Tomdio, Christine Kamgna Neba, Marbel	03
2007	Jan	Rosaline Tanyi, Helen Achaleke, Chrisantus Ntongho, Bridget Fomenky, Florence Etube, Albert Sekoh, Joseph Takang	07
2007	Oct	Linda Nkamnga, Ignatius Mbeng, Nathalie Nchoutou, Julius Ashu, Beltus Nyambi, Ernestine Shirih, Maggie Egbe, Baiye Orock, Levis Cheussom, Tah Mba Techoro, Benedicta Akaya, Charles Nkwenti, Jacqueline Nyaa Ngala, Martha Egbe, Florence [Who?], Sheala [Who?]	16
2008	Jan	Rita Ebude Ewane, Mbeko Bertrand Feuko, Johnson Ngala, Endeley Lifafa Likenye Jude, Ebenezar Tawani, Margaret Tawani née Mbakwa, Hilary Fuh-Cham, Yvette Fuh-Cham	08
2008	July	Three members (no names recorded)	03
2008	Oct	Angelina Nkoh, Atem Mbecha, Fanny Ngweng, Yacubu Mohnkong,	04
2009	April	Kizito Tekwa, Sylvester Nchende, Jackson Acha Atam, Armstrong Tita	04
2009	July	No Admissions Recorded	00
2009	Nov	Banin Bohgfen Yufanyi, Celsetine Mpang, Enongene Ekwe, Hilary Fuh-Cham	04
2010	April	No Admission Recorded	00
2010	July	Ajouah Nelson Nkemgong	01
2011	Jan	Emmanuel Nankam, Eric Ayukowo Ayuk, Catherine Siy Yungong	03
2011	July	Claire Kongep; Jules Kongep; Marie Njehge, Agbonyor Tanyi, Epizitone Anabi	05
2012	Jan	Henadez Makia, Fonderson Tataw Ashu	02
2012	July	Peter Ndifor, Jessie Ndifor	02
2012	Oct	No Admissions Recorded	00
2013	Jan	Tracy Leke, Pascaline Abongwa, Thomas Acheng, Loriane Asanga	04

Ibeagha (who had also just joined the CGAM that same day) proposing 4 times/year. Fidelis Follicfac (the sponsor of most of these people) also supported the idea, specifically calling for admissions in January, April, July and October. The (unthinking) Assembly, as usual, overwhelmingly supported the suggestion: admission of new members now occurs in January, April, July and October. The question that may be asked concerns whether these calls were just after quantity or were they also considering quality and progress? Also, one can be very suspicious of the hidden agenda behind such calls, as several portions of this book would confirm, giving you the somewhat strategic reasons for this move. But more importantly, do people ever value anything they just "pick up with their left hand" as the saying goes? In my experience, I have never seen any association that loosens all restrictions to its membership and succeeds.

And this applies as well to immigration countries like the USA, Canada, and Australia. That even gets worse in the CGAM when, as to be illustrated shortly, even those who are to be applying the laws do not know them (see Fossungu, 2013b: chapter 5). The issue of "yearly bylaws amendment" is also very thorny and contributes enormously to the vexed problem. During the January 2006 GA, Florence Ngayap Namkam sagaciously suggested that there should be a lapse period for already existing bylaws to take effect and mature before being amended, rather than amendments on a yearly basis. Prudence Ayuk suggested that bylaws should be amended when there is a change of Government. The president (Paul Takha Ayah) explained that the bylaws or constitution was being amended because the bylaws stipulates yearly amendments, that the bylaws would have to be changed on this issue to allow for a longer waiting period before amendment. The questions I often ask then are these: Do we just have to make amendments simply because there is provision for possibility/modality of amendment in the constitution? Why not then amend the amendment formula? To these queries, no answer comes forth, not even something resembling the ICAO untenable excuse (see Fossungu, 1999a: 361-63), and you then four-eyesly see the politickerization that has eaten so deeply into the CGAM fabric that even simple clear-cut admission rules are thwarted daily.

That leads us back to "elected" officials not even knowing what it is that they have been chosen to do. Take the case of Secretary-General Ibeagha who sent out an announcement on March 7, 2006 when Sarah Bessem Takang lost her sister. The communiqué invited CGAMers to the night vigil and said absolutely nothing about the process until two days later after a founding member (WT Ndonkeu) had brought it to his attention. Thus, on March 9, 2006, the S-G frankly (dove the hats here; and this is why I used to enjoy working with Aloysius Ibeagha before he sort of unthinkingly joined the midnight club) wrote to Fellow Goodwillers: "Just to bring to your attention that the bye-law [sic] stipulates that men should come along with drinks while women bring food. Mrs Follifac is also contacting the women on that aspect. The association will also donate a package to the bereaved. Bah thanks for bringing this to my attention [paragraphing altered]." People are wont to call me hard on rules but would this example (which is not unique to S-G Ibeagha, of course) not give George Washington, Abraham Lincoln and their friends a lot of reasons for laying down that only native-born Americans can assume the occupancy of the White House? Just imagine for a second Paul Biya becoming an American citizen (since he is capable of buying even that country's Immigration Department, according to Ngwa Ntonufor, as cited in Fossungu, 2013b: 34 n.31) and surreptitiously climbing into the White House: and you would have seen the logic and farsightedness of the American Founding Fathers, especially regarding the presidency. You will grasp what I am saying here as you read on, discovering along how leaving the door unguarded (through politickerizing) like the CGAM did led to people just walking in and very easily harbouring so-called regular visitors and (through so-called tree-topping democratic adhocism) also disrupting long-standing traditions like the yearly rendezvous with our out-of-town members in Gatineau/Ottawa.

The founding 8/13 majority must only have given in to the compromise on their vetopowerism idea because they could probably have misunderstood or forgotten that this majority figure could not stand still with every new admission, nor that they could all have the same feeling towards a particular applicant. Whatever it was, those were the compromises that led to the membership-entry conditions of 2/3 *majority vote*, of *sponsorship*, and of *probation*: exceptions being made only of a member's spouse (mespoutomatism). The GA of January 2006 would illustrate some of these principles as the members consider the revisions presented by the pioneer Najeme-led BRC (see Table 9). A member's spouse's admission is what mespoutomatism is all about. Sixteen new members were admitted into the CGAM at this January meeting. Although S-G Ibeagha did not put in their names as is usually the case, one of them is clearly identified from those Minutes because of mespoutomatism. We are clearly told that:

Intending new members who submitted signed application forms introduced themselves and expressed their wishes for joining the group. On other membership matters, the President reiterated that Belta Anung (Wilson Anung's wife) is an automatic member by virtue of the fact that her husband is already a member of the association. Lysly Ayah jokingly added that this applies too without doubt to women who are members of Goodwill. Jules Konguep added in reiteration that, the persons sponsoring new members should be in attendance when admission applications are being considered.

I do not think calling it automatic is correct, since these spouses still have to apply for membership, being probably sponsored by their respective partners: with just the requirement of 2/3 majority vote and probation period not standing in their way (if they even ever stand in anyone's way). Saying it is automatic means that by the mere fact of being a member's spouse makes you a CGAMer; which is not true. You find the same kind of flawed reasoning with the spouse financial contribution arguments. I cannot get into that right now but must indicate that the exact number of times the presence-'reiterated' condition from Komguep has been ignored is countless. This is very unlike the MYR camp *nouveaux* and no rights talk which is always there and vibrating. It got to a boiling point between me and a *contremaître*. I had been in room for more than three weeks when someone suddenly appeared in the camp, claiming that it was his place that I was occupying and that I should get out. I told him to remember that latecomers are always wrong and just go look for a different place somewhere else.

Seeing how adamant and audacious this *nouveau* was, the *ancient* went straight to the camp manager who came foolishly barking out that I had to leave the room because I was new and did not have any rights. The manager quickly readjusted when I held my cell phone like a microphone to him and asked him to repeat what he had just said so that I could sue the hell out of him and MYR. I have since ceased being *collective* in rights defence in MYR but no one there messes around with me as an individual and get away with it. Unlike the others with their notorious '*on a pas le choix*', I have a choice always; and that choice extends to wondering if it could not then be argued that these Africans who are habituated to say they have no choice had consciously or unconsciously made a choice between MYR's problems and its appeal? Do they really have no choice? Does that also give correctness to those who say that *AITWs* are western but un-westernized?

Are *AITWS* Western But Un-Westernized? Some 'After-Elections' Answers From The CGAM

As expected, the publication of the results of the famous CGAM December 2007 elections could not go without the losers crying foul while the winners are singing with jubilation. But that does not mean that anyone who said a thing about it was necessarily on this or that side. I will merely indicate one thing so that you could easily trace what was going on as under- or on-top currents. On December 10, 2007 the President-Elect made his victory speech without any extension of hand to the defeated. There was also no concession speech from the vanquished. Is that what we in North America, for instance, witness all the time after election victories and losses?

It is instead a lot of finger pointing that CGAMer witnessed. For example, December 11, 2007 came breaking with the big screen title *'GOODWILL ELECTION 2007, A SCAM????'* That write-up was from Charles Nkwenti Minjo who joined CGAM in October that same year (see Table 11), and shortly to be a very conspicuous member of the Najeme-led breakaway group called UNICAM. He stated:

> The much heralded Goodwill election[s] 2007 have come and gone and like many Goodwillers, I want to commend the peaceful atmosphere that reigned that night de[s]pite the pre[e]lection tension that we all witness[ed] between the two 'camps'.

Now back to the main issue. If we had had for example somebody who just returned from Cameroon, his/her opin[i]on would have been that this election was not different from what takes place back home. The rythoric [sic] about being goodwiller made me laugh and more cynical was the fact that goodwllers openly showed their stupidity in matters of administration, duty consciousness just to discredit this and that aspirant. Camero[o]nians are Cameroonians and no matter how long they live out of paye [*pays*], our mentality will never change.

From the onset, our much praised election committee flawed the election process by accepting "lists" a thing that al[r]eady brought much division in Goodwill. As if that wasn't enough, they allowed on the election night proper, the type of election mechanism that takes place back home – corrupting the minds of electorates. Was the unveiling of gifts for the children's party in the proper place and at the proper time? [W]as the committee aware of that? [A]nd did they give their blessings? At an election campaign nite anything can happen, but is there any need to call our group "Goodwill" when goodwill gestures are used for campaign purposes? If for example the gifts were meant for the children's party, were they not to be unveiled at that party? We could see the reaction of the children and to me we would have just given them the gifts that night as gratitude for their presence at all goodwill meetings.

I don't doubt the potentials of those who were elected to the various positions of authority. But using crooked means to attain a position creates doubts as to why. [W]hat I ask is that as Goodwillers we shouldn't express our goodwill only when it comes to election. I was surprised for example to know that some goodwillers know how best we can integrate in Canada, declare taxes, get jobs etc. and will not open up till an election nite. It's really hard to change a mentality especially when we are products of a corrupt society, though living in a fair one. I have also heard how those who were defeated want to leave Goodwill! I ask them, did u join goodwill because of positions? No single individual will rule goodwill forever. I advise u rather to show us that u had and still have goodwill at heart, no matter ur position in the group. Most of the great men [and women] we know in history were not presidents or kings o[r] queens.

The next two write-ups were brief and to their points; the first, coming on December 11 from Vivian Akong Tebo, indicated: "HI Charlie, Job well done. Your observations are just like that [those?] of King Solomon. MAY GOD GIVE[] YOU MORE WISDOM!!!!!!" Meanwhile Calep Nyambi on December 12 said "HI CHARLES, IT SHALL BE WELL WITH YOU AND MAY YOUR WISDOM FLOW[] THROUGH YOUR GENERATION."

Off-Staging the Briefers

The *briefers* had obviously had their interlude while the *long-crayons* were at work; but they are now ready and asking for the podium. It is therefore Michel Ntemgwa's turn on December 12:

Mr Charles,

Your observations and opinion always count[] that is why I think in democracy everyone is entitled to a vote and it seems to be the only way to go ahead. You gave many observations. In my opinion, the title of your posting did not really reflect your posting. I know you put a question mark after the word "scam" meaning you didn't really say it was a scam. However, I think that was a very hardline word to use considering the work the electoral committee did all this while. Something like "perspective" could have been kind of better. I don't know whether you have attended goodwill elections before i.e. in the past years. If so then you will be able to compare what happened during this election season and the others. This was the first time people actually opted to go in and be voted to serve this association. I think your suggestions will play a very good role in formulating any rules for our next elections. I believe we should try to strengthen our electoral committee instead of condemning it. Next I didn't see with your point that if someone had just come in from [C]ameroon, he will say there was nothing different. Everyone knows the issues of stuffing ballot boxes to even threats that happen in Cameroon. I didn't quite buy your saying that Cameroonians are always the same in your context. I believe Goodwillers are people I hold in very high esteem and being Cameroonian just makes me proud. Many goodwillers have this [country's] flag [] hanging in their cars, I am just so proud of it. I am happy you didn't say the counting was not fare [sic] but focused on campaign procedures. A few non goodwillers who were there instead told me the elections were very good.

There are many issues in goodwill that I have voted on the side that never won but I have always complied with the results of the majority. On **promises** that many people made during election campaigns. I see with you that those should not be done only on election night. However, these are promises and I think our best way [to] tackle this for those who are voted into office is to ask them at the end of their term. That is why, we have this written on paper (soft copy by emails sent out before elections) what these candidates promised. I also think we have some maturity for us to know some promises that are unachievable.

We will not be doing oursel[ves] any good by voting in somebody on promises we know are really impossible. However in democracy even in advanced (if we can call them that) ones like here in [C]anada, you see politicians saying what they will do and not what th[e]y have done. It is for the electorate now to see from those candidates who can deliver the goods. Agreed it was not a political campaign but the elections I observed here even in school boards recently you have to promise what you will deliver. I see with you that no one will rule goodwill forever and it is only us members who will vote who will be our exco. On your last point that some members are thinking of leaving goodwill, I just laugh because we have many things to think about achievements both individually and collectively that divisive tendencies for me have no place. We can only make progress collectively. If these fellows you are talking about are thinking of quit[t]ing, it is not new for goodwill to have members suspend their membership or leave. If on the other hand it is to form another association, then it is not also new since as we all know there are tribal/divisional associations even Njangis already running in parallel to goodwill but that has not changed our commitment to goodwill which reigns supreme and in my opinion should always reign supreme. Personally, I have a lot of fun in goodwill and no matter who is ruling, that person can't stop my fun.

I applaud you for your comments and I think others should give their opinions and ask questions instead of sitting home and grumbling without anyone ever knowing what you can contribute to make goodwill better. In science we say a gene that is not expressed is always hard to identify. My humble opinion though.

Pius Esambe Etube, the Financial Secretary-Elect, had been waiting patiently for Michel Ntemgwa to pass on the democracy debating stage. It is now open to his contribution that came in on the same day as Ntemgwa's:

Hello Mr. Charles

I have a few remarks to make regarding your nicely worded views on the 2007 Goodwill elections.

1) While being critical, choice of words is equally critical. In my humble opinion, a phrase like "Goodwillers <u>openly showed their stupidity</u> in ..." is rude and impolite. In future, avoid describing fellow one another with hard words as "stupid". Such approach should not be hailed for wisdom.

2) I also defer [differ?] with your view that the job of the electoral committee was flawed.

The committee did not accept "list" system of voting. Candidates for each position were individually presented and were voted not on the basis of a list system. A list system, though not used, has its own merits and in a dynamic society, do not be surprised if we revert to it in future. The work of the electoral committees remains commendable. I hope the next electoral committee will use your comment to improve on electoral guidelines, if need be.

3) You questioned! "Was the unveiling of gifts for the children's party in the proper place and at the proper time? Was the committee aware of that? And did they give their blessings?"

My comments: The gifts were a donation to Goodwill intended for the kids' party. The donation was presented to goodwill in the General Assembly (proper place) under general matters on the agenda (proper time) and not to the Electoral Committee during elections. As a donation to Goodwill, Goodwill through the president had to give blessings. I also doubt if the donation received any blessings. If not, why?

4) You also pointed out that candidates used "crooked means to attain a position" and it creates doubts as to why. You further stated "I was surprised for example to know that some goodwillers know how best we can integrate in Canada, declare taxes, get jobs etc. and will not open up till an election nite."

My remarks: Goodwillers have been ever supportive in helping new arrivals. Providing temporal accommodation, info on acquiring SIN, tips on resume etc. has been part of our ongoing integration process. Numerous emails on job postings have been circulated in our group. Individual(s) who declare taxes had sent out email communication to Goodwill to that effect, probably when you were not a member of Goodwill. In a nutshell, Goodwillers were not only opening up on the night of election. It's sad if you would term theses simple promises as "crooked" means to attain position.

The views above reflect the opinion of the writer

Revampinization and the Never-Ending Tree-Topperism in *AITWs?*

On December 13, 2007 Valentine Usongo, instead of coming into the dialogue as Valentine Usongo, tried the tree-topping thing. But God alone knows how some of these tree-trunk breakings do happen. The exact unedited title of his message is '*Advisory council recommendations*' and could tell you the amount of haste it was driving at. It came in under his personal email signature and shortly afterwards (someone must have pointed that out to him when) the same message was quickly re-sent under a hurriedly created GAC email. The cat was already out of the bag, wasn't it? This is the *Valusongo-cum-GAC* message (the first appearance):

Fellow Goodwillers

Taking into cognizance the elections that were held last week, the Goodwill Advisory Council deemed [i]t necessary to meet in-order to put fo[r]ward recommendations that will strengthen the unity within our group and move our association fo[r]ward. To this effect, the advisory council met on [W]ednesday [D]ecember 12 and made the following recommendations.

-Appeal to all goodwillers to attend the [J]anuary meeting so as to make their suggestions on how to improve our elect[]oral system.

-Appeal to all goodwillers to close ranks and put goodwills' [sic] interest first.

The introduction of a code of conduct in our by-laws that goodwillers should adhere to. Remember that goodwill is being looked upon as the pace setter within our Cameroon community, something we should all be proud of. We wish every goodwiller a merry [C]hristmas and a prosperous [N]ew [Y]ear in advance.

The Adisory [C]ouncil

I am not four-eyesing at all here, simply saying what I say because you know I do always remember; otherwise, you won't be getting the benefit of my expibasketism. To the best of my knowledge, I cannot remember ever attending a GAC gathering following the release of the 2007 elections results. Again, just to joggle your mind a little bit. Maybe Valentine Usongo met with PT Ayah? Not likely because PT Ayah was the chair of the ELECOM that people are questioning. But most importantly, in such meetings it is standard practice for such communications (even if written by the chair) to be circulated for corrections and other inputs before it is sent out to the wider audience. For instance, take the case of the CGAM *revampinization*.

As a follow-up on their auto-critiquing policy, perhaps, on October 7, 2009 the head of the Fifolefacist auto-embattled administration frankly told CGAMers that

We are human thus liable to mistakes [the Paulayahist bureau was made up of non-humans, of course], however, certain irregularities which we have witnessed in the past are preventable if team values were employed [what happened to the GA firing of a government without team spirit, as urged by Folefac in 2006 after the double resignations?].

Hence forth there will be zero tolerance to any preventable irregularities as such behaviours will be adequately exposed to the general assembly for actions. Remember that Goodwill is an institution, thus hierarchy, transparency and accountability must be strictly respected. In addition, we must promote equality and act with diligence and personal integrity at all time.

We must be responsible in our actions:

1. Be clear and honest if you are taking Goodwill Chairs on behalf of a non-goodwiller

2. Consult and get due approval, at least from the executive (not president) before using the name of Goodwill to assist third parties.

3. Be clear and follow due procedure for assistance demanded from Goodwill: number of chairs, amount for loan, honour loan payment schedule etc.

4. Renting Goodwill property which the assembly has prohibited. Food warmers are rented, not free as the chairs, prices are very affordable for members

By this friendly email, I am encouraging ALL Goodwillers to ensure that we operate as a team, in good-faith and personal integrity, refrain from making administration difficult for the executive or any individual and stamp out vested interest in our actions [So Jules Komguep was right then in the postponementolodrama arguments?].

Accountability and transparency are more than just ensuring that money is efficiently spent and accounted for. It also includes adequate disclosure of information, collective decision-making and responsibilities. Answerability and taking responsibility for our actions and above all to be able to admit a mistake when it is obvious.

We are two months to the end of our mandate and will really appreciate if Goodwillers can be proactive, I thank you all for your usual understanding.

Best regards Fidelis, President, Goodwill [this line altered]

Of course, critics have always said that a president (at the end of his/her final mandate) who has no more elections to contest often puts politickerizing in the cupboard at this period. But I would venture to tell you that this might not be the case here. From the foregoing appeal which Folefac titled *'Help us serve you better'*, you can see what I mean. After the GA manipulation that scrapped the birth/marriage social package (against Fossungu's four-eyesismatic advice) and ushered in an unprecedented general malaise in both the GA and Executive Bureau, Fifolefac had the humility and humaneness in August

2009 to appoint a Goodwill Revamping Committee (GRC[51]) with mandate to fact-find and diagnose ways to revamp and invigorate the Association so as to make it once more very grandiose and attractive to both existing and prospective members. Not many leaders would do that; let alone appoint as the committee's chair their greatest and unrelenting critic – the Najemehist very unbecoming behaviour in the January 2007 Assembly testifying fully.

The five-person GRC made its findings and Fossungu prepared the draft report which was circulated to the others on August 6 with his message: "Dear Members of the GRC, I hope you've not waited for more than long enough for the attached report. It is here at last and I hope I haven't left out anything of worth. [D]o [make] the necessary corrections etc. before we can share it with the wider audience. Thanks. PAF" Everything having been made to fine-tune it, the GRC presented its report (following) during a subsequent Assembly:

---

[51] The idea was actually suggested under 'Any Other Matters" of the June 2009 Assembly by Emmanuel Fokoua Tene (then treasurer) who clearly lamented on the lack of enthusiasm and interest demonstrated by CGAMers. As the treasurer (who had enthusiastically joined CGAM almost at inception and thus knew exactly what he was talking about) had noted, this attitude was exhibited through their absenteeism in meetings, lateness in meeting and in parties. He therefore, suggested that a committee be set up to conduct a survey to come up with solutions to curb the problem. Tene is one of the few French-speaking CGAMers who has not only stuck with the association till date but also a member who has served in diverse positions in the different administrations and, above all, he is always forward-looking and stands above emotion in his contributions during debates. I just do not know if a lot of the membership would usually understand his points. I also make mine in English but does that still sink in? A few other non-politickerizers (Pius Esambe Etube aside) that, unfortunately, quickly relocated include James T. Tambong, Emmanuel Ngwakongnwi, Tah Techero, Jules-Blaise Komguep, and Amos Sumboh Nzonji.

GOODWILL REVAMPING COMMITTEE

MEMBERS: Mrs. Maggie Ojong, Mrs. Yvette Fuh-Cham, Mr. Yakubu Mohnkong, Dr. Levis Cheussom, & Dr. Peter Fossungu.

MANDATE: Fact-finding and diagnosis regarding ways to revamp and invigorate the Association so as to make it once more very grandiose and attractive to both existing and prospective members.

The Goodwill Revamping Committee (GRC), after some preliminary individual consultations with the past and current membership of Goodwill, met in plenary session on Saturday 1 August 2009 at 6660 Mazarin for the purpose of sampling opinions and arriving at some possible solutions to the biting issue of disinterestedness confronting the Association. The GRC tabled the following findings and recommendations.

I. MEETING SESSIONS

A) **Findings**: Due to the recent proliferation of many ethnic associations within the community, time factor and scarce financial resources have become a real problem for those who want to belong to both Goodwill and their ethnic groupings and in this competition 'natural instinct' has not favoured Goodwill.

B) **Suggestions**: There is a general leaning towards the idea that Goodwill meetings be curtailed and held once every two months.

II. SOCIAL PACKAGES

A) **Findings**: A lot of people are no more interested in Goodwill because of the Association's unfelt presence in members' happy events such as births and marriages. These Social packages (Births and marriages) meanwhile have been shown to be veritable vehicles of solidarity among Goodwillers, when they were still in place.

B) **Recommendations**: Reinvigorate the Association by reintroducing these social packages as follows. Reduction of the bereavement package from $1500.00 to $1000.00 with births and marriages now each securing $150.00 per member concerned.

III. MEMBERS(HIP)

A) **Findings**: Most members have been found to lack the volunteer spirit even in regard of day-to-day activities of the Association; not to be motivating one another; and not to be progressive and respectful in their dealings with one another at the association level. Furthermore, there are a lot of members who are members only in name, with no seriousness in belonging to the group.

B) **Suggestions**: Members are encouraged to make themselves available when the Association needs their services in different capacities, and not to behave as if some particular members must always be the only ones to do so. In addition, membership criteria would need to be reviewed and strengthened so as to let in only serious and committed persons seeking membership.

IV. ELECTIONS

A) **Findings**: Two instances of elections irregularities (gifts & non-clearance of candidates financially) have kept resonating from most of the members that the GRC spoke to.

B) **Suggestions**: The elections committee should in the future stick to and follow elections rules (such as those prohibiting members from voting or presenting themselves for elections if they owe the Association a dime) without distinction as to who is concerned.

V. THE EXECUTIVE

A) **Findings**: The membership has largely been appalled by (1) the stark lack of the team spirit in the executive body and (2) the almost complete failure to defend and strictly apply association laid down rules and regulations when that was just the thing to do. The result has been the seemingly never-ending alterations of laid down principles at almost every meeting; occasioning general scepticism and 'I-Don't-Care' attitude from the general membership, most of who do simply feel as being targeted.

B) **Recommendations**: The executive must have the highest interest of the Association as their reason for being members of the executive, a body that must present some unity of purpose in its dealings and actions. Laws voted for at the beginning of the year have to be defended and strictly applied throughout the year.

Thanks for your time.

Dr. Fossungu for the GRC

From the appeal and the creation of the GRC whose recommendations you have just read, one would think that the out-going president was very desirous of what he impresses on us. The GWFC 'Crisis' (in the next chapter) would however present a completely different picture. The important thing right now though is that I just clearly could not have permitted the above supposedly-GAC message from Valentine Usongo the way it is to go out. Ndonkeu, the only other GAC member remaining then, could clearly not have met with Usongo: being the victor's strategist. Thus, whatever GAC meeting that might have taken place, I cannot tell. But I can surely tell that I was not part of it. Anyway, the point is not that sending out that message was a bad thing to do. It is that if I am putting anything out there regarding the situation at hand (or any other), I should not be doing so from a tree-top hiding spot.

The next 'after-elections' write-up came in on December 19 from Nixon Tebo with title '*The Aftermath of a Cout D'etat-Goodwill 2007!*' [Unedited] Fellow Goodwillers, it began,

History tells us that after a cout d'etat [sic], most pre-existing structures are destroyed, the ideologies of people completely change, some go on exile, others enter in to bushes and things are never the same again. Bullets ply the streets at every second and the inhabitants stay in camps for resistance and protection.

The cases of former Zaire, Ivory Coast, Rwanda, Nigeria, France (under Napoleon Bonapart[e]) and many others are glaring examples.

There is no doubt that there has been a coup in Goodwill with the electoral committee involved. As Charles wrote, it is not the issue of getting power but how you get it that matters.

The aggressive campaigns conducted by the winning team that involved high expenditure on food, drinks, transport[a]tion, social services, and the gathering and packaging of Recalled Toxic Chinisse [sic] Toys, has never been heard of in any progressing community abroad. The various interventions through questioning and expression of doubts on the election floor were already afore planned. Further, the campaign messages displayed on the net were so evil and full of lies in such a magnitude that the electoral committee should have sense[d] a danger in case of a counter action and request for a review. The over 60 days door to door knocking even though characterised by some social benefits but full of black mailing, slander and false promises, has left the community tearing apart. Was that actually meant to help the community or for hidden agenda? Never the less, the Najeme's team remained calm in order to maintain unity and peace within[] the community. Now that the elections have come and gone, there exist[s] an atmosphere of mockery and abuses in our community. My few minutes at the children's party made me thought [sic] that it was a football tonarment [sic]. Shouts of sheers [cheers?] and boos were herald [heard? in] the hall as names of children from the various camps were being read out to collect their packages.

It is a disgrace for us to institute another Cameroon in Canada. The very characteristics that led us to fled [sic] our Country are being gradually installed in our community: the rise of corrupt man killer political parties, tribal segregation, high profile gossips and others are all viruses that will continue to hunt us and our children if we don't put a stop to them. We are also setting a wrong tone to our children through our dids [sic] and what we say about others to the hearing of our children. Some of them are even being trained as spice [sic]. Our parents back home will be astonished to hear of some of our activities in Canada. Some people say and quote from the bible that the black race has been cursed which is why they never agree nor work as a team except to destroy themselves. If that is true, then following the coming [of] Christ every darkness has been put aside. Other black communities are cooperating and doing businesses together. The Ghan[a]ians, the Nigerians among others own joint and sole businesses all over Europe and North America. Only the Cameroonians are still backward abroad among popular African countries when it comes to creating businesses and wealth accumulation. We always over know!

Any Way Forward?

YES! Keep aside politics, tribal segregations, smile on face and in heart, don't seek for importance because you are already important, discuss ideas not people, brain storm on jobs and projects, respect each individual's domain, cut down excess entertainment, learn to save than to borrow, buy smaller cars enough for the family than heavy duty vehicles, and we should learn from those who have been successful. We should make better use of our short li[v]es.

Is This Realistic?

YES! There are places and countries where you can't find a black man, so any black that you meet on the way becomes your friend, brother or sister. If we think of where we come from and of those we have left behind, then we shall reshape our behaviour. The secret is that we must LOVE ONE ANOTHER as Jesus said. Without love and full of envy we shall continue to have escalating troubles in our li[v]es and communities. When children grow-up, theirs may be worse just as the case of Maryland, US.

What Should We Do Now?

Call and Apologize to those that you have stepped on their toes either directly or indirectly, intentionally or unintentionally. Accept apologies and forgive and forget as God will do to the repentant.

What Will be the Results?

Happiness, Pro[s]perity, Friends and not Enemies, Communities not Camps, More Common Initiatives that will change lives abroad and back home.

Thank you all, I am just a messenger, I have no energy but will escape if I sense trouble.

To God be the Glory. Nixon

The final message was in on December 24, 2007 with its caption being *'Together we stand; divided we fall'*. Written by Beltus Nyambi, it stated:

Dear Goodwillers,
I would like to wish you all a merry [C]hristmas and a prosperous 2008 coming up in the horizon. It is my wish that every goodwiller and their entire family enjoy this period because unto us a king is born.

Despite our ide[o]logical differences, the different diatribe of accusations and gossiping, [and] the tense atmosphere that have reign during these past months in our great association, the spirit of togetherness is still very much alive. The two baby showers is [sic] an indicator of what this spirit is. As we move into [the] [N]ew [Y]ear we all have the responsibility to keep this spirit.

The former US president Jimmy Carter once said "The bond of our common humanity is stronger than the divisiveness of our fears and prejudices. God gives us the capacity for choice. We can choose to alleviate suffering among us and around the world. We can choose to work together for peace among us and around the world. We can make these changes - and we must."

As we enter into the [N]ew [Y]ear, dear goodwillers we must choose to do the things that will promote the image of Goodwill in a positive way.

Happy Xmas and a pro[s]perous [N]ew [Y]ear to you all

All I could say at the time to myself was: 'They are only seeing now what I had seen long ago and had been trying all the while to make them see.' That could plainly explain why you wouldn't find anything in the forum on this particular election-results subject bearing my name or signature. The politickerization that a few were then condemning, using said elections, is even so blatant in the domain of the social packages on deaths, births and marriages that would constitute the rock foundation of CGAM, as you have been told already. Let us next see the way to the effective de-stigmatization of the stereotypes.

Chapter 6

From NOSIFE Into HISOFE For Appropriate De-Stereotyping And Afrikentication Techniques: Africa Must Unite Or Die

Chinese economic success is not the product of free market accidental coincidence. Rather, it is orchestrated by the State through a mixture of nationalism ('big think') and pragmatic decisions (disjointed incrementalism) in agriculture, finance and industry. Furthermore, these decisions build upon existing institutions (e.g. the Household Responsibility System, Township Village Enterprises, etc.), some dating back to pre-revolutionary China (e.g. Special Economic Zones), rather than imported ones from outside China [Gros, 2008: 56].

Once more, *NOSIFE* means *no-schooling infour-eyesism* while *HISOFE* is the *Higher School of Four-Eyesism*. As already pointed out, Africans also contribute to stereotyping Africa through not being able to utilize appropriate de-stigmatization strategies. For the effective method of tackling the issue, I will employ these three principal queries: (1) Tree-Top Habitaters Theory: Non-Africans Africanizing while in Africa? (2) Positively Using the Stigmas: Hard Choices, National Humiliation and Veperizationism, and (3) Relevantly Surprising Answers to Unnecessary Questions?

The Tree-Top-Habitaters Theory: Non-Africans Africanizing While In Africa?

This approach is entwined in a clear and simple example drawn from my rich expibasketism, a theory that developed in McGill University. As a *Je me souviens* Quebecer, I always remember this student in McGill University when I got there in

1995, roughly twenty years ago. Note well that I had been to Canada before, in 1992, and precisely in Edmonton, Alberta, where white people, from the comfort of their cars in downtown, regularly threw this at us: "Niggers, what are you doing here? Go home!" Well, at that point I could not help imagining what my fellow Blacks in South Africa must be going through. Note also that I only had to *imagine* because, unfortunately, I am yet to meet a *real* South African in Canada. I don't think these Africans too should rush to read gratuitous meanings into my use of *real* until I have explained myself with the crumbling of Carenayahism in the CGAM that takes us conveniently to the Tree-Top-Habitaters Theory.

Carenayahism Crumbling: Any Real South Africans in Canada?

I was living in the heart of downtown when I arrived in Montreal in September 1995. I am talking precisely about Metro Guy-Concordia, at the St. Mathieu exit. Don't get me wrong again. I was certainly not in any of those high-rise buildings that were full of Chinese and other Asian students. A foreign student with such huge differential fees to pay, I used to just wonder how they go about paying for those very expensive apartments until I discovered the intriguing Chinese Formula. These Chinese are really good at making maximum use of any apartment they rent. In a 31/2 in Montreal, for example, do not be surprised at the vast number of them dwelling there. I was then living in a 21/2 on Lincoln Avenue where my moderate three-storey building stood. Until a Chinese buffet around McGill University was discovered, I could give myself the pleasure then of regularly eating in a nearby McDonald on St. Mathieu/De Maisonneuve. As I was heading there one evening, this black guy approached me and asked if I could help him to eat something. His story was that he was South African and had arrived in town about two days before by ship, hidden in a container, and had not eaten a thing since. I was myself a 'Johnny Just Come', just about two weeks in town and, knowing how much I usually spent every trip to McDonald for a meal, I pulled out a 20-dollar note and handed it to the starving South African. I felt really good the rest of the day, just knowing that I had given one hungry brother a meal. Didn't I (a mere temporary visitor to the country) just give him a warm and sweet welcome to apartheid-free Canada?

The Hidden Ahidjoist-Verwoerdist Faces of Canada

Guess what! He got me! The next day at the same spot about the same time there was the same guy with the same story, probably looking forward to the same $20.00 hand-out? Is this a beggar or swindler, I wondered to myself. I am not used to judging one by the other's acts. But I think I made a general rule out of this one case: never to hand out anything to any able-bodied beggar like the myriad of them that are nicely hidden in Montreal's Metro Stations. And don't be fooled because a lot of these beggars/swindlers are welfare recipients; with plenty of the white ones having particularly easy and persuasive 'suck-your-pocket-dry' methods. For instance, they would approach you as you enter the Metro and request for some change because they want to make a phone call. It is very easy sparing fifty cents than a dollar or more. But just imagine conservatively one hundred people each care-freely handing over fifty cents (in a day) for the phone call that is never made. How much does that Canadian beggar/swindler take home daily? That is way too good and more than the factory worker (who also contributed fifty cents on her way to, and perhaps also from, work) makes a day. Extrapolate that amount, if you will, and then add to the swindler's monthly welfare cheque before asking me why I have not yet met real South Africans whereas they should normally have been so many of them in Canada seeking refuge from apartheid.

Why? What a silly question! Where do you think Verwoerd and his friends got the idea of apartheid from? Canada and its

Native Reserves, of course, provided the brain pill. Our beloved Canada is a real Hypocracy. It has even *hypocractized* in its Anthem, the first line(s) of which actually should be: *O Canada, my home **on** Natives' Land*! You think that this is not it? To properly understand the hypocracy, just hear us for decades calling anti-apartheid activist Mandela a terrorist but, before you know it, we are bestowing 'Honourable Citizenship of Canada' on him. Mandela just *might* (mark you I say might) have needed that when he was condemned to and languishing in Robin Island, not when he was already Number One South African! We are just lucky because if this rare human being with a South African tag could pardon and embrace those on the frontline actively and brutally fighting to eliminate his crusade for a just society, it is like nothing excusing the *Wallersteiners* (or behind-the-scene string-pullers) called the Canadian government.

I am very sure the Native Peoples of this country can also forgive us because being part and parcel of a just Canada is just what they are just about; and not to chase us non-Natives into the sea (like the racist regime in Pretoria had erroneously thought). Now, if the Afrikaners learnt apartheid from Canada, it is also germane that Canada should, in turn, learn forgiveness and inclusion from South Africans, one of whom is a conspicuous and vital link and special citizen of this country. Therefore, let's pay great attention to Castellano (1971) particularly and quickly 'Get out of Paternalism and into Partnership with the Native People.' That is what Nelson Madiba Mandela (the famous South-African Canadian) symbolizes or incarnates. Until that is done, rest assured that "Canada is also guilty of confusing or ambivalent multiculturalism" (Fossungu, 2013b: 151) like Cameroon, whose Ahidjo is now all over the place, and even in Canada, disturbing successors, including CGAM presidents. How come, you are asking?

Is the GWFC Crisis a Product of Fifolefacist Four-Eyesism?

Well, if your answer to this Fifolefacist title-question is 'No', then I would invite you to kindly leave your *NOSIFE (no-schooling infour-eyesism)* and follow me into the *HISOFE (Higher School of Four-Eyesism)*. I would have to try hard this time to convince you that my Ahidjoist-Fifolefacist theory explains exactly what happened to the administration of Caren Osong Ayah who I prefer to style as "CGAM's Iron Lady". From my four-eyesismatic perspective, this could be the reality which begins with *Tower-Dependence and Silent-Tradition*: Folefac's towering accomplishments (external-relations-wise) as CGAM's fourth president practically made most of his successors so dependent on him (since he is also always available, in and out of power) for this and that, that Folefac was virtually the *Wallesteiner* pulling all the strings during their term of office. It had thus become some sort of silent tradition. Bad habits die hard, it is said. Therefore, any CGAM president that would come around and do not toe this silent-traditional line is obviously, according to the fifolefacist reasoning, stepping on Folefac's precious-record toes and must be given hell, one way or the other. The Mbianyor Viperizationism below (see 'On Onafridism and National Humiliation') testifies or not? I will go for yes, adding the fact that Martha Mbianyor did not climb to the presidency as has been the tradition since Folefac (Nankam as Takang's V-P moved in; Nsom Mbeng as Nankam's vice moved into the position; CO Ayah as Mbeng's V-P became president after him). Mbianyor obviously was cleared out because she was the kind that would not allow self to be used.

If Martha Mbianyor's viperizationism was not solid enough, the Carenayahist style evidently sent a thunderous note. It is precisely because CO Ayah came into office with her own independent style of running CGAM (which is what Viperizationism was really all about) that we began having the simple appointment of the head of the GWFC becoming a "crisis", and a very baseless one for that matter. And do not think that it is mere coincidence. Like Ahidjo in Cameroon, Folefac seems to have planned his *exit-no-exit* very well before 'exiting'. That last political *joker-card* against possible phenomena like Carenayahism was very craftily (this word always pushes 99-Sensism to the foreground) put in place in November 2009. For an appetizer, I ask you: Do you recall how this guy had been so hungry of/for power, even trying everything imaginable to grab it from PT Ayah before Ayah's mandate was over? Good thing you do. Follow me then, after this last passing to *HISOFE* quiz: So, you think such a person having finally climbed into power and enjoyed it for the full maximum terms would then easily relinquish it?· A real Ahidjo, this is for sure. 80% is your mark! Get it then.

On November 29, 2009 Folefac sent out a communiqué to *nosifeans*, titled '*Goodwill property & questions*'.[52] It was clear and

---

[52] Said communiqué said:
    Fellow Goodwillers,
    In preparation for effective handing [over], a list of all Goodwill property ha[s] been established. Please verify the list and remind us if any Goodwill property has not been listed or the correct pieces.
    Furthermore, after our last meeting, some members have posed questions which I think the answers are relevant to ALL Goodwillers. Below the table are brief explanations to the three main questions.

    List of Goodwill property- in preparation for handing over to 2010 executive bureau.... [For space purposes, I have omitted the table with the list since it is not really very important to the issue here.]

    <u>2007 unaccounted-for money</u>
    After the failed mediation by some individuals of ACC permanent council, Goodwill legal adviser suggested that we needed a signed statement from ALL three Goodwill internal auditors to proceed to small claims court. The statement was prepared and signed by the lead auditor. Unfortunately, one of the

unambiguous, since these *nosifeans* would not even comprehend it, the more so as it is openly hidden at the tail-end. Would it even matter: unless these hand-picked stooges could turn around and prove not to be "docile" like Biya did? I would not want to drag you into the issue of whether the famous meeting with the GWFC TM (team manager) involved all the members of the bureau or just the out-going president. It seems to be clear it was just a two-person affair, but that is not the really crucial point. So, you are surely asking, what is it? Address your further questions now to the portion regarding GWFC, not to me. But as you are still waiting for me to continue with the *hisofe* lecturing, I ask you the query then: Why was Folefac changing/modifying the GWFC appointing rules only when he is handing over 'without actually handling over'? Remember the Ahidjo-Biya *retiring-ruling* in a previous chapter? As I did point out clearly to the politickerizers-jammed GAC, it is a non-issue, referring to the mediation (called for by GAC that was then chaired by Folefac) between then CGAM president

---

auditors was no longer a member of Goodwill and the other (RIP) could not read or write due to his medical condition. That ended the process. Goodwillers should however be proud that the[ir] determination to make elected officials accountable has raised awareness and stimulated vigilance in Goodwill and other associations.

Overdue loan
Work is in progress and you will be updated in the days ahead.
Goodwill F.C.
Following a meeting with the team management, henceforth, the President of Goodwill will appoint ONLY the team president. The rest will be elected by the players.

Please, I will be glad to clear any doubts on the functioning of Goodwill during our mandate.

Hope we are all polishing our dancing shoes for the Explosive End-of-year party

Best regards
Fidelis Folifac
President- Goodwill

and the GWFC over the former's appointment of the latter's head that GWFC rejected.

You would surely get a good grip of the folly of this 'crisis' through this other important question I have asked several times and would continue to pose: Quite apart from the silly 11th Province People concept in Cameroon (see Fossungu, 2013b: 84-87), can someone be a citizen of one of Cameroon's or Canada's provinces/territories without also being a citizen of Cameroon or of Canada? (The Quebec diehard separatists, of course, might stay as silly as they are to say *yes* here with Folefac's backing – see chapter 4.) I have been four-eyesismatically arguing, since the Paulayahist administration (during which time Folefac was pioneer president of GWFC), against non-CGAMers entering GWFC. But the politickerizers have always prevailed, pretending not to be seeing the rocky road ahead. 2013 then became Rocking Time, with Folefac playing the Rocking Tunes and the other politickerizers roughly rocking-and-rolling in spite of themselves? That is what Cameroon political dictionary calls *Dimabola-ing* or singing the supreme commander's praises.

Folefac had convened a GAC 'Mediation Meeting' on July 3, 2013 because "The current crisis in Goodwill FC warrants our immediate intervention." But I only got to know what "The current crisis" was actually about through CO Ayah's communication of 5 July 2013 to the GAC that included details of all the numerous correspondences between her and the GWFC Team Manager (Julius Ngome Ewane) who is not even a CGAMer. She essentially was requesting from the TM three nominations/suggested names from which she (as CGAM President) was to appoint the GWFC president (why all these president titles? See Fossungu, 2013c: xviii n.10). But the TM was clearly imposing or actually making the appointment himself by giving the lady just one name. After only learning of the real substance of the 'mediation' from the President-TM back-and-forth tangle (another genre of Fifolefacist Rock-and-

Roll) and CO Ayah's consequent frustration as reflected in the title of her communication to the GAC – *'Plan B In Case Everything Goes Wrong'* – I then elucidated things on 6 July 2013 in my communication to the GAC (that was out to 'immediately intervene'). For an easy comprehension of the crux of the disgusting matter being fashioned as a 'Crisis', I am putting my arguments on the relevant point verbatim and in their entirety:

Thanks [to President CO Ayah] for bringing this issue on and for letting some of us know exactly what this mediation thing was all about. I am really convinced by your write-up and would even say I am a fan of your style of rule. But I am not writing here as a fan; doing so as both a constitutionalist and the 'hardliner' that 'politickers' would say you are. If hardliner is correctly defined as someone that sees the need for compromise at times but who out rightly rejects 'politicking' with clean and clear rules, then that makes two of us.

When you govern[] an association or any other body with its constitution, you clearly do not need to rigmarole to make your points; you're on top of it, President C. Ayah, and I do not see the need for any so-called Plan B since Plan A was even a non-starter. I will briefly explain with the <u>President's Constitutional Powers</u>

The President of CGAM appoints heads (call them whatever) of sub-organs of the Association, including the GWFC. Period. Nowhere are any conditions attached, as to consultation, etc. If a CGAM president decides to consult before appointing, it is all that president's discretion, which creates no binding precedent. That is to say that, if other CGAM presidents before now had decided to exercise their discretion by actually handing over their appointment prerogative to a gang within the sub-organ whose head needs to be appointed, that does not at all bind a CGAM president who refuses to bow to such 'politicking'. The rules are exceeding clear here and I would think that GAC as [a] constitutional watch-dogging body owes the current president some excuses for not propping her up but rather even attempting to 'mediate' on her defending the constitution of CGAM and on the exercise of her powers as CGAM president.

Poutine-Doorism in the CGAM

This far you have heard more than enough of all sorts of this and that talk about responsibility, accountability, etc. in governance, especially from the Fifolefacist administration. I am clearly against not following and respecting simple and clear rules. If at this level one cannot do so then I wonder why we point fingers at the Ahidjo-Biya regime. It is very indicative to me that, with this attitude, even if the American Constitution (or any that anyone might be building up for this country)is transplanted to Cameroon, it would not have secured democracy and responsible governance there. Ahidjo might have some "justification" for trying to behave towards President Paul Biya as he did; no one else but Ahidjo put Biya there. I do not want to get into the stories circulating on the internet that the duo had a 'man-on-man' pact that the other reneged from. It is simply amazing that some people would do just anything, even if it means 'climbing' on their own mothers, just to be able to illicitly partake in the scraps from the table of power! Midnightism, it is called? Whatever the case, Biya never became the president of the republic because Cameroonians elected him.

But what "justification" would Folefac have for hindering President CO Ayah who had been duly elected by Goodwillers, and not hand-picked by Folefac, to be CGAM president? Perhaps my good friend does not know this and needs some spoon-feeding. Nothing in the CGAM Constitution prevents a former president (even if s/he has already served for the limited two-consecutive terms) from later coming back and being elected to serve again. Lyslyakoyahism in chapter 3 proves the point. If Folefac wants to be like Russia's Putin whose going is always just coming back, that is the option open to Fifolefac. I would personally and gladly vote for Folefac if he chooses to use Poutine-Doorism in the CGAM. But until that happens, it was Caren Osong Ayah (or now Julius Etaya Ashu) that was/is in office and it is the sitting president (and her/him alone) that ought to be running the affairs of the CGAM until the end of her/his mandate. Therefore, when the 2013 "conflict" was raging on, I advised Folefac to get off the neck of the woman's administration, to no avail. How was the counsel transmitted, other than through the useless GAC, you want to know?

From-the-Inside Journadictationalism

It is Funny African 'What-I-Like-Only' Journalism. The small piece in which I did so was titled "The Solution No One Is Talking About: Ahidjoism in the Cameroon Goodwill Association of Montreal". I sent it to *Cameroonjournal.com* for publication because I was truly attracted to its mission that reads: "-To serve as an independent monitor of power. To hold those entrusted with its exercise accountable. -To provide the general public with information they need to be free and self-governing in a democratic society. -To vigorously champion a return to fundamental principles of democracy and freedom, believing that it is such arrangement that can best advance the multifarious interests of citizens in a country of many nations and faiths such as Cameroon." Of course, the editor of that journal, obviously knowing Fidelis Folefac, refused publishing it. He must have thought I was writing behind the man's back, as many politickerizers like those in the CGAM would do from a tree-top position. Like several Canadian editors/publishers (see Fossungu, 2013c: xiv n.6), the *Cameroonjournal.com* editor gave very flimsy excuses like 'the article is too long and readers don't like reading long articles.' That was on August 18, 2013.

It is all bullshit but I still re-worked the piece, considerably cutting it down to the size (800 words) he had recommended. That was last year (2013) but as we speak, that piece is not yet published and I have since not heard from the publisher again. Come to think of the fact that this same journal, after publishing my "How Cameroon Should Be Governed",[53] kept reminding me (e.g. on July 7, 2013) that: "it's been long that you sent in a story for your column. Please can you supply us with a new write-up?" The unpublished piece, of course, is incorporated in this section of the book. Believe me, if I should just replace Fidelis Folefac in it today with, say, Paul Biya, and send to that very journal editor, tomorrow you will be reading it in *Cameroonjournal.com*. Call them journalists, if you care; but that is exactly what constitutes *journadictationalists* (see Fossungu, 2014: 119). Where is Africa heading to with these types of "journalists"? And the kinds of predecessors like Folefac who shine but obstructs their followers from doing same or better?

Shine and Let Shine

Fifolefac did shine because we all collaborated with and supported him; let others also shine and even surpass shining, if they can. I could see the capacity in Carenayahism to bring something unique to the CGAM. Caren Osong Ayah, our darling wife, mother, sister, colleague, twice-former First Lady and president, definitely had something to show the world. We were not supposed to be the ones to stand in her way. Could Folefac just be unwittingly concerned that someone after him, with a free hand, would beat his well-known record as CGAM president? My brother and ex-president, if that be the case (because the people surrounding you cannot be your friends

---

[53] See Peter A. Fossungu, "How Cameroon Should be Governed: The Political and administrative set up" available at: http://www.cameroonjournal.com/how%20to%20govern%20cameroon.html.

enough to tell you that it looks like it), then my advice to you is that no one (but yourself) would already be beating your record if you do not work hard on these issues I am indicating and wash your hands clean. Perhaps most people in power are great because of the patronage they exercise, I do not quite know. Most presidents do that. What makes Folefac's case different and reprehensible is the fact that he is not just doing so with his 'collaborators' while in office (*Viperizationism*, for example) but doing it to a duly elected president who is in office and is also *unwilling to be his crony or proxy*. Please, let's learn to shine and let shine.

The Gagging Doublesidism Nonsense

When Folefac calls for a GAC meeting for the purpose of "immediate intervention" and then later says he, as GAC Chair, has no powers to take necessary decision as requested by the CGAM president, what message is being sent to "his Boys" in GWFC? Any good between-the-line reader would say it is clearly telling them that 'As long as I am the Chair of GAC and in GAC, there is nothing to worry about, regarding the overt violation of the CGAM Constitution; thus *un seul mot donc: Continuez*!' (see Fossungu, 2013b: 2). Yet he would continue to endlessly convene useless GAC meetings "to find a way forward". *Doublesidism*, politickerization and similar terms have been used already too much. For a brief change, let's go this way. Hypocrisy! Hypocrisy! Hypocrisy! That is exactly what is written all over it.

Now, since the GAC has no powers over the respect of the CGAM Constitution and more, my suggestion then is that this useless Fifolefacist toothless bulldog of a politickerizing tool be scrapped as an organ of the CGAM; the more so because most (if not all) of its members (from A to Z, skipping just one F) are just playing hypocrisy or what some might want to call back-stabbing politickerization. Otherwise, where then are all the other Honourable GAC Members (Presidents PT Ayah,

Takang, Nankam, Mbeng, and Founding Member Ndonkeu) on this and other blatant sidestepping of the Constitution for personal power? I am here challenging these guys to come off politickerizing or the Politickerization Bus because, when they do, they would realize that it is then so easy to nonchalantly tell politickerizers not to politickerize with clear and clean issues or rules. When these guys do this, the community would greatly benefit and smoothly move ahead. That is the real way forward that no one has been talking about. Doing it any other way only validates Caren Osong Ayah's theory/prophecy to GAC on 5 July 2013 "that history will hold us accountable for our actions and until we begin to take responsibility for our actions we are just pretending to build a healthy community" because "If we really want a healthy community, let us put aside our personal interest. I work for the interest of the community and so shall it be."

Fossungu (the lone GACer who responded) was in total concord with the then CGAM president when he stated the next day: "Madam President, just imagine that I was ever thinking of abandoning my own creation (CGAM) and then know that you have given me one more reason to stay on. If CGAM really needs its own 'Iron Lady' in your person to rid it of the paralyzing Politick[eriz]ing that now has it flat on the floor, then so be it." Unfortunately, I have learnt that Caren Osong Ayah decided not to run for a second term, thanks to her being fed up with the politickerizers who, with this writer out-of-town and not always being around as before, have since been reigning unperturbed and unsurpassed. What a shame to Africa to be getting all this from *AITWs* belonging to an endless *list* of doctors! Is our Montreal Cameroonian community really plagued by these doctors rather than being blessed with them? Dog-Rule exclusionist politics doesn't appear to be any different from apartheid to me. Would you then say the 'South African' still having my 20-dollar note ever tested Canadian-inspired apartheid that was practised by the Pretoria gang that the racist Albertans reminded me of?

The Tree-Top-Habitaters Theory and the Likehewasians

Whatever you say in response, the important issue right now is that this is no longer Canada's Prairies but Montreal and three years later. Very full of himself, the young McGill student (certainly an American) came up to me and said: "You are from Africa where you people live on trees, aren't you?" My unprompted response was: "I am from Africa. You're damned right about that. Of course, yes also to where we live. Your ambassador's small tree is just next to my grandma's gigantic tree in uptown Yaoundé." I can proudly tell you that, till date, I am yet to find a better de-stereotyping pill for this young man. It was more effective than any angry 'fighting' (which might obviously be what he was expecting) over the matter would ever have done. He instantaneously became very humble, from just realizing just how daft he had just turned out to be. His requests for forgiveness and for friendship were as genuine as any good and effective educator could discern. This quick recognition of error is a domain in which I admire white people a lot. He thereafter learnt a lot about Africans (accompanying me to our parties and other social occasions), discovering for himself what the MIME ('Military-Industrial-Entertainment-Media') stereotypes and other topographies of stigmas had been blinding him from knowing. The strategy I employed here is as effective, as Colding (2013) would say, because it "rips the veil from the readers' eyes. One begins to see that the [South African mine] workers were husbands, fathers, and sons fighting for dignity against organized, imperial powers." My McGill student-friend in question thereafter ardently aided (on his own volition) to spread the word to others who were like-he-was-before (you can always call them *Likehewasians*, if you will).

Mark Tessier and others have been able to do the same to the likehewasians of the Islam-Democracy-Obstructing Syndrome. *Religion, Democracy, and Politics in the Middle East* is a book that tries tobridge the gap between sensational media coverage and reality, explaining many of the most important issues in the region today in a way that is historically and theoretically informed because the contributions in this volume, taken together, form a rich trove that will leave the reader better aware of the nuances and complexity behind the newspaper headlines (Byman, 2012: vii). Looking at the Data and Measures (Tessier, 2002: 342-44), Tessier's Analysis and Findings (2002: 344-48) led him to some conclusions. Among these conclusions (Tessier, 2002: 348ff) are the following. Despite a number of statistically significant relationships, Islam appears to have less influence on political attitudes than is frequently suggested by students of Arab and Islamic society (2002: 348). The study also strongly suggests that Islam should not be reified when attempting to explain Arab political orientations, and, in particular, it offers evidence that support for democracy is not necessarily lower among those individuals with the strongest Islamic attachments. On the contrary, it provides strong support for those who challenge the thesis that Islam discourages the emergence of political attitudes conducive to democracy (Tessier, 2002: 348). It also suggests that support for political Islam does not involve a rejection of democracy and that those with more favourable view of Islamist movements and platforms are no less likely than others to favour political competition and to desire mechanisms to hold leaders accountable (Tessier, 2002: 349; Göymen, 2007: 233-39; Embong, 2007: 141). If these authors are wrong in theorizing as they do, then one would have to ask whether Islam had been wiped out completely in the Arab world in order for the Arab Spring (being essentially a demand for democratization and an end to dictatorship) to happen.

Question: Would I have succeeded at McGill through arguing otherwise (no matter the quantity of it) that Africans are not *tree-top habitaters*? Make sure not to confuse this with the notorious tree-toppers that the majority of Africans are. The approach used here was not only non-violent like Ghandi's in India. It is also exactly what is necessary "as it opens the minds and hearts of men and women who truly are seeking an understanding of what 'is' African as interpreted by Africans" (Killough, 2009). All that is required to better educate in this fashion, I think, is just being bold and staying true to who we are: Africans. When you are bold and truthful, it has been christickinologized, there is absolutely no need to be struggling with your ideas or identity (Fossungu, 2014: 51-55) because only the truth stays consistent (Fossungu, 2013a: 83-86). True, it may be to say that 'while in Rome, do as Romans'. But I am certain that it is not the same thing as saying that while in Rome you have to *unAfricanize* and unthinkingly *Romanize*. Otherwise, why do Europeans in Douala not 'do as *Doualans* by, for instance, *globalizing* in Marché Nkouloulou', let alone *Africanize* while in Africa?

Chinalogizing Sovereignty and Globalization: Becoming Big Boys Is Only Way to Fight Big Boys

You certainly need the foregoing Authenticity Thesis to better understand why communist China, considered in the West as authoritarian (see Drezner, 2009; Gat, 2013; Huang, 2013; Krastev, 2013; and Jiang, 2013), "has gradually emerged from the shadow of an ideologically inspired closed economy to become a powerful global economic player in the age of globalization" (Edoho, 2011: 104). This miraculous rise of China necessarily impels my also exploring "the utility (and lack thereof) of the Chinese model in the African context, as well as the possibilities of an Africa-centred 'big think' (Pan-Africanism) capable of mobilizing the continent for development" (Gros, 2008: 56). China presents an interesting case for challenging theories that seem to tie economic development to Western-style democracy. I suspect the kind of cultural erosion that Munyaradzi Mawere draws attention to must be behind the Chinese shutting of the door to globalization from 1950 to1970, until after their Cultural Revolution meant to get them "From 'All-Under-Heaven' to a Nation-State" (Wang, 2012: 71-94).[54]

It is because only an economically strong and politically robust nation-state can really achieve some of these goals in Africa that this book is banging as hard as would be necessary to awaken fast sleeping Africans and bring them to the realization that unity is their only hope for survival in a neoliberal world order. The book, no doubt, is also putting a

---

[54] Mawere in 2012 offered a comprehensive study and erudite description of the struggle of African indigenous knowledge systems in an age of globalization, using in particular eighty-four children's traditional games in south-eastern Zimbabwe. His book is an informative and interesting anthropological account of rare African children's games at the risk of disappearing under globalization. The virtue of the book does not only lie in its modest philosophical questioning of those knowledge forms that consider themselves as superior to others, but in its laudable, healthy appreciation of the creative art forms of traditional literature that features in genres such as endangered children's traditional games. The book is a clarion call to Africans and the world beyond to come to the rescue of relegated and marginalized African creativity in the interest of future generations. See http://www.langaa-rpcig.net/The-Struggle-of-African-Indigenous.html. The issue of globalization's effects on indigenous culture has also been ably handled by J. Oloka-Onyango, Professor of Law and Director of the Human Rights & Peace Centre (HURIPEC) at Makerere University in Kampala, Uganda, and who was the Special Rapporteur on Globalization and Human Rights of the United Nations Sub-Commission on the Promotion and Protection of Human Rights between 1999 and 2003. His thesis is that globalization has diverse implications (both positive and inimical) to the promotion and protection of the right to culture in contemporary Africa. While pointing out that culture is a dynamic aspect of human evolution, his study explores what implications globalization has for ensuring that its positive aspects are protected, while the negative are not given free reign. In particular, his work pays particular attention to the concept of traditional knowledge and women's human rights and the role of the African Commission on Human and Peoples' Rights in dealing with globalization's most adverse consequences (Oloka-Onyango, 2005).

stress on some of the positive cultural endowments that Africans must not compromise under any circumstance, while advising on the negative things that must be shunned in order for the community to strengthen itself against erosion. What could make the vast difference between Africa and Asia which were both colonized, you want to know? Simple: "when Asians said 'independence' they meant it and got it" (Fossungu, 2013c: 117). For the *AITWs*, do the necessary re-writing with tree-topperism or midnightism and you will come out with this Grand Theorem: "When most *AITWs* said NO to 'Midnight Politics' by seeking asylum in Western countries, they DIDN'T mean IT, with the WEST getting *VOLUNTARY-SLAVERY* calculations RIGHT". This means in effect that (1) Africa cannot survive the extinction threats in the capacity of many mini-states and (2) it has to stay true to its own value systems (rather than inappropriate imported models) in devising means to govern its diverse populations.

It is all about being sovereign and "[w]ithout independence, sovereign equality is meaningless" (Nahar, 2008). Sovereignty has seen much ink and paper marriage in the wake of globalization. Steven D. Krasner has made some very interesting points on the issue. He thinks globalization is changing the scope of state control (Krasner, 2013: 71-72) but not that it undermines state control (2013: 71), declaring that the proponents of 'The Sovereign State Is Just About Dead' are very wrong (2013: 68). That sovereignty does not mean final authority (2013: 68-69) because The Peace of Westphalia did not produce the modern sovereign-state, it came later (2013: 69-70), making it wrong, in his view, to hold that universal human rights are an unprecedented challenge to sovereignty (2013: 70); although he concedes that, to some extent, NGOs are nibbling at national sovereignty (2013: 72; also Mathews, 1997) and that it is true that sovereignty sometimes blocks conflict resolution (Krasner, 2013: 73). His conclusion is that it is true that the European Union is a new model for supranational governance, but only for Europeans (2013: 73-74). So what are Africans waiting for to have their own model for themselves?

Developing nations, according to Dani Rodrik, have always complained that the system of globalization is biased against their interests since it is the big boys that make the rules (What else would you logically expect, except to fight hard and become a 'big boy'?). A motley collection of anarchists, environmentalists, union interests, and progressives, Rodrik has added, have also occasionally made common cause in their opposition to globalization for obvious reasons. But the real big news in recent years, he concludes, is that the rich countries are no longer happy about the rules either (Rodrik, 2010: xiv). Why are the rule-makers no longer happy about their own rules? Could it not be because some of 'the small boys' (like China and other Asian Tigers) are now able to also take advantage of the rules, to the consternation of 'the big boys'? Or, is it because, in the world of greedy people (see Achal and Tangonyire, 2012; Serwer and Sloan, 2008; Edsall, 2013), the comparative and superlative would still apply on greed? That is, that some would always be greedier than others? I will not get deep into that but instead continue this study of globalization and state sovereignty by focusing on the theme of unity.

Africa must therefore unite or die. This is then the one message I need Africans (from north to south, east to west, black, white, or whatever) to attentively listen to. This book builds on my earlier works, and demonstrates that African states have to come together in order to have any impact in the global economy, whether it is capitalist- or communist-driven. Let me repeat it over and over that Fossungu (1999a: 361) even wondered and questioned as far back as 1999 if Africa's "impending misfortune" resulting from irreversible trends in international air transport was not enough for Africa to rethink its attitudes towards meaningful federalism and the effective pooling of resources. As he went on to suggest and ask,

Could joint air transport organizations or agencies (which the Chicago Convention even implores the [ICAO] Council to encourage) not provide a better nucleus and locomotion (than the Organization of African Unity (OAU) Charter presently does) for the eventual emergence of a United States of Africa (USAF)? Would the world's complex metamorphoses outrun Africa's ability to devise new mechanisms of legal, political, and social cushions? Would Africa not be flexible enough to adjust its perceptions to changing global realities? Would Africa not be able to exchange conventional mental habits for ones more suitable for understanding unconventional circumstances or phenomena? What, if at all, could Africa learn in this regard from the European Union's experiences? Would "Mama Africa" never wake up from her long sleep? [Fossungu, 1999a: 360, note omitted]

It has to be noted that China (which is not an ethnically homogenous society) was similarly also asleep until the "Awakening [of] China" (Wang, 2012: 75-78) from the late nineteenth century in tandem with the transformation from imperial dynasty to a modern nation-state. The awakening of the Chinese people was not just a historical narrative or an education campaign; it was also a political technique for building a sovereign and independent state (Wang, 2012: 77), "one in which nationalism replaces culturalism as the dominant Chinese view of their identity and place in the world" (Wang, 2012: 75). Could it then be that the bang on the door for "Awakening Africa" has not been loud and reverberating enough? If so, then why? There is little doubt that the issue of globalization is a crucial one for those interested in questions of contemporary political economy and governance. In any talk of African political unity a study that aims at 'Understanding the Political Economy of Cameroon' (Fossungu, 2013b: 194-238) would be very important because the country is most suited (culturally, historically, geopolitically, and economically) to unite Africans.

This thesis is also seen in 'A Dream for Africa's children' in which a future wise leader from Cameroon

will want (with the people's free accord and ratification) to realize the following for a start:

The name [Cameroon] will become the capital of the genuinely open DRA. This capital (Cameroon) will be sited somewhere in the territory that Parliament will (through a well-debated law) carve out of the present Cameroon Republic's three provinces of Adamaoua, Centre, and East. The larger part of it will come from Adamaoua. (Look at our current map and you will begin to visualize what that dream is saying.) Cameroon will thus be the name for the capital territory of DRA [Democratic Republic of Africa].

That new capital (Cameroon) will have its boulevards, avenues, streets, parks, etc. – which will all be well-planned – named after the current African states (e.g. Mauritius Avenue, South African Boulevard, rue Côte d'Ivoire) and some African heavyweights (such as Place Mandela, Avenue de Klerc, Nkrumah Street). Other cities will follow suit; with the Ministry of Town Planning having then to live up to its name and tasks [Fossungu, 1998b].

In the aforementioned study on political economy (and viewing the general decline on the continent), Fossungu agreed fully with the then leading opposition party's (Social Democratic Front's) 1996 'An Economic Blueprint to Challenge 14 [now 33] Years of Unpardonable Economic, Political Mismanagement'. That is, that Africans are a frightened, opiumized and confused people (Fossungu, 1998d). Unlike others such as the Chinese (and Asians generally – see Fossungu, 2013b: 209-217) who do look forward to the 21st century and beyond with excitement, Africans look to the same thing with fear. This globalization-paradoxical fear, as the SDF Economic Blueprint explicated,

is the emotion which is shared by that half of mankind which finds itself ill-prepared for this [accentuated globalization] moment [since 1989 with the Soviet collapse] because they live in economic and social circumstances which make them believe that their future as well as that of their children is going to be worse than what it is now. It is this half that has suffered economic decline as a result of their failure to structure their societies in a manner which enables them to become efficient players in [the] emerging global economy of the 21st century. These societies have lived beyond their means for too long and now find themselves trapped in a cycle of dependency. They are ill-equipped to survive in the competitive world of the 21st century. Some are doomed to disappear as sovereign states and shall be absorbed by more economically powerful nations [cited in Fossungu, 2013b: 202].

Positively Using The Stigmas: Hard Choices, National Humiliation And Viperizationism

Is absorption then what African states are currently undergoing because of their failure to unite especially during the cold war era? Could it be happening because Africa is not one like China, and how can the awakening be done differently? Could the stereotypes be positively used? This book is more in line with what Fru Doh is calling for: dissipating rather than reinforcing the stereotypes about Africa. 'Beloved Son of God', you can now have the microphone to tell us more. Characteristically, Emmanuel Fru Doh's blurb reads, Africans in any Western country are asked so many different questions about "Africa," as Westerners love to refer to the many countries that make up that huge continent, as if Africa were a single nation state. So one begins wondering why it is that Africans, on the other hand, do not refer to individual European countries as "Europe" simply, then the trends and consequences of stereotyping begin setting in just as one is getting used to being asked if Africa has a president, or if one can say something in African. It is some of these questions that

Emmanuel Fru Doh has collected over the years and has attempted answering them in an effort to shed some light on a continent that is in many ways like the rest of the world, when not better, but which so many love to paint as dark, backward, chaotic, and pathetic.[55]

You can also pick up what Fru Doh is lecturing on from the fact that (even within the Western academia) *Nigeria* is not even seen as being included in that *country* (or region) called *Africa*: "We can also divide comparativists into those who emphasize area studies – close knowledge of a country or region (the Middle East, Latin America, Africa, China, Nigeria) – and those who stress the 'science' in 'social science,' seeking general laws of political behaviour and institutions that would apply in all areas of the world" (O'Neil and Rogowski, 2013b: 2). There is no doubt that stereotyping could be involved here. But here is what I positively see in these stigmas, which makes me to greatly wonder if every African should have to be schooled in the science known as Four-Eyesism (see Fossungu, 2014: chapter 4 & xiii-xv) for this continent to quickly awaken from the induced slumber and assume its rightful place in this world. Get it from Hard Choices Schooling.

Globalization and the Hard Choices

This book essentially provides Africa with an original, critical, and multi-level analysis of the trio (globalization, democracy, and national determination), showing that China, but not the African states, did face up with those ineluctable *political trilemma* choices. In the same manner, we have seen how the CGAM has grossly failed to make hard choices, preferring politickerization to fossungupalogy which is the science/theory of straightforwardness. This science calls for fearlessly looking at truth straight in the eye. You have

---

[55]See http://www.langaa-rpcig.net/Stereotyping-Africa-Surprising.html.

obviously seen the tragedy of that pretence; an attitude that extends to the stereotypes; s*tigmas* that are not unique to just Africa. Dabashi (2012: 44) obviously agrees with and confirms this thesis when he states that "Libraries and museums of scholarship, journalism, visual and performing arts, imaginative landscapes, and so forth, have been produced to manufacture the figure of the Arab and the Muslim as the absolute, and absolutely horrid, reversal of the white man – the white man with whom even a black man like Barack Obama identifies." Of course, Dabashi is here himself stereotyping the black man. Everyone else who is also pushed around always ends up taking it out on the black man, why? I leave that to our famous Blackologists out there. But could it not be because of their negative competition, that leads to bad community leadership, and hence no community cohesion?

There is the urgent need for competent leadership in Africa; a kind of leadership that would be keenly interested in the intersection of questions about how economic globalization is or is not affecting the connection between nation and state as cultural and political formations. We need leaders who are keenly interested in what this phenomenon might mean for democracy, given that this historically has been organized and exercised through the nation-state. No one would deny that this is a well-covered but still fruitful topic; that these are ongoing open-ended and very uneven processes. In *The Globalization Paradox: Democracy and the Future of the World Economy*, Dani Rodrik argues essentially that (economic) globalization, national determination, and democracy are inconsistent. This is basically what he regards as the fundamental political trilemma of the world economy, in the sense that

> we cannot simultaneously pursue democracy, national determination, and economic globalization. If we want to push globalization further, we have to give up either the

nation state or democratic politics. If we want to maintain and deepen democracy, we have to choose between the nation state and international economic integration. And if we want to keep the nation state and self-determination, we have to choose between deepening democracy and deepening globalization. Our troubles have their roots in our reluctance to face up to these ineluctable choices [Rodrik, 2010: xviii-xix].

Circumscribing Globalization: You cannot begin to understand or correctly assess Rodrik's argument until you have grasped the meaning of 'Globalization Paradox' that is the first part of the full title of his book. Having already seen what a paradox is in chapter 1, *globalization*, on its part, is the process by which businesses start to operate on a global scale, with global (1) relating to the whole world; worldwide; and (2) relating to all the parts of something (Hawker and White, 2007: 394). Those terms thus defined, the "use of the term 'globalization' and the processes to which it refers varies somewhat from one analyst to another" (Grosby, 2005: 17). This variation is most probably because globalization is understood as both the integration process and a buzzword, and, of course, "[g]lobalization is too important to be consigned to buzzword status" (Taylor, 2002: 24). As Matthew Sparke has advised, therefore, the two main ways of understanding globalization need to be carefully distinguished, making sure that globalization with small g be understood as a name for increasing global interdependence, while big G 'Globalization' be assigned the status of a buzzword, which he defines as "an influential key term in political speech" (Sparke, 2013: 1-10). Whatever the case (big or small), its definition "must be considered in any attempt to interpret the significance of globalization, irrespective of how this term is to be understood" (Grosby, 2005: 16). Globalization is currently defined very briefly within the academy as the contradictory and oppositional economic, political, and cultural processes of world capitalist integration (Mentan, 2013a; Oloka-Onyango, 2005: 1248-49), or the rapid integration of international markets for commodities, manufactures, labour and capital (Ferguson, 2008: 286; James, 2009: 1). What to do about hard choices in its regard?

Concretely, China chose to keep the nation-state and self-determination over the others (in the *Political Trilemma*) by largely cutting itself off from the global market from the 1950s until the 1970s (see Ferguson, 2008: 287). China had to first consolidate its sovereignty and nation-state before venturing into the globalization business. This strategy has paid off so well that *communist* China is today adding to 'the globalization paradox' with its current enviable status as the banker of the *capitalist* West. A real winner, China appears to be because of the hard choices it made. This is very unlike the African states that have somewhat failed to make the hard choices on attaining "Mimicry and Membership" in the "New World Society" (Ferguson, 2006: 155-175). Nor did they take advantage to consolidate their position by sticking together (as advocated for by President Thomas Sankara of Burkina Faso (RIP)) during the Cold War years (see Akokpari, 2001; Fossungu, 1999a). True bellyticians that the continent's leaders are (see Fossungu, 2013c: 171-74; Bayart, 1993), they instead contented themselves with eating the crumbs from the meal tables of capitalists, never foreseeing the end of that cold war and its hot consequences, one of which now revolves upon Africa's ongoing relationship with communist China (see Edoho, 2011).

Edoho's article is particularly relevant to the unity-or-die message of this book since that article not only furnishes an overview of the literature on the globalization question but also examines the current China–Africa relations by contextualizing China's economic activities in Africa. Edoho interrogates the ramifications of the evolving China–Africa relations for economic development in the region. He thinks China–Africa relations need to be understood as the logical outcomes of the marginalization of Africa in the age of globalization. China is filling the vacuum in Africa created by Western disengagement from the region since the end of the cold war. (On such disengagement Africa was simply waiting with folded arms for someone else to come rather than take its destiny into its own hands, *no bi na so?*) That Africa is embracing China, Edoho points out, is informed by the former's appraisal of the consequences of its colonial experience and the realities of its postcolonial dependent relationships with the West. He recognizes that China–Africa relations embody opportunities and threats, advising that Africa needs to utilize the new architecture of cooperation to maximize benefits and minimize threats. Africa's economic interest and quest for development could be in conflict with those of China, yet Africa must determine how to leverage the deepening relationship with China to its own advantage (Edoho, 2011).

The important question then becomes that of *how* Africa is going to leverage this relationship with China without having both legal and behavioural sovereignty (see Nahar, 2008; Krasner, 2013; Drezner, 2009)?[56] Some observers think that such sovereignty can hardly be forthcoming without Africa also 'leveraging educational quality in African educational systems' (Mawere and Rambe, 2013; Fossungu, 2013b: 90-110, 175-192). Building largely on the author's earlier studies, this book

---

[56] In the wake of the Arab spring, the Chinese regime combated the dissenting voices with a calculated propaganda campaign against the United States whose Ambassador John Huntsman interacted with protesters in Beijing on February 20th 2012. This afforded the perfect opportunity for the Chinese authorities to rile or beef up nationalistic and anti-American fervour (Kewalramani, 2012). Would China be able to even cough about this if it were not sovereign? So, Africa, stop telling me about your sovereignty when France, for instance, walks in any time any day and any how to install or throw out 'leaders' or ignite civil wars etc. Back to *Chinalogizing*, one would want to ask if this was not like the United States meddling with China's internal affairs. Again, would the latter have been able to raise a finger if it were not sovereign?

particularly seeks to advance political unity for strength and fitness in the global jungle, through meaningful federalization, as an appropriate means for such leverage. One of the underlining points made by James Ferguson, and largely shared by this book, is the ardent call for an end to the "mimicry membership" or "Pseudo-Nation-States" (Ferguson, 2006: 50-68) through "uniting Africa rather than further splitting the continent into incapable mini-states vis-à-vis the changing world stage" (Fossungu, 2013c: x). There is just no way that any of the current individual 'Pseudo-Nation-States' can ever have any leverage (without a grossly abusive or politickerized use of the word) face-à-face any of the major players of globalization, let alone an economically strong communist China, in "a competitive world in which the law of the jungle prevailed" (Wang, 2012: 74). This book therefore pursues this position of unity for strength (through a form of governmental system based on local realities). Only high quality leadership, it is useless to pretend about it, would be up to the daunting task "[i]n such perilous dog-eat-dog circumstances" (Wang, 2012:75). Africa must now listen to reason or soon die. More of such reason seems to four-eyesismatically come from Onafridism itself.

On Onafridism and National Humiliation: 3-Point Viperizationism

Onafridism refers to the 'One-Africa-Stereotyping-Disease'. I am thus inviting us to always remember at least three important things from the *stigmas* on Africa. **First Point:** that, talking of *Onafridism*, a year before Fru Doh (in *Global Shadows: Africa in the Neoliberal World Order* which virulently kicks against the stigmatization of the continent as a place of failure, etc.), Ferguson (2006: 210) also satirically talked of "African politics, so long misunderstood as backward, is starting to look very up-to-date indeed." Yet, in this "one of the most thoughtful, provocative, intelligent books written about Africa" (John Comaroff in Ferguson, 2006: back cover), Ferguson does not discuss "Africa" as a country but rather would be examining various countries on the continent to make his incisive points. One of which (from my four-eyesismatic grasping) is the underlying ardent call mentioned earlier. That is, for an end to the mimicry membership or Pseudo-Nation-States through uniting Africa rather than further splitting the continent into incapable mini-states vis-à-vis the changing world stage.

In the same vein, Glassman and Samatar (1997) do not treat 'Third-World State' as a single state in their "Development Geography and the Third-World State." That is clearly the title of their study but they (instead of a certain non-existing single state) have discussed Thailand and Botswana as two case studies. Is this not like comparing apples and oranges, according to Stegmueller (2011)? My humble response here is: *Yes*, it is, if by 'apples and oranges' you are referring to Przeworski and Tuene's 'most different systems' research design which "seeks out similarities between cases in spite of the potentially confounding differences between them" (Hopkin, 2010: 293) 'Not so fast, Stegmueller, ' Glassman and Samatar are further saying. Their choice, *inter alia*, is because

> in both countries the state has played a major role in promoting exports which can be explained with reference to the themes we identified above. Furthermore, both countries face certain definite limitations on the potential of their development strategies, limitations to which the state must now respond. Identifying critical features of those states such as their degrees of autonomy, class unity and class consciousness may help us understand the sort of responses which we seek from these states when confronted with such limitations [Glassman and Samatar, 1997:183-84].

Second Point: I have to let you know that it is the same type of 'national humiliation' (the stereotyping) – by way of one-way globalization or 'Unequal Treaties' with 'Foreign Devils' – that spurred the Chinese to seek to excel to the extent of beating their *humiliatiors*. According to the late Chinese Chairman Mao (who very skilfully localized Marxism and contextualized it in terms of China's tradition), the people, the people alone, are the motive power that creates history. I quoted the Chairman to sustain my condemnation of the Ahidjo-Biya regime for thinking that they could invent history that is not ours and impose it on us (Fossungu, 2013b).[57] You can see that because the Chinese never forget their history, shameful as they might think it was, they have been able to correctly grasp politickerized institutions of imperialism and thus be where they currently are. Yes, they have learnt to play the game only after carefully studying and mastering the rules: whether or not said rules are in regard of any of the forms or colours of the chameleon. It is indeed a *chameleon*. That is the easiest way I would explain globalization to the lay person in the open-space Marché Mokolo in Yaoundé: which is not to be confused with the grocery-store-like one in Canada on 4974 Chemin Queen Mary in Montreal (march-mokolo.foodpages.ca) that is owned by a Bamileke Cameroonian. Bamileke, thank you for our economic globalization!

Furlong and Marsh (2010: 206) think that so many authors have distinguished between economic, political and cultural

---

[57] Fossungu (2013b: 206) has, for instance, "posit[ed] that the unbending schizophrenia toward the obliteration of the history and culture of the English-speaking minority is not only inconsistent with the ceaseless singing of biculturalism (as already elaborated on above); but also principally what is (1) responsible for some African countries (with far less economic and other natural endowments than Cameroon) being ahead of Cameroon in the development or nation-building game and (2) precluding this otherwise 'Paradise in Africa' from truly advancing and assuming its legendary role as Africa's pathfinder."

processes of globalization, while acknowledging that they are interrelated. Felix Edoho and many others agree that globalization creates new markets like Montreal's Marché Mokolo and expands economic opportunities. Let me swiftly tell you that this is the part of the story that its proponents would quickly push down your 'flat-world' throat before you ever have had the time to discover how they were choking you to death, by the time those critics then go on to point out that globalization also engenders economic dislocation and accentuates global inequalities and mass discontent. These contradictions, the critics say, expose the chasm between industrialized countries, the main beneficiaries of globalization, in contrast to developing countries, embroiled in economic dislocation and social instability. Thus, globalization, they conclude, produces winners and losers (Edoho, 2011: 103; Oloka-Onyango, 2005: 1245-48; and James, 2009).

Of course, the critics are right about the fact that "The World is Spiky" and that "Globalization Has Changed the Economic Playing Field, But Hasn't Levelled It" (Florida, 2013). Globalization "generally implies that the international expansion of the market place and the technological advancements that have made that expansion possible have resulted in a cultural uniformity among at least all those who are able to participate substantially in that market" (Grosby, 2005: 17). In this regard, some commentators have then found globalization to be "such a diverse, broad-based, and potent force that not even today's massive economic crash will dramatically slow down or permanently reverse it. Love it or have it, globalization is here to stay" (Naim, 2009: 28). The inevitability theory that is implied here – an unstoppable feature for which the administration of William Jefferson Clinton is well known (see Toal, 1999: 140-141) – combines with those of 'newness' and of 'level-playing field/flat-world' to embody what is ordinarily known as 'the three myths of globalization'. Of the three, the 'flat-world' or 'borderless world' myth is clearly the most contentious, whatever the meaning of globalization that is attached. This is because this myth mixes a lot of theoretical convictions in economics with geopolitical distortions to give the impression that everybody (or the entire world) actually benefits from the overwhelming neoliberal deterritorialization agenda, whereas the unembellished reality is the creation of not only 'peaks, hills, and valleys' but also of terrible suffering, waste and violence (see Florida, 2013: 590-93; Sparke, 2013: 36, xv; Paasi, 2009: 214-225; and Toal, 1999: 142-143).

Such bristly attitude is true, especially if one also considers Europeans' insatiable lust for gold and silver (money) in Peru in earlier centuries, which led to Manco Capac's time-tested observation that "Even if the snow in the Andes turned to gold, still they would not be satisfied" (Ferguson, 2008: 21). It indicts as well Francisco Pizarro's horrendous mistreatment of Peruvians just to have his endless masses of gold and silver, not to forget the imported African slaves who took "their places as 'human mules'" (Ferguson, 2008: 23; and Ferguson, 2006: 194-210, 69). I cannot omit to also drag in the horrible plight of modern day South African mine workers (see Colding, 2013) and extraction workers of Angola, Mozambique, Congo RDC (Ferguson, 2006).

True as the stories in them are, the foregoing arguments are somewhat oblivious of the fact that in the brutal world of politics (even more so at the international level) there is going to always be a winner and loser, whether or not there is globalization, and also that sovereign equality is always illusory for the small boys. The Chinese never forgot these simple lessons that they had learned the hard way. China withdrew from international markets (globalization) because it appears to have learnt from Rodrik's *trilemma* thesis that the only countries that have managed to become rich under capitalism are those that have erected an extensive set of *formal* institutions that govern markets: "tax systems that pay for public goods such as national defence and infrastructure, legal regimes that establish and protect property rights, courts that enforce contracts, police forces to sanction violations, bureaucrats who design and administer economic regulations, central banks that ensure monetary and financial stability, and so on. The economists call them institutions of 'third-party enforcement'" (Rodrik, 2010: 15-16). Anyone supposing that there can be 'free trade' in the absence of a system "(punctuated by a neutral arbiter) is, to say the least, crazy" (Fossungu, 2013b: 6).

Paradoxical Self-Made Victim?
Russell (1987: 20) tells us that in a third-party process, the adjudicator or judge must be truly independent of both disputants; otherwise, the whole process is difficult to sustain as a public institution and becomes an open farce; with Rodrik (2010: 33-34) also saying the same thing regarding long-distance trade through colonialism or neo-colonialism. It should then be noted that the issue of 'third-party enforcement' here is highly controversial or flawed in so far as eighteenth century Victorian globalization goes. A typical illustration concerns what is commonly known in China as 'The Opium Wars' (Wang, 2012: 49-53). Like "the 'drunkard, unthinking man' adage" (Fossungu, 2013b: 200 n.200), this Opiumization Thesis relates basically to the sending of warships by the British administration to back up William Jardine and James Matheson's *opiumization* of the Chinese populace. The two rogues are more aptly described by Niall Ferguson as the buccaneering Scotsmen who had set up a trading company in the southern Chinese port of Guangzhou (then known as Canton) in 1832 and were openly engaged in the opium trade in China – a practice that Emperor Yongzheng had prohibited over a century before, in 1729, because of the high social cost of opium addiction (Ferguson, 2008: 289-92). The Chinese, who never forget national humiliation, had obviously learnt from the colonial experience

when they withdrew from one-way globalization or "Unequal Treaties" with "Foreign Devils" (Wang, 2012: 60-69) for about twenty years.

The Chinese, very unlike (forever drunken and opiumized) Africans, had discovered that, contrary to the Chinese *tianxia* system (that focused on soft power such as culture, morality, and harmony), the Western international system was based on hard power such as military and economic strength, territorial expansion, and cutthroat competition (Wang, 2012: 73). The evidence of this knowledge is reflected, *inter alia*, in the constant changing of the Chinese national anthem to mobilize the people to 'Arise and roar their defiance and March on' (Wang, 2012: 84-94). The very essence of the 'unequal treaties' has thus come to define what it means to be Chinese — to be both victim and vanquisher. (Is Africa here carefully listening?) On the one hand, Wang explains it, China was a victim of Western imperialism, forced to abandon the high culture of the *tianxia* system for the base survival-driven nation-state worldview. On the other hand, he concludes, these humiliations provided the all-consuming fire needed for China to rise like a phoenix from the ashes and overcome the West in its quest for glory (2012: 77).

Should Africa be entitled then to always take cover behind the fact that it *was* colonized and raped by the West? What have Africans done to remedy or correct the situation since 'achieving independence'? What is paradoxical is also the fact that most of the states of the South (the so-called losers) do not even know competition internally, like was the case in China between the Kuomintang (KMT) and the Chinese Communist Party (CCP) until the civil war (see Wang, 2012: 77-84). The African regimes do not permit challenges, clinging on to power forever and also creating 'human mules' out of their citizenry. Ahidjo and Biya of Cameroon (like elsewhere in Francophone Africa) are always calling in the French army to come and crush patriotic opposition. That is certainly not what

I have to be the first to tell you. So, leaving the question of sovereignty aside, how and why must they now be able to *compete* with anyone else on the international sphere? There lies our predicament, self-made, that we now want others (the winning West) to shoulder blame for? How different is this from the root of the 'whites getting richer and richer and blacks poorer and poorer' thesis noted in the previous chapter? Akokpari and other development experts tell the rest of the predicament story better, indicating how since the end of the Cold War a newly emerging orthodoxy has been changing the character of the global economy. The principles of the market and free trade have become the unflinching articles of faith. The private sector (which, I must add, was never encouraged and/or developed by the African tyrants) is accepted and projected as the engine for growth while the role of the state is being curtailed in economic development. Also, information flow has witnessed a major revolution, while multinational corporations (MNCs) and trade policies have fused the global economy into a large single market for the first time in history, with information flow now witnessing a major revolution (Akokpari, 2001: 189; Glassman and Samatar, 1997: 164; Oloka-Onyango, 2005; Edoho, 2011; and Pires, Stanton and Salavrakos, 2008).

And, the **Third Point** is linked directly to the second point, and which the CGAM's viperizationism begins to conveniently expose. As noted earlier, the only Vice-President that has actually viperizationized in the CGAM is Martha Egbe Tanyi-Mbianyor. Viperizationism deals with the replacement function of the V-P and, in the infamous *UNICAM love-affair*, turns on this famous brawl between the vice-president (as acting president[58]) and the absent president (with the

---

[58] According to Article 9 of the CGAM Constitution, "Unless otherwise stated by the General Assembly, the Vice-President assists the president in executing his/her functions; [and] assumes the functions of the president in his/her absence."

financial-secretary *connexion*). The heart of the matter relates to the V-P's show of solidarity with UNICAM that the president himself would so very much cherish in his own (tree-topperism?) dealings with these same defiant debtors of the CGAM. Don't worry if you do not get it yet because it will become exceedingly clear to you as you read the V-P.'s response to also further discover Fifolefacism.

The V-P was certainly not taking the Fifolefacist accusations and 'ordering-around' sitting down when she *clarificationingly* fired back on July 2, 2009:

Dear all, hope everyone is doing great. This mail is just a clarification to the President's mail. I will be precise[].

Yes, I did reserve chairs, tables and field for UNICAM.

Reason, as I said in my mail which I sent to the president, [t]he president of UNICAM [that is, Hans Najeme] contacted the council first before seeing me. The council told him to contact me if they want anything from the council because they only recognize one association at the time from a particular country [that is a very clear call for unity that *AITWs* clearly fail to four-eyesismatically understand: Would the LaSalle Council also be accused of *stereotyping* diverse Cameroon here?]. I contacted the council, and they did the reservation for them.

Comments: I do not think it is wrong for me to do [? the] reservation [p]ersonally for another sister association as Goodwill is practicing cordial relationship with them. I stand to defend my action and it is not a MUST that I have to contact the exco before rendering service to other sister association on trivial things. As the Sitting President for the moment (VP) [because t]he president is not [around] yes, any action I take I have the discretion to do so and defend it. The president has his own way of doing things, it must NOT be my way. I have my own way. There are many things which I have consulted the exco many times before decisions are made but not for every little thing the president or the vice needs to contact the exco before taking decisions. Then why are you the president or vice. The president or vice takes decisions and stands to defend them when need arises. That is what I just did. But the exco should be informed. For more info I had kept this issue to talk about in the next exco meeting which I have scheduled for this [S]unday [J]uly 5th at my place to let the exco know the reservation I did [make] and how they contacted me and many other things which we have to discuss at exco level.

So I do not know why the president had to make this issue public as if it is a major problem by complaining to the exco and copying members of the advisory committee. It is not an issue copying others because I do not see it as a problem at all and I took the decision as the Vice President who will be judged as an individual and NOT the whole Exco if necessary. I think issues like this need just little correction and suggestion rather than making it public for no reason.

Besides, Goodwill had already opened it[s] doors to welcome UNICAM when they came and presented their business to us openly in one of our meeting sessions, they ate and drank with us [Madam V-P, you're kind of hitting the politickerization nail right on the head here too]. Presently the president is sending a letter of congratulation for their 1st anniversary party on this [S]aturday 4 July. So is it wrong to help them when we have already accepted them in the first place[?] This was the reason why I even did the reservation and remember they had contacted the council first without me knowing before the council sent them to me.

NOTE: If we would have refused them in the first place, I would not have made the reservation. Pls I do not want this matter to look like a back biting or conniving issue. I did it with clear and clean minds with no intention of misrepresenting anybody. (This is not part of me).

Well, as I earlier said, it is not all situations I have to contact the exco to take a decision on minimal issues like reservation for few hours. [I]f it is necessary to contact the exco, I will happily do that if not, no need I will take an action if within my reach. There are serious and big issues which I have always contacted the exco before decisions are made and there is nowhere in the constitution nor by-laws that says, the exco MUST always be contacted before decisions are made. [Who ever said CGAM officials did not know their constitution?] It is just the President's way of doing things which is fine but it must not be my way. Yes we work as a team and there are many ways to work in a team. Pls Mr President do not make me feel as if I do not know what I am doing. I am adult enough to know what is right and what is wrong and my limits.

[I]f Goodwill believes in me as their Vice President, let them trust in me whatever I do because I will never betray or let them down and I will always stand to defend my actions.

I think this mail was necessary to clarify certain doubts
Regards to all

I have already made a few comments within the vice-president's eye-opening *clarificationistic* viperizationing four-eyesism. But there is both an anti-dose to viperizationism from the financial bench and a presidential response to the curable viper bite. Both of these long viperizationism-provoked pieces we need to also pay close attention to.[59] The important thing

---

[59]Titled '*Chairs Reservation for 'sister' Association*', the financial desk contribution came in on July 3, 2009 and essentially disagreed totally with viperizationism. Listen to Pius Esambe Etube:

After reading the mails from the President and VP, I feel compelled to express my opinion. The issue here is whether an Executive member can alone without consulting its [sic] Team members as is usually the case proceed to use the name of Goodwill, and expose the Association to risk or liability by rendering service to an individual or a sister association because we are fostering collaboration with sister associations?.

From VP's mail, the answer is YES, provided you defend your action after the deed. **I totally disagree with [the] VP's position** because support to her view will generate a situation in future that we may not be able to handle. Today is VP reserving chairs for UNICAM, tomorrow it could be the Financial Secretary reserving chairs for another association without consulting the team, or taking another action using [the] name of the Association.

Should I, the financial Secretary, use the association's name to render services to either an individual or another association without consultation with team members which has been our common practice in my opinion is not a trivial matter, and I will be acting in abuse or beyond the powers the Assembly entrust on me. It is not as trivial as VP puts it but in my opinion a serious issue whose legal implication is that, Goodwill is held responsible and not UNICAM nor the Vice President should UNICAM cause any damage to the chairs.

One question I will like to put to VP is whether she will be personally liable and not Goodwill if anything goes wrong with the chairs? Further, will VP stand to defend this in front of the General Assembly without support from the Executive? The President in his mail suggested to VP to formally put the issue to the Executive to formalize the common practice or procedure we have been following in order to sample opinion from the team members. The VP rather preferred to keep it for Sunday after the event. In fact, if the majority of the team should say we should not reserve the chairs using Goodwill's name, then VP cannot proceed with the action because the action is engaging the Association. Why would the VP prefer to defend her action on Sunday rather than throw it to the team?

VP mentioned that *"Goodwill had already opened it[s] doors to welcome UNICAM when they came and presented their business to us openly in one of our meeting sessions"*. We received UNICAM for its team to make publicity without assuming any risk for them. That situation and current situation are not similar at all, and the first does not imply that we should proceed individually to execute any request from any association or business entity that came to market its services to goodwill. We will not do this even for our known sponsors.

My suggestion:

The VP should put the matter to the team immediately and not wait till Sunday for [her] to defend her action in the Executive meeting. This may avert a situation now that may not have a cure in future should it go unaverted. Each team member should comment for or against using Goodwill's name to reserve chairs for UNICAM.

Thank you for reading

The Financial Secretary [bold is original]

The Financial Secretary's invitation to his team members to comment went without response: except for the president who answered back on July 3, 2009:

Dear V.P.

Thanks for your explanation. <u>Please do not get me wrong and least [sic] my email be misinterpreted by anyone of us.</u> **My concern is not that you made reservation for a sister association, it is rather the single-handed approach you followed which is not our usual functioning procedure in doing things. Together, we have condemned this procedure when Goodwill food warmers were used by another sister association. Let me be clear that Goodwill, my executive and myself have nothing against anybody or sister association.** In life it is not about doing things correctly but doing the correct things so I am not disturbed by any label when doing the correct thing.

Let me disagree with you V.P. that non-respect of procedure is a trivial matter and that one will be judged as an individual. It may be the case when everything goes right and one gets all the praises but imagine if something goes wrong. At that time it will be the liability of the Association and not the individual. The council will not come after any executive of Goodwill but all of Goodwill. An example is the church who addresses all letters of complain[t] to Goodwill and not Fidelis Folifac. This justifies why as elected leaders we MUST act with diligence and collectivity in the discharge of our responsibilities.

I agree with the V.P, and it is true that no executive is compelled to act as Fidelis, but as elected leaders of Goodwill, we are compelled to act in the BEST interest of Goodwill, to inform, consult and engage, at the very least the exco in all we do. Leadership is continuous and effective communication is paramount to that continuity. This supports the views and arguments presented by the Financial secretary. In a membership association, leadership is service, and as servants such leaders have responsibilities to build a team and work collectively and not authority to do things and defend them.

Yes, we received them in a general meeting, and I have sent a message on the occasion of the anniversary. This is in line with our fraternal and collaborating policy with all sister associations, and done with due understanding of the rest of the executive. Even adults, myself included, do make mistakes, but it is one thing to make a mistake and quite another not to acknowledge that one made a mistake more often than not by failing to engage corrective measures.

though is that Mbianyor's viperizationism was a pioneering deed meriting emulation. Yes, those who were thinking that the list system was the best for CGAM would better be rethinking now. That list system might have avoided eye-opening viperizationism and would not also have been able to furnish us with firstohocelectionism/charalicism. I think I prefer both of these new forms of friction to unthinking serenity and cronyism which are largely responsible for our not seeing that those so-called stereotypes (like asking who the president of Africa is) are in effect telling or awakening Africans (who are still failing) to clearly and four-eyesismatically see this plain fact: That if they have to ever move away from the backward, chaotic, and pathetic, tags, they imperatively need to by-pass the continent's bellyticians who are only and always interested in "Selling the Sea to Stay in Power" (Dabashi, 2012: 207-213) and have one effective voice or president who speaks for them on the world stage like "China's president, Hu Jintao, [who] was powerful not only because of the rapid growth of the Chinese economy since the 1980s, but also because China had emerged as the provider of global savings and global surpluses.

The reasons I made this known to the executive and the Advisory council (who cannot be described as a public) is to ensure that the executive and the association is [sic] formally engaged. In addition, to strongly discourage any executive member from making the same mistake in the future. Remember that if we shy from auto-critiquing ourselves, we are not helping ourselves and Goodwill.

Please exco members, even without a formal presentation of the request from our sister association from the V.P. I motioned that Goodwill be formally engaged in the provision of this service and give them all the support they need for a successful event.

Hope the two points I suggested in my last email will be considered for inclusion in the agenda for the executive meeting.

Thank you all for understanding that my point is procedure and not that the V.P should not have assisted.
  Best regards
  Fidelis Folifac
  President, Goodwill [bold is original].

He made clear that China would assert its own interests, whether on the question of Tibetan independence or on the character of the international currency regime. He held in his hand the future of globalization" (James, 2009: 4-5).

I humbly submit that this is a thing that is only possible with Africa's political unity. And it is not like the unity drums for "Awakening Africa" have not been beating very hard. As Fossungu (1999a: 359-60) warned and advised in the context of the International Civil Aviation Organization (ICAO),

[e]ven keeping this prestigious [ICAO] Council membership aside, international air transport is currently going through a period of dynamic change as a result of increasing competition, trans-nationalization of business, globalization of the world economy, and the emergence of regional economic and political groupings, privatization of service industries, and the introduction of new global trading arrangements for service sectors. Necessitated by the ever-changing technology in the field, the international air transport industry is now faced with the almost irreversible trend of oligopolization and extremely high investment. Against this scenario alone, would one not naturally think that the time may be ripe for developing countries in general, and Africa in particular, to take a more balanced and serious look at the possibility of pooling resources together in order to jointly operate more efficient, competitive, and viable air transport agencies? Only by doing this could we hope to hear of "African Tigers" that could even smell (let alone eat) the lunch and/or supper of U.S. and EU flag carriers.

Relevantly Surprising Answers To Unnecessary Questions?

That was just an example of the many and ceaseless calls for Africa to, like China, rise like a phoenix from the ashes and overcome 'the West' in its quest for glory. If four-eyesing the stereotypes is not proving enough, perhaps adding the relevant surprising answers to unnecessary questions would cement it and thus tip the balance? The second set of the experts' queries noted above would relate to the importance or relevance of case-studies. The critics' query is clear enough to me. Is one case (Africans in Canadian factories, for instance) an adequate representation of all (diverse Africa)? Quite apart from what I have already said above and would be advancing below too, this issue need not be a complicated matter at all to anyone seeking understanding and knowledge. Both of these are often distinguished by 'argumentative' political scientists. Some experts even see their endless debating as just a pretext for fencing off the "accusation that political science lacks a distinctive theoretical and methodological core" (Vromen, 2010: 250).It is just as comparative politics. "One of the greatest problems in comparative politics", O'Neil and Rogowski (2013a: ix) write, "is that it lacks an agreed upon core."

The role of comparison in political science is widely misunderstood, probably because of the entrenched American use of the term 'comparative politics' to describe what is not really comparative. That is, they merely use the terminology to describe research into 'foreign' countries; research which, ironically, "is not explicitly comparative at all, consisting instead of 'idiographic' studies (studies which are limited to particular cases or events), often of individual countries" (Hopkin, 2010: 285-86). To this extent, the comparative method shares common critiques with the experimental method whose potential "as a research method has been downplayed and underestimated in political science... [because] 'we are limited by the impossibility of experiments. Politics is an observational, not an experimental science'" (Margetts and Stoker, 2010: 308). All this would hold because all else does not remain equal (as per the *certeri paribus* assumption, that is) in social and political life when two or more variables change, and it is thus usually empirically difficult to pin causes to a particular effect. To emphasize, this is because social and political life in modern, mass societies is so complex, and any attempt to develop a reasonably parsimonious theory will neglect potentially important explanatory factors (Hopkin, 2010: 292).

With or without an agreed upon core, I think these specialists know, at least, what the debate is about. My advice here is that you should never try to debate with someone on a subject unless you know what the debate is all about. Making it clear you are not yet ready to argue with them is the wise thing wise people do to be wise. Yes China! An Afro-Chinadian obviously hears you well even if Canada refuses to listen to him. Let them further debate *understanding* before I drunklampost them.

The Battle for Understanding

Some of these political scientists have lengthily explained that foundationalists focus on *explanation* and, initially, many of them felt that the use of rigorous 'scientific' methods (quantitative) would allow social scientists to develop laws, similar in status to scientific laws, which would hold across time and space (Furlong and Marsh, 2010: 191). In contrast, they further explain, anti-foundationalists focus upon the *meaning* of behaviour, emphasizing *understanding* rather than *explanation*. Understanding here relates to human reasoning and intentions as grounds for social action. In this tradition, these sapient authors conclude, it is not possible to establish causal relationships between phenomena that hold across time and space, since social phenomena are not subject to the same kind of observation as natural science phenomena (Furlong and Marsh, 2010: 192). Stoker's (2010: 181) warning about epistemological positions not being fixed in stone is important because, while sharing much with the positivists, realists believe (like the interpretivists) that there are deep structural relationships between social phenomena which cannot be directly observed, but which are crucial for any explanation of behaviour (Furlong and Marsh, 2010: 192).

I think it is sane to agree with Leston-Bandeira (2013: 210) who argues that these political science approaches and methods should be employed as *"means* towards an end, rather than an end in itself." Liam Stanley apparently concurs when he offers an interesting critique of this understanding/explanation stuff by elaborately explaining that:

Explanation has a very specific meaning here [in political science's foundational-anti-foundational connotation], and diverges considerably from the classic concept in philosophy of social science, in which the term is conflated with prediction and contrasted dichotomously with interpretation or *verstehen* (e.g. Flyvbjerg, 2001). The usage of explanation here, in contrast, indicates an attempt to answer how or why something political happened. So, for instance, the question of why social democracy has declined is often explained through the effects of globalisation on the nation state, or the power of states is often explained by their relative military or economic strength. This understanding thus incorporates *descriptions* of how something happened without necessarily appealing to causal logics ormechanisms. Explanations are not the only aspect of first-order political science. Whether acknowledged or not, explanations are typically embedded within a particular context (e.g. cultural, temporal, geographical, etc.) and are not necessarily generalizable beyond that. However, there are, of course, strategies to increase the extent to which an explanation can be generalised beyond the immediate context. Comparative political science, for instance, aims to search for patterns invariables among a series of explanations from more than one context to purport amore generalizable *theory*. Furthermore, we can also distinguish *approaches*, such as rational choice theory or historical institutionalism, which represent pre-packaged meta-theoretical apparatus for generating explanations.

Consequently, approaches should be analysed and evaluated as second order because they, in principle, explain little about politics [Stanley, 2012: 94-95, original emphasis].

I can only say that this debate will surely continue till the end of the world; or, better, until there is "willingness of institutionalists on both sides of the Atlantic to pose again the fundamental and difficult questions of the relationship between agents and structures, between institutional architects, institutionalised subjects and institutional environments" (Hay and Wincott, 1998: 957). Let political scientists argue about understanding/explanation but the important thing here is that each of the two, as the experts have shown, is required to shun stereotypes (Fossungu, 2014; Zembylos, 2013; Reaves, 1992). I would here therefore simply avoid getting into the understandable endless debates among political scientists over approaches and methodologies etc., (for more of which, see Vromen, 2010; John, 2010; Leston-Bandeira, 2013; Hopkins, 2010; Reaves, 1992) by answering back (like I did with the McGill likehewasian earlier) to *drunklampostism* with some simple but tellingly straightforward questions.

The Theory of Drunklampotism

I know some critics could also be saying that my equalization of the few Africans I have known in Canadian factories (including the CGAM) with *AITWs* or all Africans "could more satirically be equated to the drunk looking for his keys under the lamp-post because that is where the light is" (Hopkin, 2010: 294). I will call Hopkin's thesis drunklampostism. It is clear that many Africans just do not grasp a lot of simple things. Yet, just imagine the high-sounding titles some of these people carry around with them, making me to wonder if *biggytitlemania* is Africa's own version of China's vanquished-conqueror definition. To put the drunklampostist thesis in other words, just how useful is a case-study (like this one) to social and political science? This query (like the stereotyping issue from the One-Africa-Disease that Americans suffer from) is also an excellent one, isn't it? I must again be addressing both of these interlocking issues of stereotyping and of relevance here – two sides, same coin, as I see it.

A Blackologist advised me about eleven years ago to always pay great attention to the ones we call mad and drunkards. Why do I need to? I asked. He looked at me for a while and must have thought I was just doing good journalism with him when he explained that "these people are only mad to us because they think at a level that is far higher than ours!" Wonders shall never end? What kind of bullshit was Charly attempting to feed me with? I was then wondering if that could be what is behind Bob Marley's *Kaya* in which he sings that (after taking his *médicament*, as it is called in the MYR camp) he feels so high that he could even touch the sky above the falling rain; the same rain that is the cause of his wanting to have his marijuana then. Could some of these drunks and mad ones not just be so simply as a way of staying clear of the tyrants' guillotine? Have you not even known someone who was so perpetually drunk and yet could publish three books in one year?

Whatever the case with the theory of the Blackologist, would one unavoidably need to be a four-eyesismatic expert to visualize that the drunkard is not totally foolish in beginning the search for his keys where there is light? Doesn't the mere talk of '*where there is light*' already four-eyesismatically tell us that there is also '*where there is no light*'? Can the sober person not then take the light (that is, to make sure another lamp-post is available) to the other place and find the key, if that is where it really is? You just don't still get the points and, therefore, need to be further spoon-fed? To put it differently, talking about *AITWs* (democracy) necessarily imports *AITEs* (Africans in the East) or the Marxist way of 'doing state business.' I am here inductively reasoning from the drunkard's comportment to say that if *AITWs* are not seeing the key, perhaps *AITEs* can. Again, is it not even more expedient for you to dispel the stereotypes of 'regarding many as one' by simply 'discussing one as representative of many'? By the way, the use of the CGAM in this book, like Cameroon, is a good representation of Africa that is predominantly English- and French-speaking – officially, that is. The CGAM is also a kind of 'inverse Cameroon' (with an English-speaking majority) and could also readily provide good testing ground for those theses that hold that 'Anglophones' would do better in (independently) governing Cameroon which is Africa in Miniature. How valid some of such (sweeping?) propositions are, could also be drawn from all the chapters of this book.

Conclusion

Having dug a little bit into the history of Africa, it is my belief that Africans have to start standing upright and taking their own destinies into their own hands rather than waiting for others who might not even properly understand their situation and/or cultures to do things for them [Fossungu, 2013b : 3].

I always love to see my readers drawing their own conclusions themselves from what I present to them. That is exactly what I still want them to do here. But I do not think I would want to close this book in any other way that does not involve stressing some points on China, African unity and the need for Africans to wake up and live. Because only an economically strong and politically robust nation-state can really achieve some of the pressing goals in Africa, this book is banging as hard as would be necessary to awaken fast sleeping Africans and bring them to the realization that unity is their only hope for survival in a neoliberal world order. The book, no doubt, is also putting stress on some of the positive cultural endowments that Africans must not compromise under any circumstance, while advising on the negative things that must be shunned in order for the community to strengthen itself against erosion.

I have spent a little more time on the rising Asian giant since it is very important for understanding the various positioning of the other actors (local and foreign) in Africa generally, indisputably making China a "Voracious Competitor" (Edoho, 2011: 107-108) and "New Colonizer" (Edoho, 2011: 108-109) who is "Filling a Vacuum" in Africa (2011: 109-110) since it can be "argued that given its embracing of the Western-type capitalism, China has no genuine desire to help to bring about authentic development, nor will China support the cause of good governance, encourage the rule of law, and promote respect for human rights" (Edoho, 2011: 107; also Diamond, 2013). My important and constant questions are: Why must only *others* 'fill a vacuum in Africa'? And why must there be a vacuum in the first place? AFRICANS MUST WAKE UP AND LIVE!

Rather than cleverly emulating successful people, it looks like Africans would wait on or allow these others to endlessly 'succeed' on Africans through the *distinction theses*. When the recent events in the Arab world sparked off, China distinguished them from its system of governance. This involved the enlisting of several Chinese intellectuals and other commentators who went to great lengths to draw distinctions between their one-party, socialist system and the Arab monarchies or what Owen (2000: 45-63) lengthily describes as "The growth of power in the Arab world under family rule, and the Libyan alternative." Sub-Saharan Africa is not left out here, considering the cases of Togo, Gabon, Congo RDC, and many more waiting just 'like the hungry *Biyaist* hawks' to copy them. The Arab regimes were thus described by the Chinese intelligentsia as feudal and self-serving dictatorships that failed to invest in their people, resulting in economic stagnation (Kewalramani, 2012; Gunay, 2011). Of course, from even a fleeting reading of most modernization theorists like Schnabel

(2003), Pratt (2007), Posusney (2004), and Najem (2003), it would be kind of difficult to disagree with the Chinese description. "One of the worst things about the authoritarian Arab regimes, beyond their denial of the dignity of the individual, was the contempt the rulers showed for their people" (Khalili, 2012: 13). In contrast, the Chinese authorities have argued, the Chinese state was robust (I would substitute with sovereign) with a strong central leadership (I would substitute with patriotic and pragmatic), which was premised on collective decision-making, the absence of individual monopoly over power, and the grassroots network of the Chinese Communist Party (CCP). Its success and superiority could be gauged by the rapid economic prosperity and improved standards of living experienced by citizens along with the state's ability to respond swiftly to disasters, such as the Sichuan earthquake of 2008 (Kewalramani, 2012; Huang, 2013: 2-3 of 6; Wang, 2012).

I would have to also point out that the CCP relied on a system of majority tyranny as a basis of its legitimacy (Wang, 2012: 87). This is what He and Warren (2013) have very extensively described as 'Authoritarian Deliberation'. This would make the system just as 'democratic' (majority rule) as democracy requires, compared to the one-man/family "Deadening Hand of Personal Rule" (Diamond, 2013: 299-302), I guess? Given these facts, as Wang (2012: 222) has advised, "surely it is time for the West to rethink its perceptions about China." Kewalramani obviously sees this distinction point as propaganda, but this book does not agree with that, and therefore at the opening of chapter 6 I have further called on Jean-Germain Gros, a political science professor at the University of Missouri–Saint Louis, to back up the point for the *Sleeping Dogs of Africa*.

Most Africans are out of the continent taking all the shit they have grown used to taking principally because African administrations have been erected without the welfare of the general population in mind. Trust me then that should the situation change today very few Africans would want to continue being out of the continent. This leads to the billion dollar question. Who has to effect the required change? Only Africans can fix Africa for Africans. No one else can do that for them. Africans had therefore better wake up now and take the bull by the horns and let succeeding generations be able to proudly say in their time: "We had fore-parents who thought of us." The recent shakeups in the Middle East would constitute what is generally known as 'The Arab Spring'. According to Byman (2012: vii), the Middle East was changing at bewildering speed, throwing up new challenges for its citizens and complex dilemmas from outside powers. From the Arab awakening that began in December 2010 to Iran's nuclear program and the seemingly eternal issue of Israel and the Palestinian question, he concludes, the Middle East commands worthwhile attention, whether policymakers around the globe wish it or not.

Yes. Repeat 'wish it or not'. This is especially so because "not only were a series of tyrants toppled but the strength of popular feeling, and the stubborn willingness of the demonstrators to sustain their challenge to those who remained, also sent shockwaves across the Arab world from Morocco to Kuwait" (Owen, 2012: x). Yes. Africans, it is not what others wish, but what you wish to make of your lives, that would have to prevail: provided it is what you truly wish with all your heart and soul and might (*stubborn willingness*). Yes, Michèle Oliver, you too are right: "African solutions to African problems" (Oliver, 2011). But that should not just end with the continent's dictators using that to fend off demands for human rights respect because sovereignty, to Krasner (2013: 68-70), cannot be absolute in the face of human rights. It is not just simply wishing for African unity but actually working and making it happen, and, believe you me, it will never be given to you on a platter of gold. Dabashi (2012: 92) has been quick then (and rightly so, in my view) to warn of the dangers lurking around from "the counterrevolutionary forces now watching the Arab Spring like hungry hawks", with Ross (2011) also legitimately wondering if *oillogy* (oil politics) will drown the Arab Spring. Ross' fears are shared by Dabashi (2012: 61) who further indicates that "Today, as we witness the unfolding of the Arab Spring, an entirely different economic situation pertains, one in which the ravages of neoliberal economics, unfettered greed, and an irresponsible orgy of deregulation have suddenly made Keynesian economics a plausible strategy for survival, albeit only in the short term."

On a fleeting view, it looks like most African children have been watching and emulating only the agents of voluntary slavery like the Ahidjos, Mobutus, and Biyas. Does that mean then that all hope is lost for Africa? If some think so, I clearly do not think that Africa is completely *brimatized* (filled to the brim, if you will) with only midnighters/tree-toppers. As George Bush would prefer putting it, "Make no mistake" about the fact that there are also the human dignity defenders like the Mandelas, Sankaras, Um Nyobes, Lumumbas, Tourés, Nkrumahs, etc. that Africa's children are wisely looking up to as models. The mere fact that some of us have left behind the camp of 'we don't have a choice' and made the choice to die (not with them but) for them, gives me comfort to consider that Africa will eventually get there. I personally believe Africa would get there eventually, despite the damage that this would mean for Canadian and other western factories and 'voluntary slavery' calculations. You just cannot fool all of the people all of the time, according an American president. Don't they also say that one person awake in the camp can (like this noisy multi-language-speaking Zairian in the MYR Camp called Amadi) wake up every one?

WOULD AFRICANS NOT WANT TO WAKE UP AND LIVE?

Bibliography

Achal, Lawrence Kyaligonza and Raymond Chegedua Tangonyire (2012), *Economic Behaviour As If Others Too Had Interests* (Bamenda: Langaa RPCIG).

Akokpari, John K. (2001) "Globalisation and the Challenges for the African State" *Nordic Journal of African Studies* 10:2: 188-209.

Ansari, Hamid (2007) "Foreword" in Zoya Hasan (ed.), *Democracy in Muslim Societies: The Asian Experience* (New Delhi: Sage Publications India Ltd.), 7-9.

Appleby, R. Scott (2010) "Of Fundamentalism, Secular and Otherwise" *Open Democracy* (September 27), http:/www.opendemocracy.net.

Baker, Raymond W., (2012) "The Paradox of Islam's Future" in Daniel Byman and Marylena Mantas (eds.), *Religion, Democracy, and Politics in the Middle East* (New York: The Academy of Political Science), 197-239.

Bayart, Jean-François (1993) *The State in Africa: The Politics of the Belly* (New York: Adeison-Wesley).

Behbehani, Hashim S.H. (1985) *China's Foreign Policy in the Arab World, 1955-75: Three Case Studies* (London: KPI Limited).

Boh, Herbert (2013) "FrancAfrique Deals: Colonialism is Not Over" available @ http://www.cameroonjournal.com/Colonialism.html.

Bojicic-Dzelilovic, Vesna (2001) "Transnational Networks and State-building in the Balkans" *Open Democracy* available @ http://www.opendemocracy.net.

Brooks, Stephen (1996) *Canadian Democracy: An Introduction* (2nd edition) (Toronto: Oxford University Press).

Byman, Daniel (2012) "Overview: A New Middle East?" in Daniel Byman and Marylena Mantas (eds.), *Religion,*

Democracy, and Politics in the Middle East (New York: The Academy of Political Science), vii-xii.

Castellano, Marlene "Out of Paternalism into Partnership: An Exploration of Alternatives in Social Services to Native People" in James A. Draper, ed., *Citizen Participation: Canada* (Toronto: New Press, 1971), 351–370.

Colding, Rosetta (2013) "THE TRUTH: Marikana (summons) Voices from South Africa's Mining Massacre 2012" http://www.examiner.com/review/the-truth-marikana-summons-voices-from-south-africa-s-mining-massacre-2012.

Dabashi, Hamid (2012) *The Arab Spring: The End of Postcolonialism* (London: Zed Books).

Debrix, François (1998) "Deterritorialised Territories, Borderless Borders: The New Geography of International Medical Assistance" *Third World Quarterly* 19:5: 827-846.

Derian, James Der (2009) *Virtuous War: Mapping the Military-Industrial-Media-Entertainment Network* (2nd edition) (New York: Routledge).

Diamond, Larry (2013) "The Rule of Law Versus the Big Man" in Patrick H. O'Neil and Ronald Rogowski, *Essential Readings in Comparative Politics* (4th edition) (New York: W.W. Norton & Company), 294-303.

Drezner, Daniel W. (2009) "Bad Debts: Assessing China's Financial Influence in Great Power Politics" *International Security* 34:2: 7-45.

Duncan, Thomas K. (2013) *Economizing Defense: Economics of the Military-Industrial Complex* (PhD Dissertation, George Mason University, Fairfax, VA).

Eagleton, Terry (2011) "In Praise of Marx" *Chronicle* (April 10) available @ http://www.chronicle.com/article/In-Praise-of-Marx/127027/

Edoho, Felix M (2011) "Globalization and Marginalization of Africa: Contextualization of China-Africa Relations" *Africa Today* 58:1:102-124.

Edsall, Thomas B. (2013) "Does Rising Inequality Make Us Hardhearted?" *The New York Times* (December 10), http://www.nytimes.com/2013/12/11/opinion/does-rising-inequality.

Embong, Abdul Rahman (2007) "Islam and Democracy in Malaysia" in Zoya Hasan (ed.), *Democracy in Muslim Societies: The Asian Experience* (New Delhi: Sage Publications India Ltd., 2007), 128-176.

Ferguson, James (2006) *Global Shadows: Africa in the Neoliberal World Order* (Durham: Duke University Press).

Ferguson, Michaele L (2010) "Choice Feminism and the Fear of Politics" *Perspectives on Politics* 8:1: 247-253.

Ferguson, Niall (2008) *The Ascent of Money: A Financial History of the World* (New York: Penguin Books).

Florida, Richard (2013) "The World in Spiky: Globalization Has Changed the Economic Playing Field, But Hasn't Levelled It" in Patrick H. O'Neil and Ronald Rogowski, *Essential Readings in Comparative Politics* (4th edition) (New York: W.W. Norton & Company), 590-595.

Fonjong, Lotsmart (2012) *Issues in Women's Land Rights in Cameroon* (Bamenda: Langaa RPCIG).

Fossungu, Peter Ateh-Afac (2014) *Africa's Anthropological Dictionary on Love and Understanding: Marriage and the Tensions of Belonging in Cameroon* (Bamenda: Langaa RPCIG).

_____ (2013a) *Africans in Canada: Blending Canadian and African Lifestyles?* (Bamenda: Langaa RPCIG)

_____ (2013b) *Understanding Confusion in Africa: The Politics of Multiculturalism and Nation-building in Cameroon* (Bamenda: Langaa RPCIG).

_____ (2013c) *Democracy and Human Rights in Africa: The Politics of Collective Participation and Governance in Cameroon* (Bamenda: Langaa RPCIG).

_____ (2013d) "How Cameroon Should be Governed: The Political and Administrative Set Up" available at:

http://www.cameroonjournal.com/how%20to%20govern%20cameroon.html.

_____ (2010) "Separation of Powers in Public International Law: Is the International Civil Aviation Organization (ICAO) Out of or Within the United Nations System? A Critique of ICAO Assembly Elections" *Annals of Air & Space Law* 35: 267-96.

_____ (1999a) "999 University, Please Help the Third World (Africa) Help Itself: A Critique of Council Elections" *Journal of Air Law and Commerce* 64: 339-375.

_____ (1999b) "Who Is an Infant in Cameroon?" *The Herald* (Cameroon) (10-11 February).

_____ (1998a) "The ICAO Assembly: The Most Unsupreme of Supreme Organs in the United Nations System? A Critical Analysis of Assembly Sessions" *Transportation Law Journal* 26: 1-49.

_____ (1998b) "Eve of OAU Summit: A Dream for Africa's Children" *The Herald* (Cameroon) (25-26 May), 10.

_____ (1998c) "DRA Politics and Our Unborn Children" *The Herald* (Cameroon) (9-10 September), 4.

_____ (1998d) "When Will Cameroonians Ever Grow Up?" *The Herald* (Cameroon) (20-21 July), 19.

_____ (1998e) "New Forms of Solidarity" *The Herald* (Cameroon) (12-14 June), 4.

_____ (1992) *The Judiciary as a State Power in Canada and Cameroon* (LL.M. Thesis, University of Alberta), available @ http://era.library.ualberta.ca/public/view/item/uuid:750d94be-ae0c-41b0-9c4f-6eac693c0b3e/.

Friedman, Thomas L. (2012) "Why Nations Fail" *New York Times* (March 31) available @ http://www.nytimes.com/2012/04/01/opinion/sunday/friedman-why-nations-fail.html.

Furlong, Paul and David Marsh (2010) "A Skin Not a Sweater: Ontology and Epistemology in Political Science", in David

Marsh and Gerry Stoker (eds.), *Theory and Methods in Political Science* (3rd ed.) (London: Palgrave Macmillan), 184-211.

Gat, Azar (2013) "The Return of Authoritarian Great Powers" in Patrick H. O'Neil and Ronald Rogowski, *Essential Readings in Comparative Politics* (4th edition) (New York: W.W. Norton & Company), 539-544.

Giroux, Henry A. (2007) *The University in Chains: Confronting the Military-Industrial-Academic Complex* (Boulder, CO: Paradigm Publishers).

Glassman, Jill, and Abdi Ismail Samatar (1997) "Development Geography and the Third-World State" *Progress in Human Geography* 21:2: 164-198.

Göymen, Korel (2007) "Interaction of Democracy and Islam in Turkey" in Zoya Hasan (ed.), *Democracy in Muslim Societies: The Asian Experience* (New Delhi: Sage Publications India Ltd.), 219-255.

Gros, Jean-Germain (2008) "'Big Think', Disjointed Incrementalism: Chinese Economic Success and Policy Lessons for Africa, or the Case for Pan-Africanism" *African Journal of International Affairs* 11: 2: 55–87.

Grosby, Steven (2005) "The Fate of Nationality" *Society* (Jan-Feb), 15-20.

Gunay, Cangiz (2011) "Mubarak's Egypt: Bad Paternalism, and the Army's Interest in Managed Transition" *Open Democracy* (February 3) http://www.opendemocracy.net

Hartung, William D. (2001) "Eisenhower's Warning: The Military-Industrial Complex Forty Years Later" *World Policy Journal* (Spring), 39-44.

Hawker, Sara and Maurice White (eds.), *Oxford Paperback Dictionary & Thesaurus* (Oxford: Oxford University Press, 2007).

Hay, Collin and Daniel Wincott (1998) "Structure, Agency and Historical Institutionalism" *Political Studies* 46:5: 951-57.

He, Baogang and Mark E. Warren (2013) "Authoritarian Deliberation: The Deliberative Turn in Chinese Political

Development" in Patrick H. O'Neil and Ronald Rogowski, *Essential Readings in Comparative Politics* (4th edition) (New York: W.W. Norton & Company), 509-538.

Hindmoor, Andrew (2010) "Rational Choice", in David Marsh and Gerry Stoker (eds.), *Theory and Methods in Political Science* (3rd ed.). (London: Palgrave Macmillan), 42-59.

Hopkin, Jonathan (2010) "The Comparative Method", in David Marsh and Gerry Stoker (eds.), *Theory and Methods in Political Science* (3rd ed.). (London: Palgrave Macmillan), 285-307.

Huang, Yasheng (2013) "Democratize or Die: Why China's Communists Face Reform or Revolution" *Foreign Affairs* (January/February).

James, Harold (2009) *The Creation and Destruction of Value: The Globalization Cycle* (Cambridge, Mass.: Harvard University Press).

Jaspan, Norman, with Hillel Black (1960) *The Thief in the White Collar* (New York: J.B. Lippincott Company).

Jiang, Min (2013) "Authoritarian Informationalism: China's Approach to Internet Sovereignty" in Patrick H. O'Neil and Ronald Rogowski, *Essential Readings in Comparative Politics* (4th edition) (New York: W.W. Norton & Company), 613-627.

John, Peter (2010) "Quantitative Methods", in David Marsh and Gerry Stoker (eds.), *Theory and Methods in Political Science* (3rd ed.). (London: Palgrave Macmillan), 267-284.

Kewalramani, Manoj (2012) "China and the Arab Spring" *Canary Trap* http://www.canarytrap.in/2011/05/30/china-and-the-arab-spring/ [accessed on 24 October 2013].

Khalili, Rashid (2012) "Preliminary Historical Observations on the Arab Revolutions of 2011", in Bassam Haddad, Rosie Bsheer and Ziad Abu Rish (eds.), *The Dawn of the Arab Uprisings: End of an Old Order?* (London: Pluto Press), 9-16.

Killough, Alvin L. (2009) "Review of *Stereotyping Africa*" http://www.langaa-rpcig.net/Stereotyping-Africa-Surprising.html

Konings, Piet (2012) *Gender and Plantation Labour in Africa: The Story of Tea Pluckers' in Cameroon* (Bamenda: Langaa RPCIG).

_____ (2009) "Review of *Stereotyping Africa*" http://www.langaa-rpcig.net/Stereotyping-Africa-Surprising.html.

Krasner, Steven D (2013) "Sovereignty" in Patrick H. O'Neil and Ronald Rogowski, *Essential Readings in Comparative Politics* (4th edition) (New York: W.W. Norton & Company), 68-74.

Krastev, Ivan (2013) "Paradoxes of the New Authoritarianism" in Patrick H. O'Neil and Ronald Rogowski, *Essential Readings in Comparative Politics* (4th edition) (New York: W.W. Norton & Company), 502-509.

Lakoff, George (2012) "A Framing Memo for Occupy Wall Street" *Nation of Change*, http://www.nationofchange.org/framing-memo-occupy-wall-street-1319120987

Leston-Bandeira, Cristina (2013) "Methods Teaching through a Discipline Research-oriented Approach" *Politics* 33:3: 207-219.

Lindorff, Dave (2013) "About Time American Idiocy and Paranoia Over Marxism Got Called Out" *The Nation of Change* available @ http://www.nationofchange.org-About-Time-American-Idiocy.

Maguire, Diarmuid (2010) "Marxism", in David Marsh and Gerry Stoker (eds.), *Theory and Methods in Political Science* (3rd ed.). (London: Palgrave Macmillan), 136-155.

Margetts, Helen and Gerry Stoker (2010) "The Experimental Method: Prospects for Laboratory and Field Studies", in David Marsh and Gerry Stoker (eds.), *Theory and Methods in Political Science* (3rd ed.). (London: Palgrave Macmillan), 308-324.

Marsh, David (2010) "Meta-Theoretical Issues", in David Marsh and Gerry Stoker (eds.), *Theory and Methods in Political Science (3rded.).* (London: Palgrave Macmillan), 212-231.

Marsh, David and Gerry Stoker, eds. (2010), *Theory and Methods in Political Science (3rded.).* (London: Palgrave Macmillan).

Martino-Taylor, Lisa (2008) "The Military-Industrial-Academic Complex and a New Social Autism" *Journal of Political and Military Sociology* 36:1:37-52.

Mathews, Jessica T (1997) "Power Shift" *Foreign Affairs* 76:1: 50-66.

Mawere, Munyaradzi, and Patient Rambe (2013) *Leveraging Educational Quality in Southern African Educational Systems: A Practitioners' Perspective* (Bamenda: Langaa RPCIG).

Mawere, Munyaradzi (2012) *The Struggle of African Indigenous Knowledge Systems in an Age of Globalization: A Case for Children's Traditional Games in South-Eastern Zimbabwe* (Bamenda: Langaa RPCIG).

McCain, John (2011) "Remarks by Senator John McCain on the 'Military-Industrial-Congressional' Complex" **Congressional Documents and Publications** (December 15, 2011), available @ http://www.mccain.senate.gov/public/index.cfm/floor-statements?ID=42987243-f045-7da7-6952-e32c98949a64.

Mentan, Tatah (2013a) *Assault on Paradise: Perspectives on Globalization and Class Struggles in Africa* (Bamenda: Langaa RPCIG).

_____ (2013b) *Democracy for Breakfast Unveiling Mirage Democracy in Contemporary Africa* (Bamenda: Langaa RPCIG).

_____ (2012) *Socialism: The Only Practical Alternative to Contemporary Capitalism* (Bamenda: Langaa RPCIG).

Nahar, Snigdha (2008) "Sovereign Equality Principle in International Law" *Global Politician* available @ http://globalpolitician.com/default.asp?24351-international-law.

Naim, Moisés (2009) "Globalization" *Foreign Policy* (March/April) 28–34.

Najem, Tom Pierre (2003) "State Power and Democratization in North Africa: Developments in Morocco, Algeria, Tunisia, and Libya", in Amin Saikal and AlbrechtSchnabel (eds.), *Democratization in the Middle East: Experiences, Struggles, Challenges* (New York: United Nations University Press), 183-201.

Nichols, John and Robert W. McChesney (2013) *Dollarocracy: How the Money-and-Media Election Complex Is Destroying America* (New York: Nations Books).

Oliver, Alexander J. (2009) *A Model of the Military-Industrial-Academic Complex* (M.A. Thesis, Tufts University).

Oliver, Michèle (2001) "Impact of the Arab Springs: Is Democracy Emerging as a Human Right in Africa?" @http://www.defenceweb.co.za/index.php?view=article

Oloka-Onyango, Joseph (2005) "Who's Watching 'Big Brother'? Globalization and the Protection of Cultural Rights in Present Day Africa" *Human Rights Quarterly* 27:4: 1245-1273.

O'Neil, Brendan (2009) "Green-Industrial Complex: Al Gore and his Allies Know the Color of Money" *The American Conservative* 8:11: 8-10.

O'Neil, Patrick H. and Ronald Rogowski (2013a) "Preface" in Patrick H. O'Neil and Ronald Rogowski, *Essential Readings in Comparative Politics* (4th edition) (New York: W.W. Norton & Company), ix-x.

_____ (2013b) "What is Comparative Politics?" in Patrick H. O'Neil and Ronald Rogowski, *Essential Readings in Comparative Politics* (4th edition) (New York: W.W. Norton & Company), 1-2.

Owen, Roger (2000) *State, Power and Politics in the Making of the Modern Middle East* (2nd edition) (New York: Routledge).

Owen, Roger (2012) "Foreword – Jadaliya: Archiving the Revolution" in Bassam Haddad, Rosie Bsheer, and Ziad

Abu Rish (eds.), *The Dawn of the Arab Uprisings: End of an Old Order?* (London: Pluto Press), x-xvii.

Paasi, Anssi (2009) "Bounded Spaces in a 'Borderless World': Border Studies, Power and the Anatomy of Territory" *Journal of Power* 2:2: 213-234.

Pires, Gullherme D, John Stanton, and Ioannis-Dionysios Salavrakos (2010) "The Interaction of Foreign Direct Investment with Electronic Commerce in Less Developed Countries" *Forum for Social Economics* 39:2: 127-143.

Posusney, Marsha Pripstein (2004) "Enduring Authoritarianism: Middle East Lessons for Comparative Theory" *Comparative Politics* 36:2: 127-138.

Pratt, Nicola Christine (2007) *Democracy and Authoritarianism in the Arab World* (Boulder, CO: Lynne Rienner Publishing Inc.).

Randall, Vicky (2010) "Feminism", in David Marsh and Gerry Stoker (eds.), *Theory and Methods in Political Science* (3rd ed.). (London: Palgrave Macmillan), 114-135.

Raymond, Jack (1964) *Power at the Pentagon* (New York: Harper and Row Publishers).

Reaves, Celia S. (1992) *Quantitative Research for the Behavioral Sciences* (Washington, D.C: John Willey & Sons).

Rodrik, Dani (2010) *The Globalization Paradox – Democracy and the Future of the World Economy* (New York: W.W. Norton).

Ross, Michael L. (2011) "Will Oil Drown the Arab Spring? Democracy and the Resource Curse" *Foreign Affairs* (September/October), 2-7. http/search.proquest.com/printviewfile?accountid=14789

Russell, Peter H (1987) *The Judiciary in Canada: Third Branch of Government* (Toronto: McGraw-Hill Ryerson Ltd.).

Said, Edward W. (2001) "The Clash of Ignorance" *The Nation* (October 22) available @ http://www.thenation.com/doc/2001said/print

Schmidt, Diane E. (2010) *Writing in Political Science: A Practical Guide* (4th edition) (New York: Longman).

Schnabel, Albrecht (2003) "A Rough Journey: Nascent Democratization in the Middle East", in Amin Saikal and Albrecht Schnabel (eds.), *Democratization in the Middle East: Experiences, Struggles, Challenges* (New York: United Nations University Press), 1-22.

Schwarzmantel, John (2012), "Rethinking Marxism and Nationalism in an Age of Globalization" *Rethinking Marxism* 24:1: 144-161.

Serwer, Andy and Allan Sloan (2008) "The Price of Greed" *Times* (September 29) 16-21.

Sparke, Matthew (2013) *Introducing Globalization: Ties, Tensions, and Uneven Integration* (Maden, MA: Wiley-Blackwell.

Stanley, Liam (2012) "Research and Analysis: Rethinking the Definition and Role of Ontology in Political Science" *Politics* 32:2: 93-99.

Stegmueller, Daniel (2011) "Apples and Oranges? The Problem of Equivalence in Comparative Research" *Political Analysis* 19: 471-487.

Stoker, Gerry (2010) "Introduction to Part 2", in David Marsh and Gerry Stoker (eds.), *Theory and Methods in Political Science (3rded.).* (London: Palgrave Macmillan), 181-183.

Taylor, Timothy (2002) "The Truth about Globalization" *Public Interest* 147: 24-44.

Terretta, Meredith (2013) *Petitioning for our Rights, Fighting for our Nation: The History of the Democratic Union of Cameroonian Women, 1949-1960* (Bamenda: Langaa RPCIG).

Tessier, Mark (2002) "Islam and Democracy in the Middle East: The Impact of Religious Orientations on Attitudes toward Democracy in Four Arab Countries" *Comparative Politics* 34:3: 337-354.

Toal, Gerard (1999) "Borderless World? Problematising Discourses of Deterritorialisation" *Geopolitics* 4:2: 139-154.

Vromen, Ariadne (2010) "Debating Methods: Rediscovering Qualitative Approaches", in David Marsh and Gerry Stoker (eds.), *Theory and Methods in Political Science* (3rded.). (London: Palgrave Macmillan), 249-266.

Wang, Zheng (2012) *Never Forget National Humiliation: Historical Memory in Chinese Politics and Foreign Relations* (New York: Columbia University Press).

Wiktorowicz, Quintan and Karl Kaltenthaler (2012) "The Rationality of Radical Islam" in Daniel Byman and Marylena Mantas (eds.), *Religion, Democracy, and Politics in the Middle East* (New York: The Academy of Political Science), 109-133.

Zembylos, Michalinos (2013). "The Emotional Complexities of 'Our' and 'Their' Loss: The Vicissitudes of Teaching about/for Empathy in a Conflicting Society" 44:1 *Anthropology & Education Quarterly*: 19-37.